Handbook to The Riviera

" What is this life, if it be not mixed with some delight ?
And what delight is more pleasing than to see the fashions
and manners of unknown places ? "

A NEW
HANDBOOK
TO
THE RIVIERA
FROM
HYÈRES TO VIAREGGIO

With Map of the Riviera and Street Plans of Hyères,
Cannes, Nice, Monaco and Monte Carlo,
Menton, San Remo and Genoa.

———————

SIXTY ILLUSTRATIONS

———————

LONDON:
WARD, LOCK AND CO., LIMITED
WARWICK HOUSE, SALISBURY SQUARE, E.C.4
AND AT MELBOURNE

Printed in Great Britain by Butler & Tanner Ltd., Frome and London

CONTENTS

5

THE ITALIAN RIVIERA

MAPS AND PLANS

ILLUSTRATIONS

INTRODUCTION.

" Here the Spring is longest, Summer borrows
Months beyond her own."

WHAT and where is the Riviera ?
     It is the sunniest, warmest and driest district
on the Continent of Europe. It lies along the northern
shore of the Mediterranean. It has no defined limits, but
is generally understood to extend from Hyères, some sixty
miles eastward of Marseilles, to the neighbourhood of distant
Leghorn (or Livorno), so that it is partly in France and
partly in Italy. The inland boundary is fixed by the
highlands of the hinterland, for the climate which makes the
Riviera is the offspring of sheltered, sunny lowlands, and as
the high ground is nowhere far from the sea, the Riviera
is but a narrow strip.

The Playground of the World.

There was a time when the Riviera was regarded chiefly
as a health resort, visited almost solely by those suffering
from bronchial or pulmonary troubles and able to flee from
the rigours of an English winter. Reports of the beauty of
the country, the charm of the climate, and the cheapness
of living drew to the favoured region many who had not
the excuse of sickness for their visit. The latter class has
gone on increasing out of all proportion to the former, so
that now the number of those who go to the Riviera for their
health is very small compared with the number who go
frankly for their pleasure, not only from the British Isles,
but from all civilized countries. The Riviera has become
the playground of the world.

There are race courses, golf courses, and tennis courts
galore, with a succession of tournaments in which world-
renowned players engage. Polo is played, there is coursing,
and need it be mentioned that practically all the year round
there is sea-bathing—not merely by those who would break
the ice rather than miss their morning dip ?

9

Then there are the carnivals and battles of flowers, motor races and regattas, and a ceaseless round of indoor gaieties —balls, dances, gala dinners, concerts and, at the Casinos, gambling, although one may go there, as do the great majority, to enjoy good music, and never see the gaming tables.

Yet it is not the sports and pastimes which attract increasing crowds of visitors from northern latitudes. The supreme attraction consists of the twenty-six or twenty-seven days of sunshine in every winter month. Sunshine which begins the moment the Lord of Day appears on the eastern horizon and continues until he sinks to rest in the west. Sunshine which comes from a sky of intense blue, a sky without that delicate grey veil which on a bright summer day in England almost always tones down the blue of the great celestial vault. And for the same reason that the sunshine is so brilliant and the sky so blue during the day, the moon and the stars are more brilliant than they are between the parallels of latitude which embrace the British Isles.

The French call the coast of their portion of the Riviera **la Côte d'Azur,** a name which speaks of the marvellous blue sky overhead and the equally marvellous blue sea stretching away to the southern horizon ; and the title might aptly be given to the whole of the coast.

When and Where to Go.

The answer to the first part of this question depends upon the proposed length of the visit. To avoid the English winter and its chilly autumn, one should go early in October, and remain at least until the early days of May. If it is necessary to face some cold days in England, it is better to meet them before going than after home-coming. Prudence dictates that one should, if possible, avoid returning from the warmth of the South to the chilly air of England in early Spring.

Where should one alight in the delectable land ? This also is a question to which a brief direct answer cannot be given. The climate does not suit all invalids, and those going in search of health should first seek the advice of a medical man, who will probably indicate a suitable destination. Those who are not invalids and yet not very robust should not expose themselves to the *Mistral,* a bitterly cold wind which comes down the valley of the Rhone and then turns eastward, getting less terrible the farther it goes, so that the strongest loses its bite before reaching Menton.

Those whom these considerations do not concern, and who wish to be in the midst of gaiety and at a centre of movement, should select a large town—it may be two or more, if the visit is to be a long one. On the other hand, those who prefer quietude, or accommodation making modest demands on a slender purse, will select one of the smaller resorts, some of which, as will be seen from later pages, are within easy reach of a great centre.

The stream of winter visitors begins in October. Its flow perceptibly increases in November and augments daily until it has attained its greatest volume in the first two months of the New Year. Then the ebb begins. After Easter the ebb is very pronounced. In the middle of May the first of the shops which open only for the winter season have their fronts boarded up and some of the hotels follow suit. A diminishing number of hotels, however, do this, for of late an effort has been made to create a summer season, and really it does seem strange that such a magnificent stretch of coast should not receive more of those who spend their summer holiday at the sea-side. It suits those who do not need a bracing climate and can support a high temperature even at night. Charges are reduced, there is an abundance of beautiful fruit at prices much lower than in England, and the sea bathing is delightful.

The period between the two winter seasons is a time of longer days, of an even less number of rainy days, and of a sun which raises the temperature of the Mediterranean to a point far higher than that of the seas having northern coasts. It is a temperature to be happy in. Long hours can be spent in the water, and on quitting it one is not met by a chilly atmosphere, but by the warmth of a sun in a cloudless sky and the air which it has heated.

Motoring.

An increasing number of visitors take their cars to the Riviera, or hire a car for a period. Speaking generally, the roads are less pleasant to travel upon than are the roads in Great Britain. In France off the *Routes Nationales* the surface is often local limestone, and where this is not tarred it is ground up as fine as flour. A shower of rain converts the dust into mortar-like mud. For further details *see* pp. 26–7.

Motor-coaches run in all directions. By making systematic

use of them a visitor with little time at his disposal may, in a few days, gain a good general idea of the Riviera. The competition is sufficient to keep fares at a reasonable level. Motor-bus services with time-tables are also very helpful. The railways do not offer facilities for excursions similar to those offered by the British companies.

The best way of all to see the Riviera and its hinterland is to go with a stout stick in hand and a knapsack on the back, not always on foot, but taking advantage of friendly lifts—the omnibuses, the tramways, the light railways, and even of main-line trains—to cross uninteresting bits or sections which in that way can be as well or better viewed.

Whether one travels eastward or westward along the Riviera, the builder is seen at work. Villas and many-storied houses are being erected. Infant towns are coming into existence, and towns that have come to maturity are expanding upward and outward.

Other changes are being wrought. The population is becoming less and less composed of natives, particularly along the French coast, to which Italians and Spaniards migrate to work, and English and Americans, especially the former, to live at ease or to exploit the soil. All along the Riviera are colonies of English-speaking settlers, with their churches, clubs and sports grounds, and effecting a change in the appearance of their neighbourhood by the style of the villas which they build and the lay-out of their gardens.

The Climate.

The popular impression of the Riviera is of a land of balmy zephyrs and of an ever-smiling nature. Are there not orange and lemon trees in the gardens ? Do not heliotropes, carnations, marguerites and roses flower all the winter out of doors ? Are not primulas and cyclamen bedded out in November, and cinerarias in January ? And are not the happy ladies pictured lightly clad and holding up a sunshade even on Christmas Day ? It is so, and yet the Riviera is not a veritable Avalon.

At the risk of unpopularity in certain quarters we deem it advisable to point out that there is another side to the question and that while visitors should come prepared for boundless sunshine they should also bear in mind that even on the Riviera there are occasional cold days and chilly corners against which it is necessary to be forearmed.

It is common to talk of the Riviera climate, and even this section is so headed, whereas the Riviera has a dozen climates, but all have one notable quality in common, namely the great amount of sunshine. There is something like nine times as much sunshine on the Riviera as in England, and the sunshine on the Riviera is quite different from what it is in England, where watery vapour gives a whitish hue to the sky and mitigates the power of the sun's rays.

The mean temperature during the winter months is only some 5° higher at Nice or Cannes than at Torquay or Falmouth, but at the former places there is in the sun a temperature of 75° or 80° and the English winter resorts cannot promise that. On the other hand, they have this advantage over the Riviera resorts : their daily temperature is less varied.

This is due to the fact that the higher temperature of the Riviera in winter is that of the sun. The air not under its influence is usually cold. There is often a difference of 50° between the temperature in the sun and that in the shade at midday. And at sunset, especially in places which have western hills near them, so that the sun suddenly disappears from sight, the abruptness with which the temperature falls is disconcerting and dangerous.

Those who visit the Riviera for the first time often think that summer clothing only is necessary. " Never was there a greater mistake," says Dr. Bennett, the great authority on the climate of the region. " Summer clothes are useless from December to May. Those required are the light but warm woollen clothes we wear during our cold spring and autumn with light over-garments. The latter can seldom be safely dispensed with even on the sunniest and warmest winter days, on account of the great difference between the sunshine and the shade."

To the inequality of the daily temperature as one of the drawbacks of the climate of the Riviera must be added the windiness of the region, especially in the first four months of the year. The worst of the winds is the **Mistral,** magistral or master wind, to which reference has already been made. It is due to the inrush of cold air to take the place of the rarefied air which ascends from the heated coast. The mountains bordering the French Riviera compel the cold northern currents to turn round their western flank and so become a north-west wind.

Another wind which originates in the north is the **Tramontane.** It is hardly felt in the sheltered spots. Passing over the mountains in its path, it strikes the sea at a considerable distance from the shore, where it may be seen raising big waves. Occasionally when it has passed over the coast, the atmospheric conditions reflect it, and it returns as a cold south wind.

Originating in the African deserts is the **Sirocco,** which comes as a south-east wind, and is chiefly experienced in spring and summer. When the mountains of Corsica are heavily laden with snow, the sirocco is sometimes accompanied by sleet which is called the *Neige de Corse.*

With the exception of the sirocco, the south winds are not of great importance during the Riviera winter season. That from the south-west is not a wet wind, as in the British Isles, as it has been deprived of its moisture in passing over the Spanish mountains. The east wind of the Riviera also differs from the British east wind in being less dry.

Generally welcome winds are the land and sea breezes, caused by the difference in the temperature of the land and the sea, and experienced in fine settled weather.

The mollifying influence which the sea exercises on the climate of the neighbouring land is here greater than that of the Atlantic upon the winter climate of the western coast of Great Britain, because the temperature of the Mediterranean is higher than that of the Atlantic.

Finally, by reason of the latitude of the Riviera the sun has much greater power there at all seasons than it has over the coast regions of the British Isles.

In the six months, November to April, there are, speaking generally, six rainy days per month in the south of France, as against fifteen days in the south of England. For the whole period, Nice has, on an average, 36·2 rainy days; London, 89·5; but the quantity of rain which falls at Nice during that time approaches double the quantity which falls at London. Throughout the Riviera, when it rains, it pours, but thoroughly cloudy days and days of incessant rain are rare. When they do occur, however, it is chiefly at the autumn and spring equinoxes.

We have dwelt at some length on the less pleasing features of the Riviera climates in the endeavour to counteract extravagant reports which have led to so many disappointments. If we mention cold winds, it is but to emphasize the fact that even on the Riviera in winter the rays of the sun are cut off at morn and eve by the horizon and that when the sun is not shining the air is distinctly cool. But the world-wide reputation of the Riviera has been built on the predominant circumstance that it does receive, especially during the winter months, a far greater amount of sunshine than almost any other place in Europe.

A Land of Flowers.

By reason of the dryness of the climate of the Riviera, the great characteristic of the vegetation is the evergreen nature of the trees and shrubs. And by reason of the comparatively high temperature much of the vegetation has the additional charm of being semi-tropical.

Everywhere along the coast are palm trees in abundance. They look so much at home that it comes almost as a shock to learn that they are all foreigners, as indeed are nearly all the trees which attract the notice of the visitor by their foliage, flowers or fruit.

A charming tree cultivated as an ornament is the Californian Pepper, owing its name to the pepper-corn form and taste of its red berries, which hang in pretty grape-like bunches. The leaves may cause the tree to be mistaken for an acacia, of which the Riviera has an endless variety. They are known by the general name of Mimosa, and form one of the most beautiful of the floral sights of the region, which is indebted for them to Australia. Also from Australia are the Eucalyptus or Blue Gum Trees.

Preferring stony, burnt-up soils are the Carouba or locust trees, among the most striking on the coast by reason of their dense crown of glossy foliage. Luxuriant specimens are met with between Villefranche and San Remo, either isolated on the sunny shore or in olive groves.

Of never-failing interest are the olive trees. Their riven and twisted trunks excite pity, until one has learned that they may have weathered the storms of centuries and may weather as many more. The fruit is generally harvested by being knocked down by means of long canes, a method mentioned in Deuteronomy xxiv, 20, together with an incitement to generosity towards the poor.

Not everywhere along the Riviera are both orange and lemon trees to be seen, as the latter are less hardy than the former. As the lemon tree flowers all the year round, there are upon it flowers and fruit of all ages at the same time.

As the sweet oranges grown on the Riviera are not, as a rule, of first-class quality with the exception of the Mandarines, it is the bitter variety of orange which is principally cultivated, and that less for its fruit than for its flower, used in the manufacture of perfume.

A fruit tree which the uninitiated may easily mistake at first sight for a laden orange tree is the Kaki, a native of Japan. The fruit begins to ripen in October, but it must be over-ripe before eaten, and care must be taken not to put into the mouth a piece of the skin, which is exceedingly astringent. The interior is pulp, somewhat between plum jam and apricot jam both in appearance and taste.

In striking contrast to the prevailing evergreens are the fig trees, whose great sprawling, crooked branches are naked when the winter visitors begin to arrive. One will look in vain for the bloom, as that is inside what we call the fruit.

Interspersed with the oranges and the figs there are trees of the almond, peach, apricot, mulberry, medlar, plum, cherry, pear, apple and quince, and as Dean Hole declared, " the bloom of these fruit trees amid the evergreens is a sight to make an old man young."

Hardly to be recognized on account of its size is the castor-oil plant, and those visitors who carefully cultivate an india-rubber tree in a pot will stand incredulous and amazed before the veritable forest trees in the Monte Carlo garden and elsewhere.

Mostly in stony ground and among rocks are prickly pears and other cacti. And forming a striking feature of early spring are the flowering aloes, whose spikes of orange or scarlet flowers somewhat resemble the " red-hot pokers " of English gardens. Commonly but erroneously called an aloe is the Agave, which came from South America to Europe in 1561. When, on the Mediterranean coast, it has been growing for 10 to 15 years, it sends up a flower stem which in a remarkably short time attains a height of from 15 to 20 feet, and has produced horizontal branches which bear at the extremity bunches of greenish-yellow flowers, which may expand in May. With its flowers expanded it is, as the peasants call it, God's candelabra.

Giving, when bearing its magnificent plume, quite an

[Hyères.

HYÈRES.

Bagarry.]

MONACO.

Eastern touch to the landscape in many spots is the Great Reed, the *Arundo Donax*, commonly called a bamboo.

Of the other vegetable productions nothing more can be said here but a word or two about the flowers which are in great demand for exportation and for the fabrication of perfume, so that their cultivation is general and has reached enormous proportions.

If abundantly watered, the soil, warmed by the sun, will grow almost anything. The rapidity and luxuriance of growth astonish visitors from northern climes. Astonishment and interest also will be excited by a visit to a flower and vegetable market in one of the great towns.

The Animal Life.

A feature which forces itself on the attention of visitors from the British Isles is the comparative rareness of birds. One may take long walks in the country without seeing or hearing a bird, and in the towns the ubiquitous sparrow is present only in small numbers. The principal cause of this paucity of birds is the practice which " sportsmen " make of firing at every feathered creature seen within range of their weapon. To go out shooting on Sunday is a very popular form of recreation. The birds are protected during the breeding season. The end of the close season is marked by the appearance in the markets of blackbirds and thrushes that have gone into a sportsman's game-bag and are now to form a dainty and by no means cheap dish.

In the Maure Mountains and other suitable habitats are magpies in abundance, jays, hawks, screech owls, common brown owls and nightjars, and an occasional hoopoe may be heard or seen. Swallows return in the middle of March and the nightingale a month later. The first note of the cuckoo may be heard a few days earlier than in England.

The quadrupeds include wild boars and their destruction is a necessity. Occasionally one changes places with its pursuer.

The Riviera is the habitat of a variety of snakes. One is a big fellow four feet long. It has a khaki-coloured back, along which are two black lines. Its underside is white. A foot longer grows the lizard-snake. Its upperskin is olive brown. It hisses loudly and in each jaw is a large sharp fang, but happily its bite is not dangerous.

The true lizards are innumerable. As there is no reason

Riviera (b)

to fear them, they should not be harmed. One, found on hill-sides in the open country, is often from twelve to eighteen inches in length. Its skin is of a brilliant green dotted with turquoise spots, from which it has derived its name of the Eyed Lizard.

There are pretty bright green frogs which ordinarily live in shrubs and trees, but in spring assemble in the pools, streams and tanks. As soon as the frosts are over the males begin to make night hideous by their croaking.

Of insect life, using the term in its widest sense, the whole region is full. There are gigantic grasshoppers whose marvellous appearance and leaps may afford endless amusement. There are crickets, great grey locusts, blue-black carpenter bees, praying mantis, sand-wasps and mosquitoes.

The mantis so closely resembles the twig on which it settles that it is not easily distinguished. Its forelegs being then bent, it has the appearance of praying. " Little old man, pray for me," say the peasants, to whom the curious creature is an object of superstitious reverence.

The sand-wasp, a creature with a long red and black body, may be seen in April searching among the roots of thyme for a grey grub, or digging a hole in which to place its prey after having paralysed it by stinging it. When the grub is in its grave, the sand-wasp lays in it a single egg from which will come a grub that will feed on the paralysed one.

The mosquito is more annoying than interesting. As it may carry infection, prudence dictates its being kept at a distance. Among the precautions taken are closing the windows early in the evening before the room is lighted, sleeping under a mosquito net, and placing suitable netting in the window frames so that the windows may be left open, a condition on which the English generally insist, much to the wonderment of the natives. Not all parts of the Riviera are equally infested. Those with tanks and swamps are the worst.

Here and there on wayside walls and banks may be seen the soft greenish light of glow-worms, whose tiny lamps are more brilliant than those of their kind in Britain, and with April there comes the first of the warm evenings when fire-flies flash like minute rockets through the foliage, appearing and vanishing, rising and falling.

Very interesting are the trap-door spiders. In the sides of banks and in the interstices of loosely-built walls they construct round tubes lined with silk and closed by a hinged lid. In the French Riviera they are most abundant in the neighbourhood of Cannes and Menton. The nest is more easily found in the evening, when the lid is generally half-raised and the spider is on the look-out for prey.

No less interesting are the harvesting ants, either wholly black or red-headed. On waste ground they may be seen taking to their nest seed grains, from which before storing they nibble off the embryos to prevent germination.

As may be imagined, the butterflies and moths are early on the wing in the Riviera, and comprise specimens rarely if ever met with in northern climes. If the humming-bird moth is seen hovering over flowers, the aptness of its name will be at once apparent. It is a large brown moth with mouse-like body and head, small wings, and a very long tongue usually curled up.

Neither striking nor pretty is the Procession Caterpillar Moth, the Bombyx of the pines, but the extraordinary proceedings of its progeny make it interesting. The young hatch out in September, and after feeding they reassemble on the pine needle holding their cradle. There they spin a globular gauze tent which day by day is made larger to accommodate their growing bodies. In February, or on fine days even earlier, they may be seen moving in single file. Almost imperceptible is the movement and so compact are they that they look like a long, grey, woolly catkin. The procession describes a curve which takes the strange creatures back to their nest. But in March there comes a day when the procession does not return. It has reached a sandy spot suitable for a subterranean resting-place. The leader begins to burrow and is imitated by each of his followers. They descend three inches or a little more, and then each gradually becomes enveloped in a cocoon.

Historical Note.

The history of the Mediterranean coastlands included in the Riviera is practically the same in its main features. They were inhabited in prehistoric times, as is evident by the discovery of the implements of men of the Stone Age, the caves in which they lived, and even their skeletons, some of which may be seen in the museums at Menton.

Of the greater part of the French and Italian Rivieras

the first of the inhabitants known by name were the Ligurians, who built hill forts of which there still exist important remains. In the sixth century B.C. their possession of the coast began to be disputed by adventurous Greeks, especially the Phocéens, inhabiting Phocée, one of the great cities of Ionia.

About 237 B.C. the Greeks at Antibes invited the Romans to help them to repel the native tribes. The solicited assistance was given, and then occurred what is said to have happened between six and seven centuries later, when the warriors of tribes on the east side of the North Sea had aided the Britons to repulse the Picts and Scots. The Romans liked so much the country to which they had been invited that they founded settlements in it and finally became its rulers. Of their buildings the Riviera still possesses interesting remains, and the lines of their roads may be traced by the milestones, bridges, inscriptions, tombs and altars along them.

When the downfall of the Roman Empire left helpless the territories which it had protected, a great part of the Riviera was, during centuries, the prey of a succession of barbarous invaders. The Saracens established themselves at various points along the Provençal coast—the coast of the Roman Provincia, of which the French Riviera is a great part. For some three hundred years they held the district of the Maure Mountains, at the western end of the Riviera, and there are villages of which the inhabitants show marked traces of Saracen ancestry.

The Saracens were expelled in 792, and although neither they nor any other barbarians afterwards obtained a footing in the land, yet the coast continued to be harried by pirates. Piracy was supreme in the Mediterranean until 1816, when Lord Exmouth bombarded Algiers, but it was not extinguished until the French took possession of Algiers in 1830. At the time of the British bombardment of the port, there were thousands of Europeans in slavery in the Algerine galleys. They were mostly natives of the northern Mediterranean shore, taken from fishing boats or sailing vessels, or carried off from coast towns and villages.

On account of the piratical attacks to which the north coast of the Mediterranean was so long exposed, settlements were established on the hills. Some of the hill towns are among the novel sights of the Riviera.

Books to Read.

Even if regard is paid only to books written in English, the works of fiction, history, topography, biography or natural history based upon the French Riviera are almost innumerable.

We do our best to indicate some of the more outstanding volumes in each class, but the list could be extended indefinitely. Most of the works mentioned are obtainable at any good bookshop; others must be sought in libraries or at second-hand book stores.

Among the English novels are *Mary at Monte Carlo*, by C. N. and A. M. Williamson; *The White Olive* and other romances of the Riviera, by Fato Profugus; *The Coming of Amos* and *The Town of Tombarel*, by W. J. Locke; *The Prodigals of Monte Carlo*, *Mystery Road*, and *Mr. Grex of Monte Carlo*, by E. P. Oppenheim, and numerous "thrillers" by Wm. le Queux; Alice Campbell's *Juggernaut*, J. L. Campbell's *The Miracle of Peille*, the Peille of the title being a rough mountain village a few miles north of Monte Carlo; *The World of William Clissold*, by H. G. Wells; *The Poisoned Paradise*, by Robert Service, and Grant Richards's *Caviare* and *Every Wife*; *One of these Days*, by M. Trappes-Lomax, who charmingly relates the legend of Ste. Dévote; Conrad's *Mirror of the Sea*, and *The Rover*.

Perhaps not less interesting than novels are *The Romance of Nice*, by John D. Loveland; and *The Romance of Nice*, by J. Douglas; *The Riviera*, by the Rev. Hugh Macmillan; *The Riviera of the Corniche Road*, by Sir Frederick Treves; C. Kingston's *Romance of Monte Carlo*; *Romance and Legend of the Riviera*, by Ysabel de Witte; *Romance of Monaco*, by Ethel C. Mayne; *The French Riviera*, one of the Picture Guides published by the Medici Society; *The Riviera*, painted and described by Wm. Scott; *The Rivieras*, by Augustus Hare; *Things Seen on the Riviera*; Professor Strasburger's *Rambles on the Riviera*, and *Riviera Rambles*, by C. A. Voigt; *A Book of the Riviera*, by S. Baring-Gould, gives many historical peeps at the region; *The Riviera Coast*, by Capt. Leslie Richardson, and *The Coast of Pleasure*, by Grant Richards; *The Riviera Ancient and Modern*, by Charles Lentheric; Frances M. Gostling's *Rambles about the Riviera*; *Our Autumn Holiday on the French Riviera*, by J. E. Molloy;

Along the Riviera of France and Italy, by Gordon Home ;
French and Italian Riviera, by Helen Waters ; *A Traveller
at Forty*, by Theodore Dreiser, has several pages about
Agay ; *Riviera Towns*, by H. A. Gibbons ; *Menton*, by Dr.
George Miller ; *Menton and its Environs*, by an Englishman ;
Cannes and the Hills, by Réne Juta ; *Nice and her Neighbours*,
by Dean Hole ; *The Lure of Monte Carlo*, by C. N. and A. M.
Williamson ; *In Monte Carlo*, by Henryk Sienkiewicz ; of
long ago but extremely interesting, Smollett's *Travels through
France and Italy*, and *Letters from Nice*.

For specialists are *The Flora of Menton*, by J. T. Mog-
gridge, and by the same author, *Harvesting Ants and Trap-
door Spiders* ; *Flowering Plants of the Riviera*, by H. Stuart
Thompson ; Kirby's *Manual of European Butterflies* ; Bick-
nell's *Flowering Plants and Ferns of the Riviera* ; *The Birds
of the Riviera*, by Collingwood Ingram.

Concerning the climate are *Winter at Menton*, by Augustus
Hare, and Brown's *Wintering on the Riviera* ; Dr. Bennett's
Winter and Spring on the Shore of the Mediterranean, and
Sparks's *The Riviera*.

Among books for those who read French are—*Le Calvaire
de Cimiez*, by Henry Bordeaux ; *La Fée de Port-Cros*, by
the same author ; *Jean d'Agrève*, by Vicomte Melchior de
Voguë, and Jean Aicard's *Maurin des Maures* and *L'Illustre
Maurin* ; *L'Ane de Gorbio*, by Dominique Durandy ; *Charme
Dangereux*, of which the scene is laid at Nice, by André
Theuriet, from whose pen has also come *La Maison des
deux Barbeaux* ; Chateau's *Le Secret du Docteur Ludus* has
much to say about gambling ; *Mon Pays, Villages and
Paysages de la Riviera*, by D. Durandy ; *Nice Autrefois*,
by Edouard Arène ; *Au Pays bleu*, by Henri Moris ; *Nice
d'Antan*, by Leon Sarty ; *Mon Oncle Celestin*, by Jules
Fabre, who has produced a graphic picture of country life
and country people in the south of France ; *La Turbie et
son Trophée Romain*, by Philippe Casimir ; *Contes Populaires
des Provençaux*, by Beranger-Feraud ; *La Riviera Inconnue*,
published by Les Malles de France ; *La Provence des Alpes
Maritimes*, by Bosis.

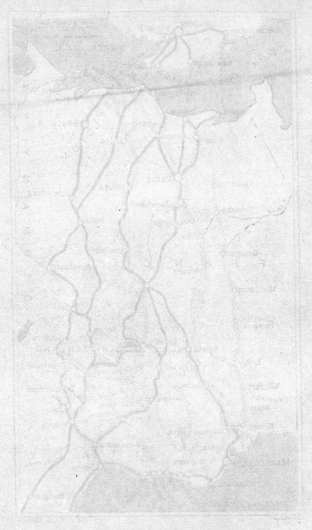

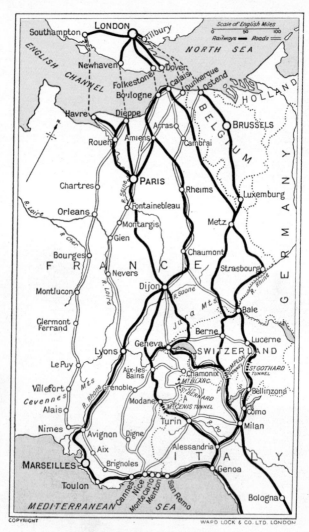

ROUTES TO THE RIVIERA.

ROUTES TO THE FRENCH RIVIERA.

MOST of the routes from England to the Riviera run *viâ* Paris. There is a choice of four routes to Paris by the Southern Railway in England and the Nord and Etat Railways in France, viz., *viâ* **Dover-Calais** or **Folkestone-Boulogne,** arriving at the Gare du Nord ; *viâ* **Newhaven-Dieppe,** arriving at the Gare Saint-Lazare ; and *viâ* **Southampton-Havre,** arriving also at the Gare Saint-Lazare. For current details as to times, fares, etc., the *Continental Handbook* and other publications of the Southern Railway should be consulted. There is also the somewhat longer route to Paris and the South *viâ* Tilbury-Dunkerque (*see* L.M.S. Handbook).

In connection with the 11.15 a.m. train [1] from London (Victoria) *viâ* Dover-Calais the Calais-Mediterranean Express (the **Blue Train**), composed exclusively of 1st class sleeping cars and dining cars *de luxe*, runs daily during the winter season, and during certain months goes on to San Remo, Alassio and Genoa. In connection with the 2 p.m. train from London (Victoria) *viâ* Folkestone-Boulogne (during summer 11.15 a.m. *viâ* Calais) a through train with restaurant facilities runs daily between Boulogne (Calais in summer) and Ventimille (Nice in summer), providing lits-salon (winter only), couchettes, and first or second-class seats which may be reserved in advance ; to this train a through coach for Hyères (providing lits-salon and first and second-class seats) is usually attached during the winter from about the middle of December.

Passengers travelling *viâ* Newhaven-Dieppe can avail themselves of a through coach to the P.L.M. Station (Gare de Lyon) and thus obviate the necessity of driving across Paris. Passengers utilizing any of the other services, not specifically enumerated above, must drive across Paris, or, if they have only hand-luggage, may reach the P.L.M. Station by Metro or Bus.

By the best trains the through journey to Nice occupies about 24 hours. Those who dislike night travelling may spend the night in Paris and the next in Marseilles, completing the journey the third day.

[1] It is understood that all references in this book to travel facilities, fares, fees, etc., are subject to verification by current announcements.

During winter the *Cote d'Azur Limited Express* (first-class Pullman cars only) leaves Paris (Lyon) each morning, reaching Ventimille (frontier) at midnight, practically the whole journey being done in daylight. In the opposite direction, Paris is reached about 11 p.m.

Those desiring " *luxe* " travel go by the *Golden Arrow* service from London (Victoria, 11 a.m.) and sleep the night in Paris, completing the journey next day by the *Cote d'Azur Limited*.

Sleeping Accommodation.—Berths in sleeping cars should be reserved in advance at the office of the *International Sleeping Car Co.*, 20, St. James's Street, London, S.W.1 ; *Lits-Salons* and *Couchettes* at the P.L.M. Office, 179, Piccadilly, W.1. Sleeping accommodation in the form of Lits-Salons and Couchettes is provided on the night Expresses and Rapides from Paris. The " Lits-Salon avec draps " (with bedding) is a compartment containing two couches placed side by side ; both of these compartments are provided with private toilet accommodation and are well ventilated. The Couchette is a compartment containing four berths, two upper and two lower ; it is much less expensive than any other form of sleeping accommodation and quite comfortable—during the day it is changed into an ordinary first-class compartment, the two upper berths being closed up.

Application for the reservation of sleeping accommodation and first- or second-class seats should be made about fifteen or twenty days prior to the departure of the passenger, and the cost of the accommodation must be prepaid.

Luggage.—Passengers, 1st, 2nd and 3rd class, on the French Railways are allowed 66 lb. of personal luggage free ; all excess to be paid for. All luggage should be clearly labelled with the name and destination of the traveller.

Customs.—Luggage registered through to the Riviera by the Calais-Mediterranean Express (Blue Train), as well as hand-luggage, is examined on the train directly after leaving Calais.

Luggage registered through to the Riviera by the Through Rapide (2 p.m. from London *viâ* Boulogne in winter and 11.15 a.m. *viâ* Calais in summer) will not be examined at the French port, the following special arrangements having been made :—

(A) From June 1 to July 31.—Baggage registered to Marseilles, Hyères, St. Raphaël-Valescure, Cannes, Nice, Menton and Ventimiglia examined at destination ; at Calais for Monaco and at Marseilles for baggage registered to all other Riviera stations. (Baggage registered to stations on the Chemins de fer de la Provence will be examined at Hyères if registered *viâ* Hyères, and at St. Raphaël if registered *viâ* St. Raphaël :—Baggage registered to Agay, Le Trayas, Théoule and Mandelieu will also be examined at St. Raphaël.)

(B) Remainder of the year.—Marseilles, Hyères, St. Raphaël-Valescure, Cannes, Nice, Beaulieu, Monaco, Menton and Ventimiglia will be examined at destination; at Marseilles for Toulon and Fréjus; at Cannes for Golfe-Juan-Vallauris, Juan-les-Pins, Antibes, Grasse; at Nice for Cap d'Ail and Villefranche-sur-Mer; at Monaco for Monte Carlo and Cap Martin Roquebrune, and at Menton for Menton-Garavan. (Baggage registered to stations on the Chemins de fer de la Provence will be examined at Hyères if registered *via* Hyères, and at St. Raphaël if registered *via* St. Raphaël:—Baggage registered to Agay, Le Trayas, Théoule and Mandelieu will also be examined at St. Raphaël.)

Baggage registered *via* Newhaven-Dieppe or Southampton-Havre to all destinations other than Paris (St. Lazare) is examined at Dieppe or Havre.

Luggage registered through to the Riviera *via* Calais or Boulogne by any other service is examined at the French port. Luggage registered to Paris only is examined at Paris Nord or Paris St. Lazare.

Customs Examination.—Travellers should be perfectly frank in their declaration concerning objects liable to duty. Dutiable articles should be conveyed only in hand baggage, not in registered luggage, as freedom of admission is accorded only to articles supposed to be for use during the journey.

No merchandise is allowed to enter into France free of duty. The importation of matches and playing cards is prohibited. The authorities usually allow men to have 10 cigars *or* 20 cigarettes, or 1½ ounces of tobacco. If more than one passenger in a party takes advantage of this, the quantity allowed must not be in one trunk or bag, but must be in the possession of each respective person.

By the courtesy of the English customs each passenger is allowed ½ lb. of tobacco, ½ pt. of spirits, ½ pt. of perfume and a moderate quantity of other dutiable articles, such as sweets and chocolate. If the permitted quantities are exceeded, the duty will be levied on the total quantity.

Cameras, field glasses, watches, silk stockings, silk dresses and all other dutiable articles taken out of Britain on a holiday visit and brought back, are allowed in free if ample proof is forthcoming that they were bought in Britain.

It is a mistake to suppose that articles bought abroad and worn for a time are allowed to pass free. *See also* p. 147.

TO THE RIVIERA BY SEA.

An increasing number of visitors take advantage of the fact that all parts of the French Riviera are linked by road or rail with the great port of **Marseilles.** Liners call here on the way to and from England, America and other countries, and as the journey from England takes several days, there is sufficient time on board to enable one to savour something of the joy of a holiday at sea.

In the Italian portion of the Riviera is the port of **Genoa**, also visited by the liners of many nations and also linked by rail and road with all the Riviera centres.

In addition, there are a number of **Steamship Cruises** which include the Riviera coast in their itinerary, with opportunities for landing at Nice, Cannes, Menton, Monte Carlo, etc.

For further particulars apply—*P. & O. Steamship Co.*, 14, Cockspur Street, Charing Cross, S.W.1 ; *Royal Mail Steam Packet Co.*, America House, Cockspur Street ; *Blue Star Line*, 3, Lower Regent Street, S.W.1 ; or one of the Agencies mentioned on p. 32.

BY AIR.

By means of the London-Paris and Paris-Marseilles services it is possible to breakfast in London and arrive on the Riviera coast in time for dinner the same day. Passengers are allowed 14 kilos (30 lb.) of luggage free ; considerably more may be taken on payment of an additional charge.

Particulars as to times of starting, etc., can be obtained from Imperial Airways, Ltd., Croydon Aerodrome, Surrey ; Airways House, Charles Street, London, W.1 ; and 38, Avenue de l'Opéra, Paris ; at Air-Union, Croydon Aerodrome, Surrey ; 52, Haymarket, London, S.W.1, and 9, Rue Auber, Paris, or at tourist agencies.

MOTORING TO THE RIVIERA.

Recent improvements in French main routes and increased facilities for the transport of cars across the English Channel have done much to popularize the motoring to and from the Riviera. By the most direct route the distance from coast to coast is about 700 miles, and the general quality of the road can be gauged from the fact that on more than one occasion a car has travelled between the Riviera and the Channel more speedily than the Blue Train. The ordinary mortal will deplore such misuse of opportunities of seeing something of France and will spend at least three days on the road. Much, of course, depends upon the time at which the car is ready to leave the Channel port ; and in this connection the Automobile Association and the Royal Automobile Club render invaluable service to members by arranging for customs-deposit formalities to be carried out in England

and by reducing the port formalities to a minimum. Motorists and others derive many advantages from membership of the *Touring Club de France*, 65, Avenue de la Grande-Armée, Paris. The fee is very small and admission is without formalities.

Rates for transport of cars across Channel vary according to the size of car, but for an average touring car the return fare is about £10. For full details *see* Southern Railway *Continental Handbook*, or apply Messrs. Townsend Bros., Ltd., Leadenhall Street, E.C.

The **direct route** (*see* sketch-map facing p. 23) lies either through or just round Paris and thence goes through Fontainebleau, Montargis, Nevers and Lyon, from which the valley of the Rhone is followed to Avignon. Then comes Aix in Provence, followed either by Toulon or by Brignoles to Fréjus on the coast, 740 miles ; Cannes, 761 ; Nice, 782.

An *alternative route*, preferred by some who are not bent on getting to the Mediterranean in the shortest possible time, has Dieppe or Havre as the port for disembarkation. Thence the way is through Rouen, Chartres, Orleans, Bourges, Montluçon, Clermont Ferrand, Le Puy, over the Cevennes Mountains and through Pradelles and Villefort to Alais, on the plains. Thence to Nimes, Avignon and Aix in Provence, and then either through Toulon and along the coast road to Fréjus, or through Brignoles to Fréjus. Thence either over the Esterel Mountains or along the beautiful Corniche d'Or coast road. The two meet at Cannes. This route is about 70 miles longer than the direct Dieppe-Paris-Cannes route, of which the length is 650 miles.

If time can be spared, an interesting *détour* is from Villefort to Nimes *viâ* Florac, the Gorge du Tara (one of the finest in Europe), Millau and Le Vigan.

Many motorists make use of the very fine *Route des Alpes*, by which Nice is reached from Western Switzerland *viâ* Grenoble.

Motor Coaches meet the boats at Boulogne and make a non-hurried journey to the Riviera. Inclusive prices are quoted for the journey, hotel accommodation, gratuity and services of a courier. A very fine run is that known over the Routes des Alpes, by which Nice is reached from Chamonix. This service is run by the P.L.M. Railway, who issue combined rail and road tickets from Paris, etc.

The principal tourist agents (*see* p. 32) can give full particulars and reserve places for all routes.

HOTELS AND TARIFFS.

So numerous are the Riviera hotels that in the following list hotels de luxe have perforce been omitted, as have also the hotels with a very low tariff. The Syndicats d'Initiative will send a complete list of the hotels in their respective districts (*see* p. 32). (Or apply to *Office, Nationale de Tourisme*, 56, Haymarket, S.W.1, for *Les Prix des Hotels en France*.) The figures enclosed in brackets ( ) indicate the number of rooms, the others represent the charge, in francs, for a room and three meals per day. In the winter resorts prices are highest during the first three months of the year and are considerably reduced at the beginning and at the end of the season. " Pension " terms are only allowed when the visitor takes the room for at least 3 days. Generally the minimum time is longer. For a room only, the charge would be about half the inclusive terms. In all cases there must be added 10 per cent. for service, or for tips if service is not charged for on the bill, and at the principal resorts there is a " *taxe de séjour* " (visitors' tax), payable during a month, and varying in each place and according to the grade of the hotel. Where the sum per day has been published it is shown below in italics. It is levied on French people as well as on foreigners. A percentage of the amount for board and lodging is also added to provide the tax which the State levies on the annual turnover. *It must be clearly understood that the proprietors are not bound by the prices quoted below or given in lists obtained directly from the Syndicats d'Initiative. They should be regarded merely as indicating what a visitor may be asked to pay. Only on application to the hotel can the actual terms be ascertained.* During the holiday season it is advisable to make arrangements in advance.

Some of the complete lists mention **Hôtels Meublés.** These have bedrooms only, so that guests must go elsewhere for meals, except for the *petit déjeuner*, the usual French breakfast of a roll with or without butter and jam, and coffee, tea or chocolate. This is not included in the charge for a room. There are also *Pensions de famille*—Boarding Houses.

The letters or word added to a place-name in the following

list indicates its department, which should form part of the address.

For list of Hotels on the **Italian Riviera** *see* pp. 148–151.

Agay (Var).

Rastel d'Agay : *fr.* 35.
Beau-Site : *fr.* 45.
les Roches Rouges : *fr.* 60.
La Baumette : *fr.* 60.

Anthéor (Var).

Flots Bleus : 35–40.
Genève-Mediterranée : 40–60.

Antibes (A.M.).

Antipolis-Mediterranée : (40) *fr.* 40.
Terminus : (60) *fr.* 45.

Beaulieu (A.M.).

des Anglais : (100) *fr.* 50.
Beaulieu : 50–80.
Empress : *fr.* 45.
Pension de Londres : (30) 40–60.
Pension O'Connor : (15) 40–75.
Royal : (40) *fr.* 50.

Beausoleil (A.M.).

New York.
Suisse.

Beuil (A.M.).

du Cians : *fr.* 35.
Nouvel : *fr.* 30.

Boulouris-sur-Mer (Var).

Grand : (40) 60–100.
Miramar : *fr.* 60.

Cagnes-sur-Mer (A.M.).

Savournin : (35) 32–40.
Golf : 30–40.

Cannes (A.M.).

(*The prices are those at the height of the Winter Season.*)
Alexandra, *Boulevard Carnot :* (50) 65–90, *1.30.*
Azur-Eden, *Boulevard Carnot :* (31) 60–85, *1.30.*
Campestra, *Boulevard Carnot :* (50) 60–80, *1.30.*
Cannes Palace, *Route d'Antibes :* (70) 65–75, *1.95.*
Regina, *Route d'Antibes :* (60) 70–95, *1.95.*
Saint Maurice, *Route d'Antibes* (25) 50–70, *1.30.*
Winter Palace, *Route d'Antibes :* (95) 75–90, *1.95.*
Luxembourg, *Rue d'Antibes :* (25) 50–70, *1.30.*
Victoria, *Rue d'Antibes :* (70) 70–120, *1.95.*

Canisy, *Route de Fréjus :* (38) 60–90, *1.30.*
Château St. Georges, *Route de Fréjus :* (40) 55–75.
Elysée Palace, *Route de Fréjus :* (60) 60–80, *1.95.*
Atlantide, *Rue Jean-Dollfus :* (35) 50–70, *1.30.*
Belle-Plage, *Rue Jean-Dollfus :* (30) 45–70, *1.30.*
Terminus, *Rue Maréchal Foch :* (30) 60–80, *1.30.*
Iles Britanniques, *Boulevard d'Alsace :* (80) 60–85, *1.95.*
Paris, *Boulevard d'Alsace :* (34) 45–70, *1.30.*
des Anglais, *Boulevard d'Italie :* (120) *fr.* 100, *1.95.*
Genève et d'Angleterre, *Boulevard d'Italie :* (30) 50–70, *1.30.*
Excelsior, *Rue de la Croix :* (40) 65–75, *1.95*
Hollande, *Avenue d'Oxford :* (45) 50–80, *1.30.*
Londres, *Rue du Canada :* (30) 50–70, *1.30.*
Balmoral, *Quartier St. Nicholas :* (50) 70–100, *1.95.*
Beau-lieu, *Hautes Vallergues :* (65) 60–80, *1.95.*
Bristol, *Av. St. Nicholas :* (65) 90–120, *1.95.*
Castleflor, *Pl. Commandant Maria :* (40) 50–80, *1.30.*
International, *Rue Maréchal Galliéni :* (43) 45–70, *1.30.*
Mediterranée, *Boulevard du Midi :* (200) 90–120, *1.95.*
Royal, *Promenade de la Croisette :* (50) 90–120, *1.95.*
There are other hotels at which the *taxe de séjour* is 1.95 or 1.30. There are also hotels at which the tax is 3.90, 2.60 or 0.65.

Le Cannet (A.M.).

Astoria : (60) 60–80.
Les Oliviers : (22) 50–75.
Roches Blanches : (40) 50–100.

Fréjus and Fréjus Plage (Var).

Grand.

Grasse (A.M.).

Belvédère : (140) 60–80.
Beau Soleil : *fr.* 35.

Grimaud (Var).

Beausoleil : (17) 35–60.

Hyères (Var).

Ambassadeurs : *fr.* 45.
Continental : *fr.* 45.
Métropole : *fr.* 45.
Chateaubriand : 60–80.
Grimm's Park : 60–70.
Iles d'Or : *fr.* 70.
Hespérides-Régina : 40–70.
Suisse : 30–50.
Maritima, *at La Plage* : *fr.* 50.
Plage, *at La Plage* : *fr.* 40.

COSTEBELLE—

Espérance : 40–80.
Mimosas : 40–80.
Montclair : 40–60.
Hostellerie Provençale and its annex
Le Manoir, *Ile de Port-Cros* : (50)
50–80.
Grand, *Ile de Porquerolles* : 36–40.
Sainte-Anne, *Ile de Porquerolles* :
28–40.

Juan-les-Pins (A.M.).

Pension la Rosaraie : (35) 55–70.
Pension du Golfe : *fr.* 35.
Terminus : (60) *fr.* 45.

Le Lavandou (Var).

de Provence : (75) *fr.* 60.

Mandelieu (A.M.).

Golf : *fr.* 55.
de Provence : *fr.* 45.

Menton (A.M.).

(*Minimum Winter Price.*)

Bristol, *Avenue Carnot* : (56) 60, *1.95.*
Excelsior, *Avenue Carnot* : (40) 55,
1.95.
Stella Bella, *Avenue Carnot* : (31) 55,
1.95.
Celine Rose, *Avenue du Careï* : (44)
45, *1.30.*
Gallia, *Avenue du Careï* : (50) 50, *1.95.*
Claridge, *Avenue de Verdun* : (32) 40,
1.30.
Europe et Terminus, *Avenue de Ver-
dun* : (60) 50, *1.80.*
Beau Rivage, *Garavan* : (60) 55, *1.95.*
Cecil, *Garavan* : (60) 60, *1.95.*
Palais des Fleurs, *Garavan* : (35) 50,
1.95.
Splendide, *Garavan* : (45) 45, *1.95.*
Albion, *Avenue de la Riviera* : (40)
40, *1.95.*
Ambassadeurs, *Rue Partouneaux* : (70)
50, *1.95.*
Colonies, *Avenue Félix Faure* : (70)
40, *1.95.*
Côte d'Azure, *Avenue Edouard VII* :
(24) 45, *1.95.*
Gay, *Place Honorine* : (30) 40, *1.95.*

Prince de Galles, *Avenue de la Madone* :
(45) 55, *1.95.*
Rives d'Azur, *Promenade du Midi* :
(30) 50, *1.95.*
Turin, *Rue Villarey* : (58) 55, *1.95.*
Annonciade, *Colline* : (50) 70, *1.95.*
There are other hotels at which
the *taxe de séjour* is 1.30 or 1.95.
There are also hotels at which it
is 2.60 or 0.80.

Monaco.

Condamine : (55) 45–65.
du Siècle : (24) *fr.* 40.

Monte-Carlo.

de la Réserve : (60) *fr.* 55.
Gourmets : (39) *fr.* 40–50.
Ravel : (45) *fr.* 50–80.
Renaissance : (45) *fr.* 40–110.
Suisse : (90) *fr.* 60–100.
Sun Palace : (75) *fr.* 50–90.
And many others.

La Napoule (A.M.).

Beau Rivage : *fr.* 40.
La Maïon Longa : (18) *fr.* 50.

Nice (A.M.).

The first figure represents the
minimum price before and after the
winter season ; the second represents
the highest price at the height of the
season.

Princes et Bellevue, *on the Sea-front* :
50–90, *1.95.*
Suisse, *on the Sea-front* : 70–90, *1.95.*
British, *At Cimiez* : 40–70, *1.95.*
Délice, *At Cimiez* : 50–100, *1.30.*
Albion, *Boulevard Dubouchage* : 50–
80, *1.95.*
Alexandra, *Boulevard Dubouchage* :
50–75, *1.95.*
Empéreurs, *Boulevard Dubouchage* :
65–120, *1.95.*
Pavillon Sévigné, *Boulevard Dubouchage* : 45–65, *1.30.*
de Liège : *Boulevard Victor Hugo* :
50–110, *1.95.*
du Louvre, *Boulevard Victor Hugo* :
55–110, *1.95.*
des Palmiers, *Boulevard Victor Hugo* :
80–120, 2.60.
Victoria, *Boulevard Victor Hugo* : 50–
80, *1.30.*
Brice, *Rue Maréchal Joffre* : 55–85,
1.95.
Busby, *Rue Maréchal Joffre* : 50–80,
1.95.
Edward's, *Rue Maréchal Joffre* : 65–
110, *1.95.*
Carabacel, *Avenue Désambrois* : 45–
70, *1.95.*
Colbert, *Rue Lamartine* : 45–75, *1.30.*

Concordia, *Rue Eugène Emmanuel :* 60–90, *1.95.*
Cosmopolitan, *Avenue Maréchal Foch :* 55–70, *1.30.*
d'Europe, *Rue Alberti :* 50–70, *1.30.*
du Parc, *Rue Alberti :* 45–90, *1.95.*
Gallia, *Rue Georges Clemenceau :* 65–100, *1.95.*
Gounod, *Rue Gounod :* 40–75, *1.30.*
Grimaldi, *Place Grimaldi :* 50–120, *1.95.*
Impérial, *Boulevard Carabacel :* 45–75, *1.30.*
de Pris, *Boulevard Carabacel :* 40–65, *1.30.*
International, *Rue Rossini :* 55–100, *1.30.*
Londres, *Rue Grimaldi :* 40–70, *1.30.*
Merveille, *Avenue Saint-Lambert :* 55–90, *1.95.*
Mont Blanc, *Rue François Aune :* 45–80, *1.30.*
Pacific, *Rue Rivoli :* 60–100, *1.95.*
Rivoir, *Rue Massenet :* 50–100, *1.95.*
Soleil d'Azur, *Rue Marceau :* 40–70, *1.30.*
Trianon, *Avenue Auber :* 45–75, *1.30.*
Windsor, *Rue Dalpozzo :* 50–100, *1.95.*
Berne-Phocéens, *Avenue Thiers :* 50–80, *1.30.*
Cécil, *Avenue Thiers :* 55–120, *1.95.*
Terminus, *Avenue Thiers :* 65–85, *1.95.*
Excelsior Funel, *Avenue Durante :* 45–70, *1.30.*
Richmond, *Avenue Durante :* 60–80, *1.30.*
Noailles, *Avenue de la Victoire :* 45–80, *1.30.*
There are other hotels at which the *taxe de séjour* is 1.30, 1.95 or 2.60. There are also hotels at which it is 3.90 or 0.65.

Saint-Aygulf (Var).

de la Plage : (40) *fr.* 45.

Saint-Martin Vesubie (A.M.).

Ideal Séjour : (26) *fr.* 45.
Regina : 45–55.

Sainte-Maxime (Var).

des Mimosas : 55–75.

Saint-Raphaël (Var).

des Myrtes : (20) *fr.* 40.
du Parc : (50) 60–90.
Select : (20) *fr.* 40.
Terminus : (35) *fr.* 40.
Touring : 40–50.
Beau-Rivage : *fr.* 70.
les Roches d'Anthéor : *fr.* 60.

Saint-Tropez (Var).

Mediterranée : *fr.* 40.
Sube et Continental : *fr.* 40.

Sospel (A.M.).

Etrangers : (16) *fr.* 35.
Golf : (80) *fr.* 80.
France : (15) *fr.* 35.

Tamaris-sur-Mer (Var).

Grand : (100) *fr.* 45.

Théoule-sur-Mer (A.M.).

Beau-Rivage : (24) 45–90.
Grand : 40–60.
de la Terrasse : (25) *fr.* 40.

Le Trayas (Var).

Estérel : (100) *fr.* 50.
de la Gare : *fr.* 40.
de la Poste : *fr.* 40.
Villa Véronese : 35–50.

La Turbie (A.M.).

Righi : *fr.* 65.
France : *fr.* 45.

Valescure (Var).

Anglais : *fr.* 45.

Vence (A.M.).

Ad Astra : *fr.* 50.
de la Conque : *fr.* 50.
Nouvel : *fr.* 50.

Villefranche (A.M.).

la Flore : *fr.* 60.
Welcome : (40) *fr.* 45.

PRELIMINARY INFORMATION.

Travel Agencies.—Full information regarding travel routes, fares, tours, hotels, etc., can be obtained in London from the *Office Nationale de Tourisme*, 56, Haymarket, London, S.W.1, or the P.L.M. Railway, 179, Piccadilly, W.1, so far as the French Riviera is concerned. For Italy apply at the *Italian Travel Bureau*, 16, Waterloo Place, London, S.W.1 (*see also* p. 141). These offices are extremely helpful and render their assistance free of charge.

Tickets and other information can also be obtained from the *Continental Enquiry Office, Southern Railway*, Victoria Station, London, S.W.1, and from *Messrs. Thos. Cook & Son, Ltd.* (Head Office: Devonshire House, Piccadilly, W.1); *International Sleeping Car Company* (20, St. James's Street, London, S.W.1); *Messrs. Dean & Dawson* (81, Piccadilly, W.1); *The Polytechnic Touring Association* (309, Regent Street, W.1); *George Lunn* (136, Wigmore Street, London); *American Express Co.* (6, Haymarket, S.W.1); *The Free Church Touring Guild* (Memorial Hall, Farringdon Street, London, E.C.4), and from the touring departments of many London and provincial stores.

Local Information Offices.—In France the traveller may obtain local information at the office of the *Syndicat d'Initiative* (Town Development Association), or in Italy at the C.I.T. or the E.N.I.T. office, that is, the office of the Compagnia Italiana Turismo or the office of the Italian State Tourist Department (Ente Nazionale per le Industrie Turistiche) (*see* p. 141).

If one writes from England, a 4*d*. International Reply Coupon (obtainable at any Post Office) should be enclosed for reply, but the leaflets and other local publications (for some of which a charge is made) may generally be obtained through the London Offices.

Clothing.—In winter one may generally wear what would be worn in April in England, but as the temperature falls at sunset, light woollen underwear is recommended as a guard against sudden chills. Warm wraps or an overcoat

ROQUEBRUNE.

A BIT OF OLD HYÈRES.

IN OLD MENTON.

should be taken for use on an occasional sunless day, and these should be carried when it will be necessary to pass from sunshine to shade, or if the hotel will not be reached before sunset. Ladies will often find a pair of long gaiters comfortable.

In summer easy-fitting light clothes should be worn. Shantung and tussore are excellent material for the outer garments of both sexes. Excellent also for men is light grey flannel. Ordinary boots and shoes are too hot for day wear. White tennis shoes are more comfortable. In an unconventional spot, rope-soled canvas shoes called *espadrilles* are recommended, but *not* for beach use. A pair may not last longer than a fortnight, but they are very cheap. A panama hat is the most comfortable headdress for a man in the sun.

When a bathing dress will be all that protects the body from the direct rays of the sun, olive oil or the inferior oil used for cooking should be well rubbed into the parts which will be exposed, in order to prevent the skin peeling. But *peignoirs* are necessary at bathing resorts, if one is not going to dress immediately on leaving the water. They can be bought locally.

At all seasons a small hat for travelling by train or for motoring is desirable, and a light dust coat of tussore or shantung is useful for train, boat or motor-coach travelling.

Soap should be taken, as very few foreign hotels provide that commodity. In the toilet compartment of a train, it is generally contained in a small machine affixed to a wall. It falls in powder when the handle is turned.

"Endeavour not to be too easily either contemptuous or scandalized at manners and customs strange to you. Especially in such small things as table manners standards are simply different. We English people pride ourselves on ours, but the Italians are ready to weep at our insult to good macaroni, and the Dutch at our ways with bread and butter, while the way in which we sit down to or get up from table without a greeting makes us barbarians in the eyes of Central Europe."—From Broadcast *Tips to Intelligent Travelling.*

Cost of Visit.—Travelling in France and Italy is not expensive. The tariffs on pages 29–31 and 149–151 will enable an estimate to be formed of the cost of living in a comfortable hotel. *Hôtels Meublés* (p. 28), furnished flats or villas and furnished rooms, which it is preferable to engage when one is on the spot, offer the means of living more cheaply than in an hotel.

Riviera (c)

Language.—While familiarity with the language of the country will of course add to the pleasure of a visit to its Riviera, those who are unacquainted with it should not, on that account, be deterred from going. English is very widely understood in the towns, especially in the hotels, and on the Ligurian Riviera French is almost a second language. At the same time a small phrase book will be of assistance and interest, and one can write what the tongue may be unable to pronounce.

Money is reckoned in France by the franc, which is now represented by a yellow aluminium coin issued by the Chambers of Commerce and for all practical purposes may be considered as worth two English pennies. Of the same metal there are coins of 2 francs and of 50 centimes (half a franc). Coins of smaller value are of white metal. They are pieces of 25 centimes (worth a ha'penny), 10 centimes, and 5 centimes. There are also in circulation old bronze coins of 10 centimes and of 5 centimes, the former looking like a penny, but worth less than a farthing, and the latter looking like a ha'penny.

The pieces of 5 centimes are called sous and the term is often used in quoting the price of articles of small value, 5, 12 or 14 sous, for example, being mentioned instead of 25, 60 or 70 centimes.

In 1928 the French Government decided to strike silver and gold coins. Even if they eventually replace the paper money, it will probably be a long time before they can do so. The **notes** in circulation are for 5, 10, 20, 50, 100, 500 and 1,000 francs. A note should not be accepted if it has not its number at each of the bottom corners.

In 1928 the franc was stabilized at 124·21 to the £, instead of the 25·2079 which was its value before the war. The value of 1 franc in English money is therefore slightly less than 2*d.* The approximate value of 5 francs is 9½*d.*; of 100 francs, 16*s.*; of 500 francs, £4; and of 1,000 francs, £8.

Prices and wages have risen to accommodate themselves to the new value of the franc, but, as in England, those living on their means are suffering from the depreciated purchasing power of their money. The French "rentiers," as this class is called in France, are especially hard hit, as their incomes are reduced in practice to one-fifth, if not less, of what they formerly were. With the exception of the rising generation of the French people, those who have to make purchases unconsciously give the franc its former value. They thus regard everything as excessively dear, and nothing makes them more angry than to hear an English or an American visitor express an opposite opinion. For the sake of international good feeling, visitors from the north side of the Channel or the west side of the Atlantic should not openly describe as cheap, because costing only so many twopences or cents, that which a Frenchman, giving its former value to the franc, must regard as dear.

How to carry Money.—Even for travellers who intend to buy tickets and meet other expenses as occasion arises, it is not necessary to carry a large amount of either English or foreign currency. The safest and simplest way of carrying money is to have Travellers' Cheques. They may be obtained either with or without a Letter of Identification, are issued free of charge by the principal banks and tourist offices and can be cashed free of charge in practically every banking town. Most hotels also accept them. They are issued in denominations of £5, £10, £20 and higher sums. Any not used can be cashed on returning home or added to one's current account.

The only foreign money a traveller need take with him is a small sum in notes of low denomination and a few coins for the first incidental expenses incurred. They can be obtained through his bank or at a tourist office. It is uneconomical to obtain them on the boat.

Passports.—Every traveller to France or Italy must be in possession of a passport. Its visa by a French or Italian Consul has been abolished for British subjects and the subjects of most other European countries, but citizens of the United States of America must have their passport viséd. The French Passport Office in London is at 51 Bedford Square, W.C.1; the Italian at 68 Portland Place, W.1.

British subjects resident in the British Isles can procure a passport direct from the Passport Offices, 1 Queen Anne's Gate Buildings, Dartmouth Street, London, S.W.1; or the Branch Passport Office, 36 Dale Street, Liverpool; or through a tourist office for a small charge in addition to the official fee, 7s. 6d. The first step is to apply to the Passport Office or to an agency for an application form. The passport should be obtained not only for France or Italy, but for any other country which may some time be visited. Passports are now generally available for five years. They may be made available for two persons (e.g. man and wife), but generally speaking it is preferable for each person to have a separate passport.

Foreigners who stay in France longer than sixty days must present themselves to the police with their identity papers and, according to the local regulations, either *four* or *five* photographs (as for a passport) in order to obtain a registration book (*Carte d'Identité*). The fee payable by a tourist is 100 francs. A wife must have her own *Carte d'Identité*.

Postal Information.—Post offices are generally open from 8 a.m. to 7 p.m. on week-days. They are closed on Sundays and on the legal holidays, which are—New Year's Day, Easter Monday, May 13 (Fête of Joan of Arc), Ascension Day, Whit Monday, July 14 (Fête Nationale—Fall of the Bastille), August 15 (Fête of the Assumption), November 11 (Armistice Day), and December 25.

In France.—For letters and closed packets posted and delivered in France the postage is 50 c. for 20 grammes, 75 c. for 50 grs., 1 fr. for 100 grs., and beyond that weight 30 c. per 100 grs. up to a maximum weight of 1,500 grs.

For ordinary post cards 40 c. ; illustrated post cards with only date, signature and address of sender, 15 c. ; with not more than 5 words in addition, 25 c. ; with more than 5 words, 40 c.

For newspapers, each paper weighing not more than 60 grs., 2 c., and 1 c. for each additional 25 grs. But half this rate for an address in the department in which the paper is printed or in an adjacent department.

For telegrams the charge is—

1. To an address in the same department or an adjacent department, 20 c. per word. Minimum charge 2 frs., and there is a sur-tax of 1 fr.

2. To other departments, 25 c. per word. Minimum charge 2 frs. 50 c. Surtax, 1 fr.

Abroad.—For letters sent abroad the postage is 1 fr. 50 c. up to 20 grs. inclusive, and 90 c. for each additional 20 grs. up to a maximum weight of 2 kilogrammes (nearly 4½ lb.).

For postcards (plain or illustrated), 90 c.

For newspapers, 30 c. per 50 grs.

For telegrams to Great Britain the charge is 1 fr. 25 c. per word ; to New York, 5 fr. 60 c.

Stamps may be obtained at tobacconists' shops. They are there compulsorily on sale.

Correspondence to be called for at a post office should be addressed to the " poste restante." To obtain it the addressee must give proof of identity. At some offices a visiting card is accepted ; at others the production of the passport is demanded. A fee of 30 c. is payable on each letter and 10 c. on each newspaper.

The name should be very clearly written and should not be followed by Esq., which is on neither a visiting-card nor a passport, and is a title unknown in France.

Another point to remember is that the name of the department should form part of the address. These are indicated in the list of hotels on pp. 29–31.

Registered letters are delivered only to the person to whom they are addressed and on proof of identity.

When handing in a letter to be registered (*recommandée*) there must be offered with it a form, obtainable at the post office, duly completed. The fee for registration is 1 fr. for a letter posted and delivered in France ; 1 fr. 50 c. if sent abroad.

The **Parcels Post** is under the administration of the railways. Parcels are not accepted at a post office, but must be sent from a railway station or from the office of an agent, who often displays the legend " colis postaux."

Railways.—Corridor coaches are the rule on the main lines of the French railways. Third-class carriages are, generally speaking, inferior to third-class carriages on the English lines.

Smoking compartments are labelled " *Fumeurs*." Some compartments are labelled " *Non-fumeurs*," and there may be ladies' compartments labelled " *Dames seules*." In compartments not labelled, smoking is permitted if no passenger objects.

The trains run on Sundays as on other days. The fastest are the " *rapides*." Some of these carry only first-class or first and second-class passengers, and most take only those passengers who are going at least a certain minimum distance. The " express " trains take all classes. The " omnibus " trains stop at all or nearly all stations. " *Trains légers* " are rail motors.

Seats from certain stations can be reserved in advance. Tourists making a long journey are advised to do this.

Luggage which the passenger cannot take with him to his seat, or from which he desires to be separated, must be presented at the station for registration several minutes before the train is timed to start. It cannot be casually handed to a porter to be put into the guard's van. If it contains valuables or expensive articles a special declaration should be made at the same time or (according to French railway law) no compensation will be payable in case of loss.

The railway " *porteurs* " who carry luggage to or from a cab and the train are entitled to payment. From an Englishman they expect at least 3 francs.

The cloak-room or left-luggage office is called *La Consigne*. Payment is made at the time of withdrawal.

Hotel porters generally meet the trains.

The principal stations have " *buffets* " where plain meals may be obtained. A " *buvette* " is a refreshment bar.

Return tickets are issued at all stations at a reduction of 25 per cent. first class, and of 20 per cent. second and third classes, on the price of two single tickets.

Time-Tables.—The complete French time-table, which covers the whole country, is the *Indicateur Chaix*, published fortnightly. It is much too heavy and cumbersome for the ordinary tourist. *Livrets Chaix* are published monthly for the various companies. The French Riviera is served by the P.L.M. (Paris, Lyon et la Mediterranée) Railway. Its time-table costs 3 fr. It is on sale at newspaper kiosks and railway bookstalls. A time-table giving main-line trains only and called *Principaux Services* can be obtained at the London office of the company (179 Piccadilly, W.1).

On the French railways time is reckoned from midnight to midnight. Thus both 0 and 24 express midnight, but the former indicates the commencement of a day and the latter its close. 2.20 p.m. English time is represented by 14.20 and 5 minutes after midnight by 0.05.

Time.—Greenwich Time is officially observed in France.

Weights and Measures.—As in money, so in weights and measures, the decimal system is followed. For the measure of length the unit is the *mètre*, and its square and cube are taken as standards of surface and capacity. The mètre may be compared with the English yard, to which it approximates. It is slightly longer than the yard, measuring 39$\frac{1}{3}$ inches, or in decimals, 39·371 inches. The *decamètre* is 10 mètres, or almost 11 yards ; the *kilomètre*, 1,000 mètres, by which distances are measured, may be taken as $\frac{5}{8}$ of a mile. Thus by multiplying a distance stated in kilomètres by 5 and dividing the product by 8, one gets the distance in English miles.

Going downward from the mètre there are the *décimètre*, or one-tenth of a mètre, nearly 4 inches, the *centimètre*, two-fifths of an inch, and the *millimètre*, one-tenth of a centimètre.

The common measure for land is the *hectare* (100 ares). It equals 2 acres 2,280 square yards, say 2$\frac{1}{2}$ acres.

The standard measure of capacity is the *litre*, about 1$\frac{3}{4}$ pints. The *décilitre* is the one-tenth of a litre, say $\frac{1}{10}$ of a gill, and the *centilitre* the one-hundredth of a litre. Going upwards there are the *décalitre* (ten litres) or 2$\frac{1}{8}$ gallons, and the *hectolitre* (100 litres) or 22 gallons or 2$\frac{3}{4}$ bushels.

In weight the unit is the *gramme*, equal to about 15$\frac{1}{2}$ grains troy, so that 10 grammes are equal to nearly $\frac{1}{3}$ of an ounce avoirdupois. The *kilogramme*, or 1,000 grammes, is the standard weight. It equals $2\frac{1}{5}$ lb. avoirdupois and is mainly used for wholesale business or heavy goods. Retail dealers often ticket and sell their goods by the *livre* (pound) or half kilo, weighing 500 grammes or $17\frac{1}{2}$ oz. For very heavy weights there are the *quintal*, weighing 220·4 lb. (within $3\frac{1}{2}$ lb. of 2 cwt.), and the *tonne*, weighing 1,000 kilos, or 2,200 lb. English, and thus approximating to the English ton (2,240 lb.).

The centigrade thermometer is used for the measurement of temperature. The freezing point is zero (0°) and the boiling point at 100°, instead of at 32° and 212° respectively, as in the Fahrenheit thermometer in general use in England. To convert centigrade degrees into Fahrenheit degrees, multiply the centigrade reading by 9, divide the product by 5 and add the result to 32, when the mercury is above zero but subtract it when the mercury is below zero.

HYÈRES.

Access.—*See* pp. 23–27. Travellers by the P.L.M. Railway leave the main line at Toulon and proceed thence by a branch line (13¼ miles). The stations are—*Hyères, La Plage d'Hyères* and *Salins d'Hyères*.

Hyères also has stations on the Light Railway (*Chemin de Fer de la Provence*) between Toulon and St. Raphaël.

Aerodrome belonging to the Aerial Navigation Service, 1¼ miles distant.

Amusements.—Concerts, dramatic performances, soirées dansantes, fancy dress balls, baccarat and boule. All in the Casino. Cinemas. Battles of Flowers. Carnival Processions.

Banks.—*English Bank* (R. J. Corbett & Co.), 26 Place des Palmiers; several French banks.

Distances.—By rail, London, 880 miles; Paris, 593¾ miles; Nice, 98¼.

English Consulate.—28 Rue d'Algier, Toulon, and every Thursday, Grimm's Park Hotel, Hyères, 2–4 p.m.

Hotels.—*See* p. 30.

Inquiries.—Syndicat d'Initiative, The Grand Casino. For inquiries by post, *see* p. 32.

Library.—Anglo-American, 40 Avenue des Îles d'Or.

Motor-buses.—To Toulon, Presqu'île de Giens, etc.

Motor-coaches.—P.L.M. and Mediterranéene services between Marseilles and Nice. To the Gapeau Valley; the Chartreux Monastery of Montrieux; the Gorges of Ollioules; along the Coast of the Maures; to Toulon, Tamaris, the Sablettes, etc.

Population.—22,000.

Post Office.—4 Avenue de Belgique. (*See* p. 36.)

Sports.—Golf at the Golf Hotel, 1½ miles east, and at Costebelle, 2 miles south. Both courses have eighteen holes and are on public motor-car routes. There are at least twenty tennis courts and several croquet lawns. Tournaments from October to May, and an international champion tournament in December. Squash racquets at Costebelle.

Sea- and sun-baths. A bathing establishment has sea-water baths.

Sea-fishing. Fresh-water fishing in the Gapeau.

Trams.—To Toulon, La Garde, La Valette, every 30 minutes.

HYÈRES, the western gateway of the Riviera, is 880 miles from London and the most southerly of the Riviera resorts. Time was when, next to Montpellier and Aix-en-Provence, it was the most famous health resort in the south of France. It was sometime the residence of Robert Louis Stevenson. From the chalet "La Solitude," on the road from the old town to the castle, he wrote to a friend: "My house is in the loveliest spot in the universe."

Also he wrote: "I sing daily with my Bunyan, that great bard, 'I dwell already next door to Heaven.' If you could see my roses, *and* my olives, *and* my view over the plain, *and* my view of certain mountains as graceful as Apollo, as severe as Zeus, you would not think the phrase exaggerated."

40

He had previously stayed at the Hôtel des Îles d'Or, since modernized, but retaining a chair and other furniture used by him.

The Maure Mountains protect Hyères from the north winds, but it is exposed on the east and south-east, and also on the west and north-west, whence comes the unpleasant mistral, which blows here with greater violence than elsewhere on the Riviera.

Hyères was the port at which crusaders embarked and to which they returned, and in the fourteenth century it was larger and more important than Toulon. Now it is a good 3 miles from the sea, but its suburb, **La Plage,** is on the coast and has a sandy beach shaded by pine trees.

When the construction of railways enabled travellers to reach in comparative comfort spots which were at once picturesque and at the seaside, Hyères very naturally failed to retain its pre-eminence. It still, however, has its faithful admirers.

Being away from the sea, palms grow freely at Hyères, and the town likes to be called "Hyères les Palmiers."

The **Town Station** of the P.L.M. railway is on the south-eastern border of the town. Avenue Edith Cavell leads to Place du 11 Novembre, whence the palm-planted **Avenue Gambetta** leads to the centre of the town.

Avenue Gambetta takes one past another main thoroughfare, the **Boulevard de Beauregard,** leading to the English Church. Farther along, the narrower Avenue Carnot leads on the right to the **Casino** in Boulevard Jean Jaurès ; then, also on the right, comes a thoroughfare which has changed its characteristic name of Avenue des Palmiers for Avenue de Belgique. This is the site of the principal **Post Office,** of the **Hotel de Ville** and *Grimm's Park Hotel*, a building of historic interest. It was originally a country seat, constructed in the eighteenth century in the midst of 18,000 orange trees on a site which until then had been part of the land attached to a royal residence which still exists in the curious Rue des Porches. Napoleon was entertained in the new mansion, and Joséphine resided in it during Napoleon's absence in Egypt.

Only a short distance farther the Avenue Gambetta meets the great thoroughfare—a portion of the Route Nationale—going to the left as the Avenue des Îles d' and to the right as the Avenue Alphonse Denis, which p

Place Georges Clemenceau, the **Museum** and **Library** and a large public garden.

At the top of a flight of steps mounting from the Place is a statue of a son of Hyères, *Jean Baptiste Massillon* (1663-1742), the greatest of French preachers. His published sermons were much read in England. On the right in the rear of the statue is the thirteenth-century **Church of St. Louis.** Behind the altar is a large picture of the landing of St. Louis (Louis IX) at Hyères in 1254 on his return from his first Crusade. The pulpit, a row of canopied stalls and the confessionals are all of walnut, beautifully carved.

Rue Massillon, going westward from Place Georges Clemenceau, and Rue Portalet, which continues the line of Avenue Gambetta, and at once has on the right Rue des Porches, lead to **Place Massillon,** where are a covered market and the Hôtel de Ville, originally a Commandery of the Templars. Massillon was born at No. 7 in the adjacent Rue Rabaton. Westward of the Place named after him is the **Church of St. Paul,** built in the eleventh or twelfth century and badly restored.

Rue St. Bernard, going westward from the church, turns northward to **Porte de la Souquette.** Turning sharply to the left at the gate, and keeping to the right at a fork, one is led by the winding Chemin de St. Pierre to the ruins of the **Castle** in which Louis IX was entertained in 1254 and François I nearly three centuries later. The principal points in the extensive view from this spot (652 feet above the sea) are indicated on an orientation table.

La Plage d'Hyères, the seaside quarter of Hyères, has a station on the branch line which connects Hyères with Toulon, and there is a motor service. The way out to the Plage is by a road which goes off on the left from Avenue Edith Cavell and leads over a level crossing near the stations (*see* Town Plan). The beach is of the finest sand and is shaded by beautiful parasol pines.

The *Rade* (roadstead) of Hyères, which faces the Plage, is much visited by yachts in summer.

From La Plage d'Hyères the branch railway goes northeastward along the coast for 2½ miles to—

The **Salins-d'Hyères,** where salt is obtained from the sea by the natural evaporation of the water which from time to time is allowed to flood a prepared area. The production of salt in this way was, in ancient times, the chief source of the wealth of Hyères. Of more importance now are the early vegetables, the fruit and the flowers cultivated on the great Plain of Hyères.

The aristocratic suburb of **Costebelle,** S.S.E. of the town, is approached by way of the Avenue Victoria, leading out of Boulevard de Beauregard (*see* Plan). There is a motor service. The suburb is situated in a valley among the pine, olive and cork trees of Mont des Oiseaux. It has excellent hotels, attractive villas, an English Church, and a golf course. In 1892 it was the residence of Queen Victoria. It has been well described as " a tiny self-contained England, easily the least cosmopolitan of all the winter resorts."

Above Costebelle is the thirteenth-century pilgrimage chapel of the Ermitage, with a modern tower surmounted by a gilded figure.

Excursions from Hyères.

There are numerous easy and pleasant excursions by field paths, by motor, by the P.L.M. railway, the light railway, electric tramways, and by boats.

Among the nearer spots which can be thus visited are :
The Maurettes, the heights immediately behind the town.
Mont Fenouillet, the highest point of a spur of the castle hill. A path to it from the castle runs through woods and thickets of arbutus. The view from the highest point, 900 feet, is finer and more extensive than from any other height in the immediate neighbourhood.
Mont des Oiseaux, 750 feet. A short walk leads to the Trou des Fées (the fairies' hole), a cave with stalactites.
St. Pierre d'Almanarre, a ruined convent 3 miles from Costebelle, from which a road goes southward, passing on the way the extensive but indistinct remains of the Roman town of *Olbia.* The return can be made by the Chemin de Fer de la Provence.
Les Salettes, a small fishing village between Hyères and Toulon.
Carqueiranne, a small summer resort in the same direction. It has a station on the light railway and gives its name to this part of the coast. There are remains of aqueducts and baths of the Roman Pomponiana.
The Peninsula of Giens, 7½ miles distant, is about 2 miles long. An excellent description of it is contained in Conrad's *The Rover,* most of the scene of which is laid on the headland of Escampobarion. This name signifies capsizer of casks, and has reference to the rough sea raised here by the meeting

of the mistral with the current coming from the east. A long stretch of salt marsh lies between the mainland and the town of Giens, at the extremity of the peninsula. Eastward of Giens is La Tour Fondue (the sunken tower), from which boats start for the Île de Porquerolles, one of—

The Islands of Hyères,

"The Isles of Gold" as they have been called on account of their mica-like rock which glitters in the sun. To the Romans they were the Stoccades, and were so named from the profusion of a kind of lavender, the *Lavandula Stœchas*. Its scent is strong but does not much resemble that of the true lavender. At the top of each spike is a large bunch of bright purple bracts. These are sterile. The true flowers are below and so dark as to seem almost black. The plants are in full flower at the end of March.

The most important of the islands is the **Île de Port-Cros,** to which have been given the poetical names of Île du Paradis and Boquet dans la Mer. It is both a winter and a summer resort. The principal accommodation for visitors is provided by the *Hostellerie Provençale* and its annex the *Manoir*. There is a regular daily service of boats between it and *Les Salins* (p. 42). Pines dip their branches in the sea and wild flowers grow down to the water's edge of the little bay, on which is an old fort. "Nowhere in Europe can one find such a sea of peacock-blue and green, nor such a wealth of wild flowers and beautiful vegetation as at Port-Cros of the Golden Isles" (Leslie Richardson : *The Riviera Coast*).

There are sandy coves with good bathing ; boating to the neighbouring islands, and some of the best sea fishing on the French Riviera.

Île de Porquerolles, about 4 miles long and half as wide, is the largest of the islands. It has many sandy beaches shaded by pines, and receives both summer and winter visitors, for whose accommodation there are hotels (*Îles d'Or* and *Sainte Anne*), and several boarding-houses. Boats run between the island and La Tour Fondue on the Peninsula of Giens (passage about 20 minutes), which is in communication with Hyères by motor-bus.

Levant is a large and barren island, and the remaining two islands are unimportant.

Inviting to—

Longer Excursions from Hyères

is the region of mountain and forest which motor coaches traverse daily. It is a region of which poets have sung and to which many legends are attached.

First there is the **Valley of Sauvebonne,** which at 7½ miles

N.W. from the town is overlooked by **Solliès Ville,** an ancient town nearly a thousand feet above sea-level. It has a twelfth-century church standing on the foundations of a Roman temple and protected as an historical monument. Another possession is the " Oustaou " (château) of Jean Aicard's amusing *Maurin des Maures,* and now containing the Museum commemorating the poet.

Then begins the charming **Valley of the Gapeau,** in which fruit is largely cultivated. Through it a picturesque road leads by rocky defiles to the **Chartreuse de Montrieux,** 17 miles, in a vast forest belonging to the State. Much farther to the north-west is **St. Maximin,** the reputed burial-place of Mary Magdalen, Lazarus and his sister Martha, their servant Marcella, Sidonius and Maximinus, a martyred bishop of Aix. Over their graves was built an oratory which attracted pilgrims. Then there arose a Benedictine Abbey. This, in the eighth century, was destroyed by the Saracens. The relics of St. Mary Magdaleñ, the most precious possession, were carefully hidden, and are now said to be in the crypt of the magnificent Gothic Church, an historical monument. The choir is profusely ornamented in the style of the seventeenth and eighteenth centuries. The altar dates from 1683. The stalls, 94 in number, illustrate the life of St. Dominic.

From St. Maximin the road rises gradually to the chain of the Sainte-Baume mountains, with an altitude of from 2,296 feet to 3,786 feet, and containing the grotto of the penitent Magdalen, who is said to have spent the last part of her life in it. It is in the face of a fine cliff, has been converted into a chapel, and since the end of the thirteenth century has been a famous place of pilgrimage. The climb to it is fairly stiff, along a zig-zag path and up flights of steps. Rising above the grotto, which must not be confounded with the grotto Sainte-Baume of Cap Roux (p. 57), is **St. Pilon** (2,952 feet), with the ruins of a chapel on a spot to which angels are said to have daily carried the saint to pray. The view from St. Pilon is very beautiful. On the summit is an orientation table.

Those who care to spend a few days at the hostellerie de La Sainte Baume can enjoy delightful rambles along the innumerable paths through the splendid forests.

Another route is by way of the village of **Ollioules,** from which there is a delightful view over the town of Toulon and the roadstead. From the village the road crosses the Reppe stream and then descends to the **Gorge d'Ollioules** in Mont Evenos. The cleft is 2½ miles long. On each side cliffs rise to a height of 300 feet, and the torrent flows in a series of lovely cascades. Thence the route is through the austere **Ravin du Destil,** in which are prehistoric caves, to the picturesque hamlet of Géménos. Soon afterwards the route enters the fertile valley of St. Pont, from which there is a steep ascent, necessitating many corkscrew turns, to the top of the **Col de l'Espigoulier** (2,183 feet). On the right is the loftier **Col de Bretagne** (2,628 feet), affording magnificent views.

Here is **Sainte-Baume,** protected by its own chain of mountains.

The return journey is full of charm, the route leading through the defile of the *Loube* and then through the forest of St. Julien.

The Maures

may be made the scene of innumerable excursions from Hyères. They are traversed by picturesque roads revealing marvellous views, and passing interesting spots connected with the history of the region when it was held by the Moorish pirates.

Fierce controversy rages over the name. Does it mean the mountains of the Moors or only the Black Mountains ? The inhabitants say that the name comes from " mauron," meaning black, and has allusion to the dark forests covering the hills.

The mountains lie between the sea and the main railway, and extend eastward from Hyères to the neighbourhood of St. Raphaël. They are composed of granite, gneiss and schist. In the early days of the French Revolution the golden dust of the mica schist sadly deceived a Representative of the Department, who hurried off to Paris with a handful of it to show to the Convention that at its disposal was untold wealth lying neglected through the ineptitude of the administration.

The inhabitants of the Maures live chiefly by the cork industry maintained by the great forests of cork oaks. The crown of these trees resembles that of evergreen oaks, but the leaves of the cork oak are ovate in form and have serrated edges. The stripping of the trunks gives the trees a most singular appearance. " The trunks are peeled till they look like red stockings," to quote Julius Hare. The newly stripped parts are almost blood-red in sunshine.

Spanish chestnuts are largely cultivated, and alternating with the cork woods are woods of Maritime pine to which much of the charm of the region is due.

The Coast of the Maures also can be easily and pleasantly visited from Hyères, as it is served by the P.L.M. motors and the Provence railway. Along it are many attractive little tourist centres, described in the next chapter.

THE LITTLE RIVIERA.

Access.—By the P.L.M. line to Hyères or to St. Raphaël-Valescure. At the former the P.L.M. and Provence Stations are quite close (see plan) at the latter they adjoin one another. All the little centres are on or near the light railway—the *Chemin de Fer de la Provence*—connecting Hyères and St. Raphaël; and Bormes, Le Lavandou, Le Canadel, Le Rayol, Cavalaire, Gassin, Pardigon, La Croix, are on the *Corniche des Maures*, the route of the P.L.M. motor-coaches. Seats on these should be reserved, as the number is limited (P.L.M. Office: 1 Avenue Gambetta, Hyères).
Hotels.—*See* pp. 28–31.

IT was a happy inspiration which gave this name to the district between Hyères and St. Raphaël. It is a region for those who wish to enjoy the winter sunshine of the Mediterranean coast in conjunction with country life, or to spend a summer holiday alternately sea-bathing and sun-bathing under free-and-easy conditions. There are charming bays and coves, fine scenery, a wealth of flowers, wonderful woods, and a multitude of strange and quaint sights, and the water along the coast is much cleaner than it is in the neighbourhood of great towns.

Starting from Hyères, the narrow-gauge line traverses a rich and highly cultivated plain. The little old town of **Bormes**, 8 miles from Hyères, is perched on a hill, 2¼ miles from the sea. It calls itself " Bormes-les-Mimosas "—how aptly only springtime visitors can realize. In the chapel of St. François is a modern statue of the saint—St. François de Paule—who came to the town in 1481 when it was stricken by a plague which he subdued.

St. François had landed, it is said, at **Le Lavandou,** a fishing village only 1½ miles farther along the line, where he was given a dish of freshly-made bouillabaisse, every morsel of which he ate, and then expressed his gratitude by blessing the village and the fishing, with the result that the fish taken off Le Lavandou excel those caught elsewhere on the coast.

Bouillabaisse is a dish for which every Provençal longs when he is living in a part of France where it cannot be procured. The proper cooking of it is alone sufficient to establish the reputation of an hotel. Here is a recipe obtained at one hotel. Mix together garlic, laurel leaves, white pepper, and olive oil. Fry the mixture in a casserole. Then pour over it a glass of white wine and add fish,

47

lobsters and small crabs, and water sufficient to cover the whole.
Then add more pepper and salt, boil for twenty minutes and finish
with a pinch of saffron.

The village owes its name to the abundance of lavender
of the same kind as that which grows so freely in the islands
of Hyères.   It is the centre of a bay along which pines grow
almost to the water's edge.   A sloping sandy beach offers
safe and pleasant bathing.   To the right, forming the western
horn of the bay, is **Cap Bénat,** with a lighthouse and a seventeenth-century castle.   During summer motor-boats maintain
a regular service with the Île-de-Port-Cros, and there are
always motor and sailing boats for hire.

Eastward of Le Lavandou is the beach of **St. Clair;** but
on account of holes, the bathing there is only for strong
swimmers.

Aiguebelle, 1½ miles north-east of Le Lavandou, consists of
little more than a station and an hotel (*Grand*; 37 bedrooms).

The next station is at **Cavalière,** which must not be confused
with a place farther eastward.   It is a flower-growing centre,
backed by heath-clad hills and facing a sandy cove so closely
shut in by pines that in rough weather the trees are washed
by the sea.

Cap Nègre separates Cavalière from **Le Canadel,** a charming
little winter and summer resort, 25 miles from Hyères.   It
has a sheltered, hard, sandy beach, excellent for bathing,
and on which cricket is played at low water.

Le Rayol is another small summer and winter resort, with
good sands which, with other attractive features, are re-
sponsible for great efforts to make the adjective " small "
inapplicable to the place.

Then comes **Cavalaire,** beautifully situated in a pine
forest on a large bay which has a beach of fine sand.
One may freely ramble in the adjacent forest.   Sea trips
and land excursions are organized.   Among the attractive
walks is that to the Sommet-des-Pradels, the highest point
(1,720 feet) of the Maures.   Inquiries may be addressed to
the President of the *Syndicat d'Initiative de la Baie de Cavalaire*, at Cavalaire (Var), *see* page 32.   The President will
also give information respecting **Pardigon** and **La Croix**.
The former has a station, an hotel and sands ; the latter is
a winter resort a mile from the sea, upon a hill golden in spring
when the mimosa is in flower.   The nearest beach is the
Plage of Héraclée, on the Bay of Cavalaire.

The next station serves the quaint hill village of **Gassin,** 650 feet above sea-level, with ramparts and an ancient church.

From the following station, **La Foux,** go two short branch lines—one to St. Tropez, the other to Cogolin-Grimaud.

St. Tropez, a quaint, picturesque, commercial town of 4,500 inhabitants, has changed little since the eighteenth century. Since the Great War it has had a colony of artists. It stands on a gulf named after it and over-looked by a citadel. In its church is a bust of St. Torpetius or Tropez. He suffered martyrdom under Nero, and his body was sent adrift in a boat with a dog and a cock, which were to feed upon it. But they left it untouched, and an angel steered the boat to what is now Tropez. On the quay is a statue of Vice-Admiral Pierre André de Suffren (1729–88), a great opponent of the English in the Indies. He was killed in a duel. The first turning beyond his *right* hand leads to the office of the *Syndicat d'Initiative* (p. 32) ; the next, to what remains of Suffren's château, marked by a tablet on the landward side. In the thoroughfare are an elaborately carved door and the Hôtel de Ville, and at the far end is an arch giving access to *La Ponche* (the point), where is the fisherman's port, attractive to artists. From May 16th to 18th an annual fête, called the *Bravade*, com-memorates the repulse of the Spaniards in 1637. In the Hôtel de Ville are three pictures representing the contest.

Less than 2 miles from St. Tropez is **Plage Pampelonne,** a sandy beach nearly 3 miles long. By the bus carrying the mails one can reach the village of **Ramatuelle** (7 miles), which retains its ramparts and the gate in them—the Portail des Sarrasins—from which the population repulsed the pirates by casting down upon them swarms of bees. The ancient church is decorated in the Spanish style.

Daily motor-bus services between St. Tropez and St. Raphaël *viâ* Ste. Maxime.

At **Cogolin** there is an oriental carpet factory open to visitors. Other industries are cork-cutting and the manu-facture of briar pipes. In the Romanesque Church is a triptych of 1540.

Grimaud (Grimaldi's town), 1½ miles north, was a strong-hold of the Grimaldis.

Five miles from Cogolin is **La Garde Freinet,** with the ruins of the fortress called Frascinet or Freinet, from which the Moors ravaged Provence and neighbouring regions.

Guerrevieille-Beauvallon station serves the village calling itself **Beauvallon-sur-Mer,** on the north side of the Gulf of

St. Tropez, and mainly important from its possession of an 18-hole golf course. It is 1½ miles from—

Sainte Maxime, the site of the next station. It has a population of some 2,500, and is becoming increasingly popular as a winter and summer resort. (For inquiries by post, *see* p. 32.) It stands at the foot of wooded hills, on the north side of the Gulf of St. Tropez, and faces south. It has a fine sandy beach sloping gently and more than a mile long. The stone pier forms a convenient diving platform, and on the shore is a bathing establishment. Motor and boating excursions are arranged, and in the summer a motor-boat service is maintained with St. Tropez. The *Casino* is used for concerts, dramatic performances, balls and cinema shows, as well as the customary boule and baccarat. Various fêtes are organized. There are tennis courts and the ease with which the golf course at Beauvallon can be reached counts for much with many visitors.

One of the best walks from Ste. Maxime is through woods to the semaphore on the hills. (Magnificent view.) Directions for this and other walks, as well as particulars of the excursions by rail or road, are given in a local guide obtainable gratuitously at the office of the Syndicat d'Initiative in the bank called the *Comptoir d'Escompte du Golfe.*

Ste. Maxime is only 13¾ miles from St. Raphaël, which has a station on the P.L.M. line, and in summer there is a service of P.L.M. motors between the two places.

Midway between Ste. Maxime and St. Raphaël, and served also by the P.L.M. motors, is the small, but growing, **St. Aygulf,** on a creek at the foot of the final slopes of the Maures. It has a sandy beach and commands fine views over St. Raphaël and the Esterels. Roads have been made through the adjacent woodlands and many villas have there been erected.

Between St. Aygulf and St. Raphaël is—

Fréjus,

the successor of Forum Julii (the market of Julius), named in honour of Julius Cæsar, who founded it that he might be independent of Marseilles, whose inhabitants had displeased him by siding with Pompey. The area was five times that of modern Fréjus. The harbour was so capacious that in it were placed 200 captured galleys. Under the Emperors of Rome it was the most important naval base on this coast.

But the debris brought down by the *Argens* silted up the harbour, over which the railway now runs.

The town is mainly of interest on account of the **Roman remains**. Briefly, these are portions of the ramparts—the Butte St. Antoine, which guarded the Porte of Agrippa, through which the railway runs ; the Porte-des-Gaules near the station ; the Platform, a citadel which commanded Cæsar's Porte, where is now the Chapel of St. Roch ; the Lantern d'Auguste, a landmark and signal station ; Porte Dorée, a narrow arch (much restored), once a water-gate, with the remains of the Baths near it ; the remains of the Porte-de-Rome, near remains of the aqueduct, 24 miles in length, and of which some of the arches were 60 feet high.

Steps opposite the station lead to **Place Agricola,** named in honour of the Roman general who completed the conquest of Britain, A.D. 80, and who was born at Fréjus. On the Place is the church of **St. Françoise de Paule,** dating from the fifteenth century. Over an altar is a statue of the saint, and on the adjacent wall are numerous votive offerings including a model ship and two muskets.

St. François de Paule came to Fréjus in 1482 and freed the town from a plague. His landing is commemorated on the third Sunday after Easter, when the incidents connected with his arrival are represented. The house in which he stayed three days is in the Place-de-l'Eveché, where are also the old fortress palace of the bishops, now the Hôtel de Ville, and the chief building in Fréjus, the **Cathedral,** originally erected in the eleventh or twelfth century. On the door (*gratuity to sacristan who uncovers it*) are carvings representing the life of the Virgin. In the choir is sixteenth-century woodwork. Other objects of interest are a sixteenth-century painting of the Holy Family, a triptych, statues of two kneeling bishops, at the west end of the north aisle, and against the pulpit a boat representing that used by St. François de Paule. Adjoining the Cathedral are a beautiful octagonal baptistry and thirteenth-century cloisters with a (restored) fifteenth-century painted ceiling. (*In the porch of the Cathedral ring for the guardian.*)

On **Fréjus Plage** is a naval hydroplane station. St. Raphaël (2½ miles) can be reached by the P.L.M. line, the light railway, in summer by P.L.M. coaches, or by motor-boat.

ST. RAPHAËL AND VALESCURE.

Access.—By the P.L.M. main line (*see* p. 23) and the Chemin de Fer de la Provence. The Stations adjoin and are together called St. Raphaël-Valescure.

By P.L.M. and Mediterranéene motor-coaches.

Amusements and Sports.—From December to May the Casino offers a round of entertainments. Performances in the Palace Theatre. Venetian and other fêtes. Battles of Flowers. Sailing-boat regattas. Tennis. Golf at Valescure.

Bank.—W. F. King's, 10 Rue Charles Gounod.

Distances.—*By rail*, Nice, 40 miles ; Paris, 640½.

    By road, Cannes, by the Corniche-d'Or, 25 miles.

Inquiries.—*Syndicat d'Initiative*, Place de la Gare, and for those who do not speak French, W. F. King's bank and tourist office, 10 Rue Charles Gounod.

Hotels.—*See* p. 31.

Library.—W. F. King's, 6 Rue Charles Gounod.

Motor-buses.—To Fréjus, Valescure, Ste. Maxime, St. Tropez, Agay and Anthéor.

Motor-cars.—P.L.M. and Mediterranéene between Marseilles and Nice. Other cars provide for day and half-day excursions which include Cannes, Nice and Monte Carlo, St. Tropez and Grimaud, Grasse, La Côte des Maures, Les Gorges de Pennafort, Les Grottes de St. Cézaire, and Les Gorges du Loup.

Population.—Exceeds 10,000.

Water.—Brought in covered canals from the source of the *Siagnole*.

ST. RAPHAËL, situated on the Gulf de Fréjus (or of St. Raphaël), may be said to have been a suburb of the Roman Forum Julii, for it was here that the rich merchants and officers had their villas. It owes its rise from the fishing village to which it had declined to two French authors, Alphonse Karr and Charles Gounod, who revealed the charms of the spot to literary and artistic Paris.

Against the railway station is the Place Maréchal Galliëni. From its western side, **Boulevard Felix Martin,** the chief thoroughfare of the modern town, goes southward, passing the new church of **Notre-Dame-de-la-Victoire.** On the opposite side of the church is the Quai St. Tropez, on which Napoleon landed on his return from Egypt. The Boulevard continues southward to the **Casino** and thence goes eastward along the shore until it gives place to the **Boulevard du Touring Club de France,** the beginning of the **Corniche d'Or.**

A red porphyry rock on the beach is the *Lion de Terre*. A similar rock in the sea is the *Lion de Mer*.

Immediately westward of the northern end of the Boulevard Felix Martin is Rue Maréchal Petain, which leads under the

ST. RAPHAËL.

Ballance,]   [Menton.

LA NAPOULE.

6

railway to **Place Carnot,** the site of the Mairie. From the
north-west corner of the Place, a thoroughfare leads to
the **Eglise-des-Templiers,** now disused. The Knights Templars followed the Romans, and it was they who, in the
ninth century, built the square tower used as the belfry.

St. Raphaël is both a summer and a winter resort. It is
cooler than places farther east, has a clean sea-front with
a sandy beach pleasant for bathing, and there is a very good
bathing establishment. An English club on the sea-front
is one of the indications of an important English colony.

It is a walk of about 2 miles along the western flank of
the hills to—

Valescure,

charmingly situated amid parasol pines and Mediterranean
heath. Its name is said to be derived from its Roman
name, *Vallis Curans,* the vale which brings health. To it
Romans retreated from Forum Julii, when the heat there
became uncomfortably great, and now it is becoming increasingly popular with English people. Its land and sea
views are exceptionally fine ; it is largely sheltered from the
mistral, has good hotels, charming villas mostly built by
Englishmen, an English Church, an 18-hole golf course,
and as a centre of excursions it is equal to St. Raphaël.
Unusual features are a Chinese temple and monastery, and
a cemetery in which were buried many natives of Indo-
China brought to France during the Great War.

Another pleasant short walk from St. Raphaël is under
the shadow of parasol pines along the beach to Fréjus. A
third is up the ravine through which the *Garonne* flows
between ridges of the Estérels.

A longer walk is that to **Mont Vinaigre** (*see* p. 54). In a
couple of hours one reaches the ranger's house of Malpey
(" bad neighbourhood "), a name reminiscent of the days
when travelling here was unsafe. From Malpey the route
has first an easterly direction and then winds up the south
slope of the mountain.

Again, from Malpey one may go south-eastward to **Agay**
(p. 56), or by continuing along the St. Raphaël-Malpey
road and turning eastward along the Cannes road one comes
to the **Auberge-des-Adrets,** where criminals escaped from the
galleys of Toulon used here to waylay travellers. An inscription over the door records that the inn was rebuilt in 1663.

St. Raphaël and Valescure are two of the best centres for
exploring—

The Estérels,

one of the most beautiful and picturesque groups of mountains in South Europe.

They are separated from the Maures by the valley of the
Argens. Their picturesque charm is due to the porphyry of
which they largely consist. It crops up in bare rocky masses
resembling ruined castles or assuming more fantastic shapes,
while the gorgeous colouring, due to iron in different chemical
forms, defies description. The loftiest summit, *Mont
Vinaigre*, has an elevation of less than 2,000 feet. It is said
to owe its name to the sour wine made from grapes formerly
grown on its flanks.

The variety of soil in the Estérels leads to a charming
variety of vegetation. There are vast woods of pines, of
cork trees, and of oaks, and plantations of mimosa. There
are juniper trees, myrtles in abundance, whole hill-sides covered
with *Lavandula Stœchas* (p. 44) ; there are great bushes of
rosemary and tracts of the tree-heath, which in favourable
positions is a veritable tree.

The pines greatly outnumber other trees. They are the
Parasol Pine with its noble crown ; the Maritime Pine with
its reddish trunk, and the Aleppo Pine, less pyramidal than
the Maritime and also distinguished from that by its grey
stem.

Except where the light is too much excluded, there is beneath
the pines a wild tangle of undergrowth, locally called the
Maquis, and consisting largely of aromatic herbs and shrubs.

The tree-heath is in perfection at the end of March. In
April there are golden masses of the thorny broom, the strong
thorns being poisonous. Later there blooms the more beautiful summer broom, which has reed-like branches.

The Maquis is full of bulbs of many kinds. It also has
many orchids and several varieties of everlasting flowers.
Notable also is it for vile-smelling plants, among which are
the ·rues, the stinking goose-foot, and the pitch clover,
which has dark-green leaves and a blue clover-like flower.
The Estérels have flowers even in winter.

The region has considerable mineral wealth—sulphate of
lead, iron and coal—but this is little exploited.

The Estérels are national property. The cork is sold to
private companies, and some of the scanty population find
profitable occupation in dragging out of the forest the half-
charred wood resulting from the summer fires.

The Romans dedicated the whole of the great forest, of

which that of the Estérels was then a part, to Diana, but the Estérels had also their special nymph, the fairy Estrella, not always a good fairy. She bestowed fertility on mothers, but the shepherd who, yielding to her entreaties, kissed her, lost his reason and became obsessed by one idea.

Two Roman roads led through the Estérels. The earlier one followed the coast from Cannes, turned inland up a valley at the most southerly point of the region, and reached Fréjus from a westerly direction. The later road went straight over the mountains, its course corresponding, more or less, with that of the present high road between Fréjus and Cannes.

The French Touring Club has made roads and paths in all directions, and set up finger-posts. But those who intend to explore the region must bear in mind that one may go for miles without seeing any other dwellings than the scattered cottages of the *gardes forestières*.

The best map of the district is *La Carte de l'Estérel au* 1/20,000ᵉ by E. A. Martel, revised by P. Boissaye and published by the Touring Club de France.

ALONG THE CORNICHE D'OR.

THE Corniche d'Or is a marvellously beautiful road, 25 miles in length, following the coast from St. Raphaël nearly to Cannes. Its name is justified when the mimosas are blooming, and not only gardens but whole hill-sides are ablaze with golden flowers and the road is bathed in perfume. Sometimes the road runs close to the sea, and sometimes it passes between villa gardens set with palms, orange trees and mimosas, while roses and geraniums run wild along the boundary and hang down in masses of colour. But always on the inland side are the Estérels, with their fantastically shaped and gorgeous coloured crags and varied vegetation.

The route is alongside that of the P.L.M. railway between Marseilles and Vintimille, so that the villages and small towns along the Corniche either have their own station or are within easy reach of one. For hotels, *see* pp. 28–31.

Boulouris,

a suburb of St. Raphaël, is the first point reached by the Corniche d'Or on the eastward way. It is situated among the pines, has a sheltered beach, and mainly consists of villas in gardens. Although but 2 miles from St. Raphaël, it has its own railway station and hotels.

Quarries of blue porphyry in the neighbourhood were worked by the Romans, whose exploitation of them would seem to have been abruptly terminated, as blocks which they had prepared were not removed.

Between 6 and 7 miles from St. Raphaël is **Agay,** straggling around a little bay on which the Greeks established an important trading station which they named *Agathopolis*.

Nature has made Agay a sheltered spot for human beings, as certain artists have discovered, and its bay, often full of vessels in stormy weather, is a harbour of refuge for coasting-vessels and fishing-boats. The *Agay*, flowing into the bay, is attractive to anglers. The little town is supplied with water from the source of the *Siagnole*. At the office of the *Syndicat d'Initiative*, opposite Hôtel du Rastel, may be obtained particulars of the excursions by motor cars.

Cap Dramont is one of the horns of the bay ; the other is the **Pointe de la Baumette.** The tour of either makes a charming walk. The ascent to the highest point of the **Rastel d'Agay,** about 1,000 feet, means a toilsome hour, but the toil is recompensed by a beautiful prospect.

Motorists should note that the new road connecting Agay with St. Raphaël *viâ* Valescure and the golf links not only avoids the heavy traffic of the Corniche, but opens up a part of the Estérels until recently accessible only to pedestrians.

The **Gorge-du-Mal-Infernat,** "a fairy-tale in stone," and " one of the marvels of the Riviera," is only a short 4 miles from Agay, along a smooth forest road, which has the stream beside it most of the way. But the spot which forms the goal of the excursionists is a pass, not a gorge, a pass beautiful in the way it curves, forks and opens out, and in the variety and modelling of its sides.

It is in the neighbourhood of Agay that the scenery of the red rocks is most famous, but perhaps the most striking view of them from the road is just eastward of—

Anthéor,

a new winter resort of artists and of those needing rest. It lies on the far side of the Bay of Agay, where is a small beach of fine sand, on a coast of red crags and splinters and spits of rock, running out into the sea. "Flame-red rocks shooting up from a sea the colour of a peacock's neck," wrote Baring-Gould. Agay station is about 3 miles west, but motors meet all trains. Anthéor, however, has become so popular that it is to have its own station.

Cap Roux, at the foot of which Anthéor straggles, is pierced with caverns, which seemed to holy men of old inviting dwelling-places. One, the Sainte Baume, served as the habitation of St. Honorat, before he founded the Abbey of the Lérins (p. 67). Formerly it was much frequented by pilgrims, but now it is hardly visited, except by tourists. The cape attains its greatest height in the **Grand Pic** (1,360 feet), affording an extensive and beautiful view, of which the principal features are indicated on an orientation table.

The office of the *Syndicat d'Initiative* is at the Hôtel des Flots Bleus.

Even more boldly and picturesquely situated than Anthéor is—

Le Trayas,

midway between St. Raphaël and Cannes, and having a
station on the main line. It is sheltered from the mistral
by Cap Roux. One portion of it is along the shore, where are
charming little beaches, another, *Le Trayas Supérieur*, is from
150 feet to 600 feet above the sea. Both parts are peaceful
and restful and face south.

Le Trayas is an excellent centre for the exploration of the
Estérels (p. 54). In a booklet published by the *Syndicat
d'Initiative*, Grand Hôtel de l'Estérel, directions for a dozen
walks through the district are clearly given, and there are
also as many itineraries for motorists.

On the coast, about 1½ miles from Le Trayas Station, is
the pretty little village of **Miramar,** 2½ miles beyond which
is **Théoule,** on a bay noted for the abundance of fish and with
a sandy beach, excellent for children and sea-bathing.
Théoule is in the extensive commune of Mandelieu, which
also comprises the hamlets of Mandelieu, Les Thermes and—

La Napoule,

at the eastern end of the Corniche d'Or. It has a station
on the P.L.M. line, and is connected with Cannes by two roads,
along one of which trams run. It is sheltered on the north
and west by the Estérels and has a large and much-frequented
beach. There are boats for hire for sea-fishing or excursions,
and trout fishing in the *Siagne* and the *Riou*, which here
enter the sea. A great attraction to many is the proximity
of Cannes, of which La Napoule and Mandelieu are aristocratic suburbs. A large part of the commune consists of
an alluvial plain, an admirable "playing field," upon which
are the 18-hole and 9-hole golf courses, the race-course and
the polo ground which draw to Cannes a large proportion
of its visitors.

Mandelieu, which gives its name to the commune, and
Les Thermes (the Thermæ of the Romans, who used its
hot springs), which stands between it and La Napoule, are
not on the Corniche d'Or, but on the Route Nationale.
Mandelieu, at the foot of the Estérels, is both a winter and
a summer resort. The beaches of La Napoule and Théoule
are within easy reach.

For information respecting the places in the commune
apply Syndicat d'Initiative, the Mairie, Mandelieu.

CANNES.

Access.—By the main line of the P.L.M. railway or by P.L.M. and Mediter-ranéene coaches (see p. 23).

Banks.—*Barclays,* 7 Rue Maréchal Foch; *Lloyds and National Provincial,* Place des Iles, etc.

Consulates.—British, 7 Rue Maréchal Foch.
American at Nice (see p. 84).

Distances.—*By rail,* Marseilles, 121 miles; Nice, 19½; Paris, 660.
By road, Antibes, 7½ miles; Cagnes, 13¾; Fréjus, 22; Golfe-Juan-Vallauris, 3⅞; Grasse, 11½; Hyères, 73¾ by the Estérels and Cogolin; 81¼ by the coast; Juan-les-Pins, 6¼; La Napoule, 6¼ *via* Mandelieu, 5 by the coast road; Marseilles, 130; Menton, 40; Nice, 21¼; Paris, 516¼; St. Raphaël. 23¾ by the Estérels, 25¾ by the Corniche d'Or; Toulon, 89¾.

Hotels.—*See* p. 29.

Inquiries.—Syndicat d'Initiative, at the Mairie (see p. 32).

Libraries.—*The Lounge,* 16 Rue des Etats-Unis; *Aux Beaux Livres,* 55 Rue d'Antibes; *Galeries Litteraires,* 11 Boulevard Carnot; *Public,* Hôtel de Ville.

Motor-buses.—From the Hôtel de Ville to Pointe de la Croisette; to Juan-les-Pins, Antibes; Mougins and Valbonne; Pégomas and Auribeau; Le Cannet; Grasse; Golfe-Juan; La Bocca, Mandelieu, La Napoule, Théoule.

Motor Services.—To Nice, Monte Carlo and Menton.

Population.—Resident, about 45,000. Half as many again in the height of the winter and summer seasons.

Post Office.—Rue-du-Bivouac-Napoleon (so named because Napoleon halted on the vacant spot then here, after landing from Elba).

" CANNES was born of a smile of spring and the caprice of a gentleman," says a French writer. The gentle-man was Lord Brougham, who in 1832 was travelling along the south coast of France eastward to Nice, at that time an Italian town. Owing to cholera, the Italian frontier was closed to him, so he halted at Cannes, " a little fishing town agreeably situated on the beach of the sea," wrote Smollett, after passing a night there forty-one years earlier. Lord Brougham was so pleased with the climate and the neigh-bourhood that later he built for himself a residence in which he spent every winter for 30 years, and where he died in 1868. That other people endorsed his opinion of the place may be gathered from the fact that land prices quickly rose from 25 centimes the square metre to 60 francs—6,000 centimes—the metre.

A century has passed, and Cannes has become the " Pearl of the Riviera," the world's most fashionable winter resort. " Princes, princes, everywhere princes," said Maupassant in speaking of it, and a more recent writer has remarked that

" Looking round the tables (of the Cannes Casino) is like opening a picture paper : one is sure to see a row of well-known faces."

Modern Cannes is largely a town of villas, spreading itself along the crescent-shaped eastern bay—the Rade (roadstead) de Cannes. The villas on the heights above are largely in the hands of English people.

On the western side of the bay is the **Jetée Albert Edouard** (the late King Edward VII), whose statue stands at the entrance. Here, too, are the Square Merimée and the **Municipal Casino,** open from December 1 to May 1. Excellent theatrical and operatic companies are engaged and there is a round of other indoor entertainments.

From the Casino there runs along the whole length of the bay (1½ miles) the **Boulevard de la Croisette,** taking its name from the promontory which forms the eastern horn of the inlet. The Boulevard, lined by palm trees, is the main promenade and the site of the Carnival processions, battles of flowers, etc. On the landward side are the villas and various centres of interest. The first of these is the **Galeries Fleuries,** a narrow square surrounded by a colonnade of shops, comprising branches of leading Paris houses and fashionable tea rooms. Less than four hundred yards farther east is the **Cercle Nautique,** a favourite haunt of King Edward VII, and the club most used by English and American visitors. Some ¾ mile farther are the **Palais des Sports** and the **Stade des Hesperides.** Farther still, at the extremity of the promontory, is the **Palm Beach Casino,** a summer establishment. " From the outside it resembles nothing so much as a pale pink ice pudding," wrote an English journalist. Within are a theatre and concert hall and provision for dancing, gala dinners, baccarat and boule. Neither here nor elsewhere in France may Chemin de Fer or Trente et Quarante be played, as they are held to be games of chance. How they differ in this respect from the permitted Baccarat and Boule is a mystery to common minds.

From the **Palm Beach** there is a magnificent view, especially over the Estérels. The boulevard on the eastern side of the promontory connects with the Route d'Antibes, which passes through the centre of Cannes as the **Rue d'Antibes,** with shops of fashionable dressmakers, furriers and jewellers. It gives place to **Rue Felix Faure.** Between

CANNES.

CANNES.

[Paris.

Patras.]

8

CANNES 61

the southern side of this and the **Allées de la Liberté**, alongside the harbour, is an open space, the **Cours.** At the western end is the **Hôtel de Ville,** in which are the Information Office, the Municipal **Library** and the **Rothschild Museum** (9–12 ; 2–6), containing a Natural History Collection and a Fine Arts Exhibition. Running southward from it and bordering the Harbour is the Quai St. Pierre. From the Hôtel de Ville, motor-buses go to the Pointe de la Croisette.

To the west of the harbour is **Le Suquet,** the low-lying part of old Cannes, of later date than the protected portion on the adjacent **Mont Chevalier.** Pedestrians can ascend by a steep but convenient street, but vehicles must follow a thoroughfare which winds round the old town.

On the mount is the **Church of Notre Dame d'Espérance,** built in 1633. Contrary to custom, it stands north and south. It has eight chapels. Over the altars of seven of them are paintings, but the most interesting object is the coffer which once contained the body of St. Honorat. It was given to the monastery by François I as a souvenir of a night passed there in 1525, when he was a prisoner of the Spaniards.

On the summit are the ruins of a **Castle** and a Tower built by the monks of Lérins, who owned the town for several centuries. Indeed, the inhabitants only obtained complete municipal freedom a year before the French Revolution swept away the feudal system. The **Tower** was begun in 1070, but was not finished until 1305. Originally there were no openings in the lower part and entrance could be gained only by a movable ladder. Its summit commands a fine view. In the castle are the Lycklama and Regional **Museums** (9–12 ; 2–6 *except Sundays, holidays and in August*), with pictures, engravings, antiquities, Oriental curiosities, collections of the mineralogy of the Estérels and prehistoric objects. Near the Romanesque Church of Ste. Anne, which was the castle chapel, are some round walls built by the Romans.

The earliest of the modern buildings were erected westward of the old town. Here now is the **Boulevard Jean Hibert** along the coast, and passing **Square Brougham,** a sheltered public garden. Above the boulevard and parallel to it is the **Route de Fréjus,** whence one may reach **Villa Eléonore,** Lord Brougham's historic residence.

The Route de Fréjus is one of the principal English quarters. Another is **Californie,** the shoulders of a low range of hills,

about 2 miles eastward, covered with pine trees, amid which
are villas and large hotels and sheltering Cannes from the
east wind. Californie runs sharply down to the sea with
the promontory of the Croisette as its projecting arm. In **St.
George's Church** is a copy of the Duke of Albany's tomb at
Windsor. The youngest son of Queen Victoria, he died at
Cannes in 1884 and below the Villa Albany a pretty fountain
and a pillar were erected to his memory. The church can
be reached by the Boulevard du Roi Albert, which runs up
from the Route d'Antibes. The thoroughfare is continued
to the right alongside the church, while to the left the Boulevard St. Georges goes up to the fountain and the villa and
on to **Super-Cannes.**

Amusements.

Cannes offers its visitors a wide and constant choice of
indoor attractions of which the Casinos are the centres, but
it is pre-eminently an open-air resort. Owing to the safety
of its harbour and roadstead, and to the ease with which one
can land upon its quays, boating and yachting are very
popular. On some days the water immediately in front of
the town is crowded with pleasure craft of all sizes and pro-
pelled by motor, steam or sail. Nowhere else on the Mediterranean coast is there such a display : indeed Cannes is
probably the only place in the world where so many luxurious
yachts can be seen. During the high season the International
Regatta takes place, but there is yacht racing all the year.
Three times every week there are races for the little sailing
dinghies known as MMM's—*the Minima Monotypes de la
Manche*. There are several sailing clubs, and motor, sailing,
and rowing boats can be hired.

For land sports also, Cannes is an important centre.
Tennis, golf, polo, horse-racing and other sports are here
enjoyed under excellent conditions. With regard to tennis,
Cannes admits only the superiority of Wimbledon. The
importance attached to the game is demonstrated by the
fact that, although ground is very valuable, nearly all the
principal hotels have tennis courts. There are several tennis
clubs. Tournaments take place every week. Five of them
are International during the winter season, and two during
the summer season.

At **Mandelieu** (p. 58), some 5 miles west of Cannes, with
which it is connected by motor-buses, are **Golf Links** (18-holes

and 9-holes), and at Mougins (motor-buses) is the 18-hole course of the Country Club. The racing season opens at the end of January and closes in March. Cannes has an automobile week, during which there are various displays and competitions.

Each of the two bays is bordered by a sandy beach from which there is bathing all the year round. On New Year's Day it is made a great event, but the period from April to October is regarded as the bathing season, and then the beach is gay with multi-coloured tents. At the Palm Beach Casino are a hundred bathing cabins with hot and cold water. Water polo and other sports are organized, and there are four or five centres for physical drill, combined with sun-bathing. Four bathing establishments cater for those who prefer to bathe under cover. As the sea-bathing draws visitors from the inland towns and from abroad, Cannes has an important summer season. The windiness, which is one of the features of the climate of Cannes, makes the air distinctly bracing, a great advantage during the warmer days.

Cannes is not only the Pearl of the Riviera, the Cowes of the Riviera, and the Queen of Sports, she is also the Town of the Flowers, a title she owes to the gardens which sprang up on the completion of the Siagne Canal, which made possible the regular and copious watering of the crops which are largely flowers for sale to the perfume factories of Grasse.

Walks and Excursions.

The immediate neighbourhood of the town teems with charming spots which may be reached on foot, and here, as elsewhere, the public means of conveyance will put the pedestrian within easy reach of more distant points and enable him to combine itineraries. The Syndicat d'Initiative, at the Hôtel de Ville, distributes gratuitously a publication in English minutely describing the walks around the town. Numerous motor services go to all the interesting places within a day's run. There is also the highly popular excursion to the Îles de Lérins (pp. 66-7).

Le Cannet.

Hotels.—*See* p. 29.
Inquiries.—*Syndicat d'Initiative*, 6 Boulevard Carnot (p. 32).

Le Cannet is a small town some 250 feet to 500 feet above sea-level, in a sheltered valley north-west of Cannes, with which it is connected by bus services along the fine Boulevard Carnot. It is favoured by those to whom sea breezes are injurious, as it is some 2 miles from the sea, and on other grounds it is attractive. There is a wide and pleasant prospect from **Place Bellevue,** reached by the narrow Rue Victorien Sardou, which goes off on the left, just past the highest point of the main road, in ascending from Cannes. On the right side of the main road, a very short distance beyond the public school for girls, is the **Villa Sardou,** where the celebrated tragedienne Rachel died in 1858. It may be recalled that Matthew Arnold made her death the subject of a beautiful poem, and that her memory is also preserved by the great portrait of Vashti in *Villette*, and in an essential episode of *Pendennis*, but she was no placid doll like the Fotheringay. The **Church of Ste. Catherine** (1610) treasures an arm of St. Honorat. The Chapel of Notre-Dame-des-Anges was built by the monks of Lérins.

Super-Cannes

lies to the north-east of Cannes. It commands a magnificent panorama, and boasts an Observatory. One can easily walk to it or it may be reached by a funicular railway. The lower station is some 650 yards above Rue d'Antibes, a little east of the crossing of that street and Boulevard d'Alsace. But a more direct route to it is by the Boulevard de Strasbourg, which leaves the Boulevard d'Alsace westward of the crossing and goes to the Gallia Palace Hotel. Thence the route is to the right to the Hôtel Mont Fleuri. Those who wish to walk all the way should take the Boulevard du Roi Albert, which leaves the Route d'Antibes some 750 yards east of the crossing. From the upper station two routes are indicated by coloured arrows. The blue opens out views over the sea, the red is turned towards the neighbouring mountains.

La Croix-des-Gardes.

Here, as at Super-Cannes, walks can be taken in rural surroundings and there are fine views from the summit of the slope, 500 feet above the sea. It is reached by a walk of 40 minutes. One can go by the Avenue Belle-vue (a branch from the Route de Fréjus) which is continued by a country road, or one can go by the Boulevard Vallombras, nearer the eastern end of the Route de Fréjus, turning to the right at the end of the boulevard and almost immediately to the left. The **Roquebillère Crags,** a mile beyond the Croix-des-Gardes, form an even finer view-point. In February and March, La Croix-des-Gardes is a forest of flowering mimosas. The return can be made by La Bocca and the sea.

Ballance,]

THE HARBOUR, CANNES.

[*Menton.*

NOTRE DAME DE VIE, CANNES.

ST. CASSIEN.

Mougins.

Hotels.—*de France ; Café de la Paix.*

Mougins is an ancient village on an isolated hill passed by the road (bus route) between Grasse and Cannes. In summer it becomes uncomfortably crowded. It is the site of a golf course and has relics of olden times. The church is a historic monument. The *Chapel of Notre-Dame-de-Victoire*, 10 minutes distant, is a place of pilgrimage and contains interesting votive offerings. Those who arrive by bus in order to make the village the starting-point of a walk, should alight at the Baraques and take the first road on the left after passing the public fountain. It is 20 minutes' walk to the abandoned Chapelle St. Barthélemy, from which the panorama is magnificent. Returning to Mougins, one may enjoy another grand prospect. A road goes from the east end of the village to Le Cannet.

Golfe-Juan.

Hotels.—*Central ; Riviera.*

A gently sloping sandy beach attracts bathers and makes the little village a lively place in summer. The French Mediterranean squadron and other war vessels are often seen in the roadstead. It was here that Napoleon landed on his escape from Elba. Golfe-Juan shares with Vallauris a station on the P.L.M. main line, and buses connect it with Cannes, 3¾ miles ; Juan-les-Pins, 2½ miles ; and Vallauris, 1½ miles.

Vallauris.

Hotels.—*France, Renaissance et Voyageurs.*

Vallauris is a small pottery town and the centre of a flower-growing district north-east of Cannes, from which it is about 5¼ miles by tram or bus, but a little less distance on foot across Californie. Its name is thought to be a corruption of *Vallis-aurea*, the name the Romans gave the place, probably on account of the fruitfulness of the soil or on account of the yellowish red clay found in the neighbourhood, and of which they made artistic pottery, widely renowned. After the fall of the Roman Empire the art became lost. Some centuries later the manufacture was revived and it is to-day the leading industry. In 1501, the town, which had fallen into a ruinous condition, was re-planned and rebuilt by its lords, the monks of Lérins. In the work of restoration was included the **Castle,** built early in the twelfth century as a summer residence for the Abbot of Lérins, and destroyed by Raymond de Turenne towards the end of the fourteenth century. In the **Hôtel de Ville** is a collection of ancient and modern pottery.

Riviera (e)

Pégomas and Auribeau

are picturesque villages on the banks of the *Siagne* about 8 miles north-west of Cannes, among tall poplars, fields and olive woods. They may be reached by bus. A delightful picture of the rural life of Pégomas is given in the biography of Annie Keary (died 1882), who there spent the last winters of her life and wrote one or two of her novels. In the church of **Auribeau** are a sixteenth-century chalice and a fifteenth-century reliquary containing part of the jawbone of St. Honorat. Both chalice and reliquary are protected as objects of historic interest.

Les Puys and St. Cassien.

These are north-westward of Cannes. The walk may be shortened by taking train (Grasse line) as far as Ranguin halt, thence following the Pégomas road to the **Puys,** a wooded hill. By the Villa Estérel-Terrasse is a fine view-point from which one looks upon the green plain of Laval, the river Siagne, the Estérels, the old town of Cannes and the sea. Then descend to **St. Cassien,** an isolated hill beautifully clad with trees. It was probably one of the high places of Baal or Phœnician worship. Then it became the *Ava Luci*, the altar of the sacred grove of the Romans, who erected on the summit a temple of Venus. The temple was destroyed by St. Honorat, who used the stones in the construction of a convent which was destroyed by the Lombards in 578, and there followed a succession of convents and destruction. The present building was erected in the fourteenth century. How the hill came to be known as St. Cassien is uncertain. St. Cassien is the patron saint of Cannes and a fête is held in his honour on July 25. It is the custom to picnic on the hill and to dance to the beating of tambourines.

Cannes can be re-entered by the Route de la Roubine and the boulevard along the coast.

The Îles de Lérins.

Excursions daily by motor-boats at 10, 11 and 2 from near the Jetée Albert Edouard. Returning at 12.15 and about 4.30.

On the Île Ste. Marguerite are several restaurants and the *Hostellerie du Masque de Fer.* On the Île St. Honorat is a restaurant.

Of this group of islands only **Ste. Marguerite** and **St. Honorat** are important. Both are covered by luxuriant vegetation traversed by wide paths. Ste. Marguerite is the nearer to the mainland (about ¾ mile). Its greatest length is about 2 miles, breadth ½ mile. In its fort is the cell which for 11 years was the prison of " the Man in the Iron Mask," who is generally believed to have been Count Mattioli, minister of the Duke of Mantua. After having been honoured and rewarded by Louis XIV for persuading his master to cede to France the fortified town of Casale, he betrayed the plans of Louis, who caused him to be kidnapped and then secretly held him prisoner. The mask he was compelled to wear was not of iron, but of silk or velvet. Much of the romantic story associated with him was due to the imagination of Alexandre Dumas.

In 1873 the fort was made the prison of Marshal Bazaine, condemned as a traitor for having surrendered Metz to the Germans in the war of 1870–71. At the end of 9 months his cell was found empty and a rope was dangling from the window. As he was a heavy man and at that time not agile, it is easier to believe that he passed from the doorway, and not from the window, to the steam yacht which took him to Spain, his escape being facilitated by Marshal MacMahon, then President of the Republic, who had been Bazaine's brother officer, and knew his comrade had been the victim of political passion.

Originally the island was the site of a convent established by the sister of St. Honorat. It was named after Margaret, the saint of Antioch, who vanquished the fiery dragon.

The island of **St. Honorat** is named after a monk who settled there about the year 410, and established a monastery which for centuries was a centre of sacred learning and missionary enterprise. In the year 690 the monastery is said to have held 3,700 monks, but when it was closed in 1788 there were but four.

St. Honorat is about ½ mile from its sister isle. After having passed through various hands, it returned to the possession of the Church and in 1859 was conveyed to the Cistercians, who restored and used the ancient monastery near the landing-stage. The transept of the chapel and the cloister are remnants of the ancient building. On a wall of the refectory, a picture shows St. Patrick, said to have been a follower of St. Honorat, ridding the island of snakes. Women may land on the island, but are not admitted to the monastery. They may enter the fort on the south coast, built in the eleventh century, as a refuge for the monks on the approach of pirates. It was restored in the twelfth and fourteenth centuries, and altered in the eighteenth, by a French actress, who for a short time had the idea of living on the island. Along the shore are the remains of ancient chapels.

ANTIBES.

Access.—On the main line Marseilles-Vintimille (*see* p. 23). On the route of the P.L.M. and Mediterranéene coaches between Marseilles and Nice. Connected with Cannes by tramway and motor-bus services and with Nice by motor-bus services.

Distances.—Paris, 667 miles ; Marseilles, 128¼ ; Nice, 12¼ ; Cannes, 7 miles.

Inquiries.—*Syndicat d'Initiative*, Place Macé (Grand Hotel), reached from the station by following Avenue Robert Soleau (*see* p. 32).

Hotels.—*See* p. 29.

Population.—Exceeds 20,000.

ABOUT 400 B.C. a band of adventurous Greeks left Massilia, now Marseilles, which their ancestors had founded, and sailed eastward to found a new trading station. They landed on the promontory between the Golfe de Juan and the Baie des Anges, overcame whatever opposition the natives offered, and on its eastern side established a settlement which they called Antipolis—" opposite the city "—the city which has become modern Nice. The name of their town became modified to Antiboul and later to Antibes.

The Romans made Antibes a naval base. On the downfall of their empire the town was pillaged and burnt by successive raids of barbarians, whose treatment of it was rivalled later by Christians. It was sacked by the Emperor Charles V, bombarded by the English in 1751, and by the Austrians in 1813.

The *Var* having ceased to be the boundary between France and Italy, the ramparts which surrounded Antibes were in 1898 either levelled or converted into boulevards, and a new town arose around the old one.

Dominating the Baie St. Roch, below the station, is **Fort Carré,** a great square tower of the seventeenth century. On the opposite side of the haven is the old town, closely packed around two towers. Although built of Roman stones, they are not Roman work. One serves as the belfry of the seventeenth-century **Church** which stands between them and contains a good altar-piece.

From Place Macé, in the centre of the new quarter, and from the parking-place of the motor coaches, Rue Georges Clemenceau leads through Place Nationale (the site of the **Post Office** and of a column commemorating the

repulse of an attack by an Austro-Sardinian force in 1815)
to the Market Place and to the **Mairie,** a modern building.

To the right of the latter is the approach to the church,
and to a flight of steps leading up to the old château of the
Grimaldis, protected as an historic monument, and used as a
Museum (10–12, 2–5, 1 fr.). Among the interesting contents
is a plaster cast of the **Terpon Stone,** which for safety has
been confided to the proprietor of the land on which it was
found. It is almost black, and bears in archaic characters
an inscription which has been rendered : " I am Terpon,
servant of the august goddess Aphrodite ; may Cypris
reward with her favours those who have placed me here."
" It seems," says Baring-Gould, " to have been one of those
mysterious sacred stones which received worship from the
most remote ages." On a slab formerly on a wall of the
Mairie is an inscription " to the manes of the boy Septenirion
aged 12 years, who danced two days in succession in the
theatre and pleased the public." Nothing more is known
of the poor little fellow than that which was engraved about
him some 1,500 years ago. Another inscription shows that
at Antibes there were boatmen who used craft sustained by
bladders, common on lagoons and rivers, but rarely met
with on the coast. A third was erected in memory of a
horse by its sorrowing master.

From Place Macé Boulevard Albert Premier, named in
honour of the King of Belgium, runs southward and is continued by the Boulevard du Cap. At 1 mile is the **Villa
Thuret,** which, with its park and garden, was bequeathed to
the French nation by the celebrated diplomat-botanist whose
name it bears. The grounds (*open Tuesdays,* 8–6) are used
for study and research. (By turning westward here, one
soon reaches the road leading to Juan-les-Pins.)

The beautiful grounds of the Villa Eilenroc used to be open
to the public, but after the War the proprietor sold the estate.
The price paid was a little over a million francs. After a
while, the new owner put the property up to auction, and the
price it then brought was 22½ million francs, a striking
example of the great and rapid appreciation of the value
of land on the promontory.

About 500 yards along the Avenue, beyond Villa Thuret,
Boulevard Notre Dame goes off to the left for **La Garoupe.**
A wonderful view rewards those who climb to the vicinity
of the lighthouse. Close by is the little ancient chapel of

Notre-Dame-de-Bon-Port, which can also be approached
from the Chemin du Hermitage by the Via Crucis, the Way
of the Cross, along which are groups representing incidents
of the Passion. The chapel contains curious *ex-votos* offered
by sailors, and is a great place of pilgrimage.

But the glory of Antibes is its **Cap,** the promontory $2\frac{1}{2}$ miles
long and $\frac{1}{2}$ mile broad on which it stands. Grant Allen
described it exactly as "a promontory made up of little
promontories jutting into the sea at all possible angles, with
endless miniature bays and mimic islets." And few of those
who visit Antibes at sunset will be unable to re-echo the
opening words of Guy de Maupassant's little novel, *Madame
Parisse* : " Je n'avais jamais vu d'aussi surprenant et d'aussi
beau."—I had never seen anything so surprising and so
beautiful.

Again, from no other point on the coast can be so well
seen the chain of the Maritime Alps, from Mont Mounier
on the north-western horizon to the Baisse de Ste. Véran at
the opposite end. That background of snow-capped peaks,
setting off the delicate tints of the nearer heights and the blue
of the bays, forms one of the most beautiful sea-side views
in France. "It is the Riviera and the Bernese Oberland
rolled into one."

There is not a great deal for the visitor to do at Antibes.
It is rather a place for basking in the sun and loafing than
for doing, and therein doubtless lies a great part of its charm.
For the rest there are deep pools of crystal water into which
swimmers can plunge from rocks, and shallower water in
which the less expert can bathe in safety. The rock bathing
at Antibes is unrivalled.

There is no part of Provence fairer than the Cap d'Antibes.
Like other promontories, however, it is somewhat exposed,
and it has been well said that residence upon it is much like
passing a winter on the deck of a ship in genial sub-tropical
seas. On the other hand, there is comparative freedom from
the brusque changes of temperature experienced at sunset
at Cannes and Nice.

More trustworthy testimony to the geniality of its climate
than either words or figures are its flowers. The cultivation
of flowers, especially of carnations, roses, stocks and ane-
mones, is the great industry of the promontory. There are
nine or ten large horticultural establishments and a full
thousand of small producers. The early morning flower

Ballance,]   [Menton.

ANTIBES.

Riviera.   11

JUAN-LES-PINS.

market is one of the sights of Antibes, and another consists of the thousands of baskets of flowers daily sent away.

The town of Antibes and the Cap d'Antibes are not the whole of the commune. This also includes that young and vigorous summer and winter resort—

Juan-les-Pins,

whose rapidity of growth has been almost spectacular. In three years the price of land rose from 15 francs the square metre to 700 francs. If the place has something of the appearance of a young American town, that is not due to the structures but to the thoroughfares. The buildings are solid and for the most part are in the Provençal style. There is a good choice of hotels (p. 30), boarding-houses and furnished villas, good shops and restaurants, a casino open all the year, and a sea-bathing establishment. The water supply is good and the sewage system puts to shame certain older and larger resorts. It still retains many pines, although it is much less worthy of its name than formerly.

The development of the place dates only from the Armistice, and in the short time that has elapsed it has gained an enviable reputation. It is a pity that a little " town planning " did not give it a front worthy of a resort which dares to call itself the " Beach Queen of the Mediterranean." The beach is of sand, quite free from pebbles and of a slight and regular gradient. In summer it takes on somewhat the aspect of the beach at Lido, but the regulations governing undress are stricter here than there.

Canoeing, motor-boat racing and water gliding are among one set of amusements, and in another there is plenty of tennis. Antibes is but 1½ miles distant. A walk of 6½ miles takes one all round the Cap and back again. For **Biot** (p. 74), 5 miles distant, the way is along the Route Nationale towards Nice and the left-hand branch at the fork at the Chasseurs' barracks. **Vallauris** (p. 65), 6½ miles, is reached by going along the coast to Golfe-Juan, turning to the right by the port, going over the level-crossing and thence following the road which goes inland.

CAGNES-SUR-MER.

Access.—By the main line of the P.L.M. railway. By the light railway from
Vence.
By the P.L.M. and Mediterranéene motor-coach services between Mar-
seilles and Nice, and by bus from Nice, Cannes, Antibes, Vence, Grasse, etc.
Inquiries.—*Syndicat d'Initiative*, at the Banque Nationale de Crédit.
Golf.—A course of 18 holes.
Hotels.—*See* p. 29.
Population.—About 8,000, and increasing.

ON a hill midway between Antibes and Nice, about
7 miles from either, is the old village of Cagnes,
forming a very picturesque feature of the landscape. Crowning the summit of the hill is a **Castle** (*open daily; 5 frs.
Ring*) built in the early years of the fourteenth century by the
Grimaldi who was then proprietor of Monaco, and who had
been given the lordship of Cagnes by the King of Naples.
More than once it has been restored and the interior modified.
There are a staircase and a balustrade of marble, a beautiful
mantelpiece, and on the walls and ceiling of the large drawing-
room are paintings representing the history of Phaeton ;
that on the ceiling shows him being precipitated to earth.
It is signed by Carlone (*d.* 1677). The ancient chapel has
been converted into a boudoir. The view from the summit
of the tower is magnificent, as indeed is that from the terrace
adjoining the Castle. Rue Carnot passes through the base
of the church tower to Place Grimaldi, with buildings supported on arches, a double flight of steps concluding the ascent.

The **Church,** dedicated to Notre-Dame-la-Dorée, has an
exceptionally dark interior.

Having levelled its ancient walls, the village has crept
down the hill and is growing fast along the high road and
on the fertile plain watered by the *Cagnes*, the *Malvan*
and the *Loup*. As the newer site is rather low and damp,
mosquitoes are troublesome at times, but the golf course
fills the hotel, and villa residents find advantages which
counterbalance the winged pest.

The variety of aspect afforded by the neighbourhood, and
the oddities of the village, have attracted writers and artists,
so that Cagnes has a colony of painters of all nationalities,

who by the subjects chosen and the method of treatment have evolved "the Cagnes School." Also among the residents there are always to be found men of letters.

The golf course is at **St. Véran,** between the railway and the sea. The spot is named after an early bishop of Vence, who had been a pupil of St. Honorat. He founded a convent at the mouth of the *Loup,* and there are still slight remains of the little church.

Since the village began to draw nearer to the coast and found the sea-bathing there appreciated by strangers, it has called itself **Cagnes-sur-Mer.** It is a quiet winter resort. Various fêtes are organized, and besides the obvious Nice, Antibes, Juan-les-Pins, Golfe-Juan and Cannes, there are several interesting places which can easily be visited. Among them are Biot, 3¾ miles ; La Colle, 3¼ ; St. Paul, 4½ ; Vence, 7½ ; Villeneuve-Loubet, about 2 miles ; Grasse, about 15, all by bus or light railway.

The adjacent **Cros-de-Cagnes,** on the road to Nice, is a small fishing village with important Zoological Gardens, in which is a restaurant providing lunches and teas.

La Colle

(From Cagnes by the light railway ; from Nice, by buses)

is a small picturesque village in the midst of meadows, orchards, and fields of roses, on the road between Cagnes and St. Paul du Var, 3¼ miles from the former, 1¾ from the latter. It offers fishing in the *Loup.*

At ¾ mile is **Ospedaletti** with a twelfth-century church. West of La Colle is the **Castle of Canadel and Montfort,** called also Gaudelet, containing a fine chimney-piece and ancient decorations. **Canadel Chapel,** eleventh century, is an historic monument. About a mile from La Colle is the beautiful park of **St. Donat,** famous for its tall trees. A little farther are **Barres de la Bargarrée,** the lower gorges of the river.

Between La Colle and Villeneuve-Loubet is the marvellous **Cagnon** (cañon) **de St. Donat,** reached by an intricate route, for which a native should be taken as guide.

Villeneuve-Loubet.

Access.—Bus from Nice.   Light railway between Cagnes and Vence.
Hotel.—*du Loup*.
Population.—1,200.

Many centuries have rolled away since Villeneuve-Loubet was a "new town," and it is now a typical Provençal village.

The distinctive part of its name has been given to it because the *Loup* flows under the bastions of the castle. The keep was built in the twelfth century by Dante's "noble Romeo," whom the poet places in Paradise. The tradition that his Moorish slaves were the actual constructors is supported by the spur-like shape, by the small square stones used and by the ornamentation near the top.

From the summit, 90 feet above the ground, there is a fairy-like view. One can walk not only around the walls but inside them, as in their thickness there runs a flagged passage. A mural slab gives the history of the castle from its foundation until its restoration in 1842. It has been so modernized that there is nothing in the interior to recall the days of Romeo, or even those when François I lodged within its walls, while awaiting the conclusion of a treaty of peace with Charles Quint, in 1538.

Biot *(be-ot)*.

(Hostellerie Provençale—*Le Mas-des-Orangers*.)

The old-world village of Biot is situated on a rocky height above the valley of the *Brague*, 3¾ miles from Cagnes, 13¾ miles from Nice, and a short 2 miles from its station on the P.L.M. main line.

From the station the road to Biot, and onwards through Valbonne to Grasse, is one of the most picturesque in the region. Fringed with Lombardy poplars, it winds between meadows which even in early spring are spangled with flowers, and on the hill-sides are flaming thickets of mimosa. After a spell of dry weather, pedestrians may follow the footpath up the east bank of the river.

Biot still has its walls and square tower (fourteenth century), and two gates dating from the middle of the sixteenth century. Most of the enclosed streets are almost as they were in the fourteenth or the fifteenth century, and the doorways of some of the houses are charming. At the far end of the **Place des Arcades** one passes into a small court and down a steep flight of thirteen steps into the **Church,** built in the twelfth century and reconstructed in the fourteenth. It is famous for two pictures of the School of Provence, but they are hung in such obscurity that it is difficult to examine them. The most treasured, the Virgin of the Rosary, an altar-piece having eight compartments, was shown at the Paris Exhibition, 1900, as a specimen of the art of the Middle Ages.

Ballance,]

JUAN-LES-PINS.

[Menton.

13

TOURETTES-SUR-LOUP.

GRASSE.

To the old village has been added a new one in which are factories producing all sorts of vessels of clay. The most renowned are jars used as holders of oil, similar to those in which the forty thieves hid themselves. For centuries their manufacture has been carried on at Biot.

St. Laurent du Var.

At 2½ miles from Cagnes, double that distance from Nice and less than a mile from a station on the main line of the P.L.M. railway, is the village of **St. Laurent du Var,** containing some 3,500 inhabitants. It has been called the Fruit Garden of Nice, and the cultivation of flowers is as important as that of fruit.

All who pass by rail or road between Nice and Cagnes cross the River *Var*, 84½ miles in length. In summer its bed is almost dry; in spring it is deeply covered by a torrent produced by the melting of the snow on the mountains which drain into it. On account of this great irregularity of volume, the Romans named it the *Varus*. To prevent very destructive inundations, twenty miles of the lower part of its course have been confined between dykes rather more than 300 yards apart.

Not until the end of the eighteenth century was there a bridge across the *Var*. Previous to its construction the river was forded about a mile north of the present bridge. Towards the end of the twelfth century, a band of monks established themselves on the western bank, entertained travellers and guided them across the river. The occurrence of scandals led the Bishop of Vence to suppress the hospice in 1648 and inhabitants of the neighbouring village of St. Laurent undertook the work.

Each morning the fords of the previous day were examined, and, if necessary, fascines were set up to indicate safer passages. "At the village of St. Laurent," wrote Smollett, "there is a set of guides always in attendance to conduct you in your passage over the river. Six of those fellows, tucked up above the middle, with long poles in their hands, took charge of our coach, and by many windings guided it safe to the opposite shore."

To facilitate the passage of troops, the French army in 1792 built a wooden bridge at the spot, and it continued to be used until the construction of the railway led to the erection of a bridge where the river is now crossed. When in 1860 the *Var* ceased to be the boundary between France and Italy, and Vintimille replaced St. Laurent as a frontier town, the latter declined in importance.

Just westward of the present bridge, a mile nearer the mouth of the river than the original bridge, and carrying both road and railway, a new settlement has arisen with a new industry, indicated by a line of petrol pumps, which give a supply free of the octroi tax imposed on the fuel sold in Nice.

VENCE AND GRASSE.

VENCE.

Access.—By the Chemin de Fer de la Provence. By bus or charabanc from Nice.

Distances.—Antibes, 12½ miles; Cagnes-sur-Mer, 6¼; Cannes, 18¾; Grasse, 16½; Nice, 13¾.

Inquiries.—*Syndicat d'Initiative*, 16, Place du Grand Jardin (*see* p. 32).

Hotels.—*See* p. 31.

Population.—Exceeds 5,000, and the town is growing.

VENCE is nearly 1,100 feet above the sea. Behind it are precipitous heights giving shelter from north winds. In front is an undulating fertile tract descending to the Mediterranean. Its climate is temperate, both summer and winter, and the town is generally full of visitors. It is of inexhaustible interest to artists and to all who love to recall the past.

The Romans, having dispossessed the aborigines, founded a city which they called *Ventium* and which, in the words of the late Sir Frederick Treves, became " a kind of Canterbury in the backwoods of Provence rather than a military station."

Of its palaces, its forum and other Roman structures there are no traces, but there have been found inscriptions enabling some idea to be formed of what went on within the walls of the city when the Romans were its masters. Christianity is thought to have been introduced in the second century. In 374 Vence was made the seat of a bishop, and it continued to be so until the French Revolution.

The ancient **Cathedral,** now the parish church, was erected in the tenth century, but is now mainly of the period between the twelfth and the fifteenth centuries. On the exterior and interior walls are Roman inscriptions that have been unearthed. It is entered from Place Clemenceau. In the outermost of the double aisles on each side are the chapels, all ancient and beautifully decorated. One has as its altar the tomb of St. Véran (*d*. 492). It was originally a Roman sarcophagus, and it still bears Roman sculpture. In the pillar facing this chapel is a Roman statuette. Another is on the wall between St. Véran's chapel and the chapel of the Sacred Heart. The last chapel of the aisle on the left side contains a beautifully carved door from the Chapter House. The Baptistery is probably on the spot where the baptism of blood was offered to the goddess Cybele. Upon a grating over a deep pit, a bull was slaughtered. Its blood fell upon a silk-robed priest, who emerged with it dripping from him, and the worshippers then knelt before him. By the blood shed, all sin and impurities were washed away from penitents.

At the west end is a gallery, a once common feature of Provençal Cathedrals, in which was accommodation for the choir and the bishop. That at Vence still contains the bishop's throne, a fine fifteenth-century lectern and beautifully carved stalls. Some of the carvings are amusing, a few quite irreverent. To enter this gallery and the treasury, which should not be missed, one must be accompanied by a priest. (While in his company there will be apparent more than one opportunity of contributing to a church fund.)

Behind the Cathedral was the burial ground. It is now **Place Godeau,** named after a bishop. Around it are ancient houses. In the centre is an ancient column of unknown origin. The modern **Mairie,** in Place Clemenceau, is on the site of a wing of the bishop's palace. Two picturesque arches are remnants of the court of the palace.

From this square a gate (1863) gives admission to the Boulevard Marcelin-Maurel, following the course of the **Ramparts** on the south side of the town. The ramparts were constructed in the thirteenth and fourteenth centuries. On the northern side a considerable portion remains and forms a promenade.

At the point where the road from Nice enters is the **Signadour Gate** (fourteenth century). Towards the north is the **Portail Sevis** with a fourteenth-century pointed arch and the grooves in which the portcullis worked. It communicates with **Rue de la Coste,** one of the oldest thoroughfares of ancient Vence. Handsome windows and fine entries in some of the dark, narrow streets indicate dwellings once belonging to wealthy and important persons.

Small as was the area of Old Vence, it once had 7,000 inhabitants, reduced in number from time to time by plagues, regarded by the orthodox as a visitation of God due to the Huguenots, who suffered in consequence.

Interesting excursions in the vicinity of Vence include the Chapel of Ste. Anne, the Chapel of St. Lambert, the ruins of a Commandery of the Templars, the Baous- (rocky mountains) des-Blancs and des-Noirs (orders of monks), the village of the Tourettes-sur-Loup, St. Paul du Var and St. Jeannet.

Motors run to Nice and to Grasse.

Tourettes-sur-Loup.

From Vence, 3¾ miles ; Grasse, 13 ; Nice, 19½.

By the high road to Grasse or by the light railway, one may reach the ancient hill village of **Tourettes-sur-Loup,** which scrambles up along a ridge and still retains portions of its old walls and one of the towers from which it derives its name. Besides the interest of the village there are fine views across the *Loup* to the sea and to the Estérels.

Close by the Place, shaded by elms, is the modern portion of the village in which are the Mairie, the schools and the Post Office. From the Place one enters the **ancient village** by two vaulted gateways, one of which is still covered by a sort of bastion transformed into a clock tower. The other bears traces of the machinery by which the drawbridge was raised and lowered. Having passed through the gateways, one is in the little ancient fortress. The streets make the usual labyrinth through which it is difficult to find one's way. Here and there are sixteenth- and seventeenth-century doorways, Gothic windows and rounded arches of the Norman type.

St. Paul du Var.

The 3 miles or so of road which connect Vence with St. Paul du Var make a delightful promenade, and there is a tram, running at long intervals, for those who cannot walk in both directions.

The road crosses the Valley of the Malvan on a fine viaduct just over 200 yards long and as many feet above the stream, which winds between wooded slopes, making a charming picture.

St. Paul du Var is a small, ancient town around which François I constructed ramparts which were strengthened by Vauban, the great military engineer of the reign of Louis XIV. They still form a continuous wall and there are the gates, towers, bastions, barbicans, and the path along the parapet which the sentry patrolled. This commands a magnificent view. The walls enclose narrow streets bordered by ancient houses, of which some have an old nail-studded door, a sculptured door, or a doorway surmounted by armorial bearings, for the town was once a winter resort of the nobility. In many streets may be seen at least one medieval shop, now used not as a shop but as an entrance to the house. Beside the door, under a wide arch or in a square opening, is the former shop window, closed by a shutter.

In the main street, which runs from the Nice gate to the Vence gate, is a draw-well. In an aperture in the exterior of the wall, immediately to the right of the Vence gate, is a long, narrow, sixteenth-century brass cannon called the **Lacan.** Its origin is unknown.

The **Church,** a fine Gothic structure of the thirteenth or fourteenth century, is famed for its own sake and also for its exquisite wood-carvings and priceless old silver. The high altar dates only from 1818. That which it replaced is in the chapel of Ste. Anne, to the left of the entrance to the church. To the right is the seventeenth-century chapel of St. Clement, a magnificent work of art protected as an historical monument. Under the altar are the bones of the saint in a glass case shown to visitors.

But the chief glory of the church is its treasury. The contents include eight important silver reliquaries, a black Virgin with a flowing robe of silver-gilt, a fifteenth-century silver figure of St. Sebastian, having in its feet linen stained with his blood, a figure of St. John the Baptist containing some of his ashes, and an arm of St. Antoine du Désert. The best of the treasures are classed as historic monuments. (*If it is convenient for the curé to open the Treasury and to act as cicerone, an offering can be made to him for his poor.*)

Two towers near the church are of the thirteenth and fourteenth centuries respectively. The modern one is the belfry; the other belongs to the town.

For centuries St. Paul du Var had no thought of spreading outside its circling ramparts, but now it is beginning to spatter itself over the hill-slopes in villas, and just outside the walls are hostelleries and restaurants.

St. Jeannet.

It is a walk of some 5 miles from Vence to St. Jeannet, towards the north-east. The first portion of the route lies through fertile fields and then descends to the gorge, through which flows the *River Cagne.* From the bridge the road mounts the steep ascent of St. Jeannet, a picturesque village on a precipitous slope at the foot of an old coral crag which rises abruptly to a height of more than a thousand feet. Near the seventeenth-century church is an open space which offers a fine panorama of sea and land. The vine is the chief object of cultivation, and the grapes are renowned, especially

those known as *St. Jean-tardifs*. To obtain and guard these
no care is considered too great.

The ascent from the village to the summit of the rock takes
about an hour, but the view is less grand and extensive than
one would expect.

St. Jeannet is about 2¾ miles from *St. Jean la Gaude*
Station on the Provence light railway.

La Gaude is the name both of a quiet village, which hardly
repays a visit, and the great rock on which the village is
situated and which faces the rock of St. Jean. Between
the two rocks flows the *River Cagne*.

The Gorges-du-Loup.

From Vence the road goes eastward through the village of
Tourettes to the **Pont-du-Loup,** where the road is at the foot
of the **Viaduc-du-Loup,** about 180 feet high and having eleven
arches, each spanning 65 feet. Here is the entrance to the
famous **Gorges-du-Loup,** ravines 6 miles long with huge
masses of limestone and a vast quantity of water running,
leaping, falling. Fully to enjoy the scene ascend the gorges
by the footpath at the bottom, and not by the easier track
high up on the cliff. Opposite the point to which the lower
path leads is a small chapel, built by the Lord of Grasse, in
fulfilment of a vow. In mid-torrent rises a pile of rocks
surmounted by a crucifix. Beyond is a succession of magnificent scenes and increasingly fine falls.

The high road ascending the gorge passes through dense
thickets and reaches the **Cascade-de-Courmes,** or the Pas-de-
l'Echelle, as it is also called. This comes from a height of
some 130 feet. Beyond a short tunnel is the **Pont-de-Courmes.**
Then follow the Tunnel-du-Revest and the fall (1 fr.) called
the **Saut-du-Loup** (the Wolf's Leap), where the rocks rise to
some 1,200 feet above the torrent. Beyond this, the road
to Grasse turns to the left and zigzags up a one-way road to
the village of—

Gourdon,

le nid de l'aigle, " the eagle's nest," as it is nicknamed, perched
2,590 feet above sea-level on the **Dent-du-Loup**—the Wolf's
Tooth—which projects above the deep valley through which
the river struggles.

Gourdon is a poor little typical hill village of narrow ways,
dark arches, a few ramshackle houses, a modest little seventeenth-century church and a château, which has been most
unsympathetically " restored."

A tablet in a wall of its Cour d'honneur says it was constructed in 1710 by the Lombards, an ancient family
who held high offices. Over the door of the fortress are the

THE GORGES DU LOUP.

Ballance,]

[Menton.

THE VIADUCT, GORGES DU LOUP.

16

arms of the Gordons, of whom the village is said to have
been the birthplace. It is said also that from some Gordon
of the dim past the place took its name, but there is neither
legend nor historic evidence to support the story.

From behind the church a wonderful panorama unfolds.
All the rolling country is at one's feet, and the coast is spread out
as on a relief map. To the right is the hazy line of the Estérels ;
the Cap d'Antibes juts into the blue water ; to the left are
some of the buildings of Nice, and still farther to the left
are the promontories of the coast of Menton and Bordighera.

From Gourdon one drops down to Grasse.

GRASSE.

Access.—By the P.L.M. main line to a junction 12½ miles west of Cannes and
thence by a branch line. Grasse Station is 1½ miles by road from the town,
20 minutes by a steep path, and 3 minutes by a funicular railway.
By the Chemin de Fer de la Provence (light railway).
By motor-coach and bus from Cannes, Cagnes, Nice, etc.
Distances.—*By rail.* Paris, 672¼ miles ; Marseilles, 133¾ ; Nice, 30½.
By road. Cannes, 10½ miles ; Nice (*viâ* Villeneuve-Loubet), 21¼.
Inquiries.—*Syndicat d'Initiative*, 12, Boulevard du Jeu-de-Ballon.
Hotels.—*See* p. 29.
Motor-bus Services.—To Cannes, Nice, Gréolières, Saint Auban, Thorenc, etc.
Population.—About 25,000.
Water Supply.—Excellent and abundant.

Its flowers and perfumes have made Grasse widely known
by name. Its air is less exciting than that of places
on the coast. Lofty hills behind it make it a more sheltered
and less windy place than Cannes.

All the year round Grasse has resident visitors, although
it is not primarily a health or pleasure resort but is, as it
has been for many centuries, a manufacturing and commercial
town. Its principal productions are perfumes and scented
soaps. On an average the distilleries use yearly 2,000 tons
of orange flowers, 1,500 tons of roses, 1,200 tons of jasmine
flowers, 400 tons of violets, and an enormous quantity of
other flowers both wild and cultivated. Visitors are admitted into some of the distilleries and factories, but excursionists interested in the past will probably derive more
satisfaction from the exploration of the old town, which in
great part retains its medieval aspect.

It is assembled at the foot of the **Tour-du-Puy,** erected
in the eleventh century on Roman foundations. Upon it is
a tablet commemorating a son of Grasse, Bellaud de la
Bellaudière, a sixteenth-century Jekyll and Hyde, for he
was both a poet and a robber. As the former he was

Riviera (f)

honoured, as the latter he was hanged.   Adjoining the tower
is the **Mairie,** formerly the bishop's palace.   In it is a library
(10–12 ;   2–4) containing interesting MSS. and pictures.

Close by is the **Parish Church,** formerly the cathedral, a
small, low building partly of the twelfth century.   The choir
dates only from the earliest years of the eighteenth century.
The restoration of the church in the seventeenth century
was accompanied by the addition of two crypts cut out
of the solid rock.   In the south transept is the beautiful
chapel of the Holy Sacrament.   An unusual structure behind
the high altar was erected by a bishop for the accommodation
of himself and his clergy.   The most interesting of the
pictures are the *Assumption* by Subleyras, Fragonard's
Washing of the disciples' feet, and a fifteenth-century triptych.
In the Treasury is a reliquary which once contained the bones
of St. Honorat.   It is carved from a solid block of walnut
and is covered with silver plates, on which are archaic representations of scenes in the life of the saint.

Steps at an angle of the Cathedral Square lead down
to Rue Tracastel, which, followed to the right, leads to Rue
du Cours (left) and **Rue Droite** (right), the main thoroughfare
of the old town.   This passes near the Market Place (right),
and its line is continued by Rue Charles Nègre, from which an
archway on the right gives access to a small square.   At the
lower end of a descent from it is *Porte Neuve,* from which
there goes to the right *Place Neuve,* on the line of the eastern
rampart.   Here is the **Post Office.**   At the farther end is
Boulevard Fragonard, commemorating the famous painter,
born at Grasse, 1732.   No. 16 was the eighteenth-century
town house of the Marquis de Cabris and his remarkable wife,
sister of Mirabeau.   It is now the **Musée Fragonard** (closed
Mondays), and contains interesting souvenirs and paintings.

The boulevard winds round the public garden, in which is
a bust of Fragonard, to the **Place du Cours,** a charming
promenade commanding a truly magnificent panorama.   The
funicular railway has its upper station on the Cours.   The
farther end of the Place is connected with **Boulevard
Victor Hugo,** one of the fine thoroughfares of modern
Grasse and the site of the **Hospital du Petit-Paris.**   In the
chapel (*donation expected*) are three early paintings by
Rubens and three works of the eighteenth-century French
painter Natoire.

Walks and Excursions.

These constitute the principal charm of a holiday spent at Grasse and are both varied and numerous.

At 1¼ miles from the town, on the high road to Castellane, is **Le Plateau Napoleon,** a halting-place of Napoleon after landing from the Isle of Elba. It commands a delightful view.

At 3¼ miles on the road to the Pont-du-Loup is the village of **Châteauneuf de Grasse.** In the Grand' Rue, reached from the Place des Bosquets, are houses of the seventeenth and eighteenth centuries and also the Castelet, probably an ancient dependance of the castle.

Le Bar-sur-Loup, 5½ miles towards the east, is a village near the Gorges-du-Loup. Its Grand' Rue is only just wide enough to permit the passage of a laden animal. A great part of the modern quarter is around the château, once belonging to the Lords of Grasse and Bar. The most famous member of the family was that Admiral de Grasse who at the battle of Saintes had all his silver melted down and cast into bullets, but they did not save him from being taken prisoner by the English. After a victorious campaign a ball was given in his honour at Versailles. Only eleven years later the château at Le Bar was pillaged by the villagers who were supporting the Revolution. The **Church** has a beautiful Gothic doorway and contains a picture of the *Dance of Death*, said to have been painted to perpetuate the remembrance of the consequences of a ball given by a Lord of Grasse and Bar in Lent, in spite of the remonstrances of the clergy.

Less than 3 miles from Grasse, on the road to Le Bar-sur-Loup, is **Magagnosc.** Near it is the **Pre'-du-Lac,** a field forming a natural shallow basin which the winter rains convert into a lake.

Ten miles west of Grasse is the village **Saint-Cézaire,** built on the edge of a precipice at the bottom of which flows the *Siagne* in a wild and picturesque defile. At 1¾ miles north-east of the village is the entrance to **grottos.** They are lighted by electricity and can be visited in comfort.

Thorene, 23¾ miles, is situated amidst forests at a height of 4,000 feet above sea-level. The maximum summer temperature is about 77° Fah. In the coldest months there are winter sports.

Vence is 16¼ miles from Grasse, and **St.-Paul-du-Var** 13¼.

NICE.

Access.—*See* pages 22–7.

From Italy and Switzerland by the Nice–Coni (Cuneo) line connecting with Turin, Berne and Bâle.

From Italy also by the P.L.M. line from Ventimille (or Ventimiglia).

From Grenoble *viâ* Marseilles; or by the P.L.M. line to Digne *viâ* St. Auban, and thence by the Chemin de Fer de la Provence.

Aerodrome.—At the mouth of the Var.

Banks.—These include *Barclays*, Promenade des Anglais; *Lloyds and National Provincial*, Jardin du Roi Albert I; *National City Bank of New York*, Avenue de Verdun.

Consulates.—Great Britain, 95 Rue de France.

United States of America, 35 Boulevard Victor Hugo.

Distances.—*By rail.* Aix-les-Bains, 405 miles; Biarritz, 590; Boulogne, 839½; Calais, 864½; Cannes, 19½; Dieppe, 805; Digne, 94½; Grasse, 32; Grenoble *viâ* Marseilles, 356½; Hyères, 98¾; Marseilles, 140½; Monaco, 10; Menton, 15¾; Paris, 679½; San Remo, 32; St. Raphaël, 40; Vichy, 465; Vintimille, 22.

Golf.—At St. Véran, near Cagnes-sur-Mer, reached by motor-bus. *See also* Cannes, Monte Carlo and Sospel.

Hotels.—*See* pp. 30–31. The leading hotels are on the Promenade des Anglais, Boulevard Victor Hugo, Avenue Georges Clemenceau, Boulevard Carabacel, and at Cimiez. Nice has an immense number of hotels and boarding-houses (pensions) of all grades. A list with charges can be obtained on application to the Director of the Syndicat d'Initiative.

Inquiries.—Syndicat d'Initiative, 1 rue Paradis (at the junction of that street with Avenue de Verdun).

Libraries.—*English-American*, Rue de France; *Lounge*, 16 Rue Maréchal Joffre; *Barnoin Frères*, 5 Rue Honoré Sauvan; *Public*, Boulevard Dubouchage.

Motor-buses between various parts of the town and to neighbouring towns and villages. A time-table is on sale.

A bus goes daily to Ventimiglia, Bordighera, Ospedaletti and San Remo. On certain days it continues to Alassio, Varazze, Genoa, Portofino Vetta, Santa Margherita and Rapallo.

Population.—Approaching 200,000. Doubled at the height of the season.

Post Offices.—A new building nearly opposite the P.L.M. railway station in Avenue Thiers; Place Wilson, Avenue Georges Clemenceau, Place Grimaldi, Rue Parmentier, Place Garibaldi, Boulevard de Cimiez, etc. There are several auxiliary offices in banks and shops. *Poste Restante*, p. 36. There are two boxes just outside the principal railway station. Stamps are sold by the tobacconist just inside the station.

Railway Stations.—P.L.M. line. *Nice*, Avenue Thiers. *Nice–Riquier* (eastward), served only by the omnibus (slow) trains to and from Vintimille. *Nice–Saint Augustin* (westward), *Nice–Saint Roch*, on the Nice–Coni line. Chemin de Fer de la Provence. Avenue Malausséna.

Water.—Nearly all the town is supplied by water from the River Vesubie, first filtered and then purified by ozonization. Other water is purified as at Paris.

T HE greater part of Nice is situated on a semicircular area of flat or gently rising land. In front is the Mediterranean. Elsewhere are low ridges and shallow valleys backed by higher hills, which have behind them the Maritime Alps.

" I am at Nice," wrote an Englishman in December, 1782, " where I am lodged in a charming house situated in the country and at the coast, but halfway up a hill. The peas are in flower ; one finds in the gardens the rose, carnation, anemone, jasmine, as in summer. Oranges and lemons hang from thousands of trees, scattered about the open country or in enclosures."

Where the gardens remain, the flowers and the yellow fruit may still be seen at Christmas-time, but the popularity of the site has led to the destruction of its rural charm. " One comes to Nice as a tourist for a week, or as a winter resident for some months and one remains for life," wrote the poet Théodore de Bainville in 1860, and countless visitors have become residents. In 1860 the population numbered 50,000, and twenty years later, 82,000. In 1901 it was 143,000. Now it is little, if any, less than 200,000.

Even when Nice had half its present population, the modern portion of the town consisted of villas and cottages in gardens bathed in sunshine, but those residences have been replaced or are being replaced by buildings seven or eight stories high, divided into flats and cutting off the sun from their neighbours, so that there are streets that are but deep gorges into which the sunshine never falls. The lamentable transformation is being intensified by the addition of stories to houses lower than their more modern neighbours, and by building on any small garden that was spared a few years ago.

A hundred years before Théodore de Bainville wrote of the charm of Nice, it was the temporary residence of a few foreigners, including the Scottish doctor and novelist, Tobias George Smollett. He arrived in 1763, remained about 1½ years, wrote letters which drew attention to the town and surrounding district ; and in spite of the acerbity of some of his remarks, they induced Britons to visit the sleepy old town, where the sky was almost always blue. In gratitude the Nicois called one of their streets after him, and it still bears his name, although it is not spelt as he spelt it, but appears as Smolett.

The blue sky Nice shares with the rest of the Riviera, but the beautiful bay facing the town, the " Bay of the Angels," is its very own. Its shore is an immense curve, low on the right where it goes on and on towards Cagnes and Antibes, but rising on the left where is the precipitous rock whose summit was the birthplace of the town. Farther away are the slopes of Mont Boron, dotted with trees and houses, and the landscape ends at the extremity of Cap Ferrat, marked by a lighthouse.

The beach is of rounded pebbles, everywhere open to bathers in sea or sun. During the warmest months of the year portions are enclosed by slight barriers within which clusters of cabins are erected for those who prefer privacy for undressing and dressing. Within the enclosures also are deck-chairs and tables, and afternoon tea and other refreshments are served. There may even be found an enclosure with a floor for dancing. Many bathers, however, prefer the cleaner water on the same beach farther west, or at Cagnes, Antibes or Juan-les-Pins.

Overlooking the beach are an aquarium, a bathing establishment, and the **Palais de la Jetée Promenade** in Oriental style, one of Nice's three casinos. It stands on iron piles and is joined to the shore by a short bridge.

Bordering a long portion of the bay is the—

Promenade des Anglais,

one of the finest esplanades in Europe, and the most charming part of Nice. It owes its name to having been in great measure constructed at the expense of the British at Nice in 1822, 3 and 4, in order to provide occupation for unemployed men. The growth of the town has led to the continuation of the promenade westward, and one can now walk along the shore to the mouth of the *Var*, a distance of some $4\frac{1}{2}$ miles. Recently a portion of the promenade was widened, by extending it seaward, to provide increased facilities for motor parking.

The Promenade des Anglais is the haunt of visitors and of those residents who have leisure. Here they assemble in their thousands to bask in the sun to which it is exposed all day long, and to enjoy the superb prospect. Far away to the west is Cap d'Antibes, above which are the hillocks of Vallauris, Cannes and Grasse, and much more distant are the Estérels. Eastward are Cap Ferrat and its lighthouse and Mont Boron, of which mention has already been made. Northward along the curving high ground there will be seen the ruined Fort St. Alban, a great square building marking a good view-point. A little farther along the curve is the

[*Topical.*

QUAI DES ETATS UNIS, NICE.

Riviera.   17

Giletta.]

NICE, FROM MONT BORON.

[*Nice.*

dome of the **Observatory** on Mount Gros. (Visitors admitted on certain days.)

Upon the Promenade des Anglais take place the Battles of Flowers which appear in each winter season's programme. A line of palms and other trees, planted between the road and the pedestrians' path, extends along the promenade. Upon the side farthest from the sea are fine bright buildings comprising some of the largest and most luxurious hotels —the **Palais de la Mediterranée**, the most sumptuous and fashionable of Nice's casinos, opened in 1929; and the **Palais Masséna,** the property of the Prince d'Essling until it was bought by the town and converted into a Museum.

André Masséna, duc de Rivoli, prince d'Essling (1758–1817), born at Nice, where his mother was on a visit, was the son of a small innkeeper at Levens (p. 108). Having served as a non-commissioned officer in the Italian army, he was given the rank of major when he enlisted in the army raised by the French Revolutionaries. He quickly rose and became one of the most illustrious marshals of France. Napoleon named him " l'enfant chéri de la Victoire," but recalled him from the Peninsula for failing to expel Wellington.

Almost opposite the Jetée Promenade is the **Jardin du Roi Albert I,** laid out with palm trees, other ornamental trees and flower-beds filled with a succession of blooming plants, including, during the coldest months, primulas, cyclamen and cinerarias. The grass of the surrounding lawn, as in all other gardens in Nice, is but an annual, sown towards the end of October or early in November, and " dug in " some seven months later. The site lies fallow until seed-time returns.

Adding to the adornment of the spot are a pond with water-fowl, bronze and marble statues, and the *Fountain of the Tritons*, a Greek work brought from Constantinople in the eighteenth century by a descendant of Théodore de Lascaris, Emperor of Constantinople. In the garden also is a bandstand, occupied daily during the winter season. On two sides of the garden is the **Avenue de Verdun,** with very fine palms and with luxury shops mostly closed in summer.

The **Quai des Etats-Unis,** which goes eastward from the Promenade des Anglais, is named in recognition of the part taken by the United States of America in the Great War. It is continued by the short **Quai Rauba Capéu** (rob hat), in allusion to the winds often encountered at the extremity of the cape. Near its farther end is the **Harbour.**

At the meeting-point of the two principal portions of the

sea-front is the mouth of the *Paillon*, a torrent of which the lower part has been covered and on which are now **Place Masséna,** on the eastern side of the Jardin du Roi Albert I, the **Municipal Casino,** and a long area behind that building embraced between Boulevard MacMahon and Avenue Felix Faure, leading to the very large modern Lycée, just beyond which scores of women may be seen washing clothes in the stream. In the rear of the Casino are a garden (Square Masséna) and a statue of the marshal.

The line of Boulevard MacMahon is continued north-eastward by the Boulevard des Italians and the Boulevard Risso. In the latter, No. 60 is the **Natural History Museum** (*open daily, except Sundays and Mondays*). Boulevard MacMahon and the Boulevard des Italians run along the northern side of the old town (p. 91), which also can be entered opposite the eastern side of the Jardin du Roi Albert I, and from the Quai des Etats-Unis.

Running inland from Place Masséna is the wide **Avenue de la Victoire,** one of the principal shopping centres. On each side is a line of giant plane trees whose branches almost meet over the roadway. Similar trees line other important thoroughfares. Arcades are a striking feature in front of the Municipal Casino and adjacent buildings, and are seen also in the lower part of the Avenue de la Victoire.

From the foot of the avenue there goes westward (to the left) the narrow Rue Honoré Sauvan, continued by the narrow, but very busy, **Rue de France,** the ancient highway leading towards the French frontier when that was the *Var.* In it stands a marble cross erected in 1838 to commemorate the presence in Nice of Pope Paul III, as peacemaker between Charles Quint and François I (p. 74).

Opposite is a column erected in 1822 to commemorate visits of Pope Pius VII in 1809 and 1814. A fine building beside the column is called the **Palais of Marie Christine,** in remembrance of the wife of King Charles Felix (of Sardinia, 1821-31), who inhabited it during her stay in Nice.

It was in this neighbourhood that previous to the nine-teenth century visitors found accommodation in the scattered private houses. The Duke of York was here in 1764, and his brother a few years later. The suburb grew rapidly, and in it some of the most distinguished persons in Europe took up residence.

A few yards from the marble cross are the **English-**

American Library and the principal **English Church** in Nice.
Both can be entered from the inland parallel thoroughfare.
In the burial ground (not now used) is the grave, marked
by a large white marble cross, of the Rev. Henry Francis
Lyte (d. 1847), many years vicar of Brixham, Devon, and
author of various hymns, including that beginning "Abide
with me." The present English cemetery is near the town's
great cemetery of Caucade, a mile westward.

Continuing along Avenue de la Victoire, one almost at
once has on the right Rue de l'Hôtel-des-Postes, leading to
the **Post Office** in Place Wilson. A little farther, the Avenue
crosses a very fine wide thoroughfare which on the right is
Boulevard Dubouchage, containing the **Public Library,** and on
the left is Boulevard Victor Hugo, the site of the **American
Church.**

Halfway along the next section of the Avenue is the large
Church of Notre-Dame, the most modern of the parish churches
of Nice. In Avenue Notre-Dame, facing the church, is the
Salle Bréa, used for courses of lectures by University professors
and for exhibitions of pictures. (There is a permanent
exhibition of pictures and sculptures in a Museum in Avenue
des Baumettes on the western side of the town.)

From the head of the Avenue de la Victoire there goes
to the left the Avenue Thiers, the site of the principal **Railway
Station** and the new **General Post Office,** while the line of
the Avenue de la Victoire is continued beyond the railway
viaduct by the equally wide Avenue Malausséna, in which
is the station of the Chemin de Fer de la Provence.

At 1¼ miles from the sea the Avenue ends at **Place Gambetta,**
the site of a statue of that statesman and of one of the several
daily morning markets.

Gambetta was buried in the Château Cemetery (p. 92). Named
in memory of him is a boulevard extending seaward from Boulevard
Joseph Garnier, which runs westward to it from the statue. On
the western side of Boulevard Gambetta, just north of the railway
viaduct, is Boulevard du Czarewitch, leading to the **Russian Cathedral** (*open to visitors*) and an adjoining chapel, commemorating the
Prince Imperial of Russia, who died in a villa here in 1865. The
chapel was built on the site of the villa. A portion of the grounds
remains as the **Parc Imperial,** the site of tennis courts.

Northward from Place Gambetta, Avenue Borriglione runs
to the populous quarter of St. Maurice, to the west of which
is the quarter **St. Barthélemy,** with a church and monastery
founded on the site of a church destroyed by the Turks in

1543. An inscription under the sundial asserts that "The passing hour wounds us : the final one kills us." The spot can easily be reached by way of Boulevard Auguste Raynaud, which runs northward from the centre of Boulevard Joseph Garnier mentioned above. At the top of the boulevard one bears to the left and almost at once to the right. The burial-ground, now only used by families having tombs in it, is the last resting-place of many aristocratic Nicois. Farther north is the St. Sylvestre quarter.

The Boulevard Carabacel, to which lead all the thoroughfares running eastward from the Avenue de la Victoire, lies on the south side of elevated **Carabacel,** one of the most bracing parts of Nice, and favoured by those loving a quiet life. The boulevard is continued northward by the Avenue Désambrois, from which rises the Boulevard de Cimiez, affording fine views and having at its upper end a **Statue of Queen Victoria.** This is at the foot of the grounds of the immense *Hotel Régina*, where, and at the neighbouring *Grand Hotel*, Her Majesty stayed.

Cimiez, the most fashionable part of Nice, occupies the site of the Roman *Cemenelum*, the capital of their province of the Alpes Maritimes. It is said to have had a population of 30,000. Having been burnt by the Lombards in the sixth century and afterwards used as a quarry, there are very few Roman remains.

On the opposite side of the road to the Grand Hotel is a remnant of the **Amphitheatre.** Just beyond it a road on the right leads to a fifteenth-century **cross** (note the six-winged seraph that appeared to St. Francis of Assisi in a vision), the cemetery, church and ancient monastery.

The **Monastery,** now belonging to the town, was founded in 1543, after the destruction of an earlier building. In the church are fine ceiling frescoes, a carved and gilded screen behind the high altar, and, classed as "historic monuments," a triptych and two other pictures by one of the sixteenth-century Bréas of Nice. The monk's garden, open to the public, commands extensive and beautiful views.

A steep road at the extremity of the avenue leads down to **St. Pons,** an industrial quarter, taking its name from the Christian named Pons or Pontius beheaded in 259 because he refused to sacrifice to Apollo in the temple close to the amphitheatre. On or near the site of the execution was founded the Abbey of St. Pons, in 775. The existing building is used as a lunatic asylum. St. Pons had also a house for nuns. A very interesting story in *Legendes*

[*Eclecta and Patras.*

NICE.
Promenade des Anglais—Jardin Albert I—Palais de la
Jeteé Promenade.

A STREET IN OLD NICE.

and Contes de Provence, by Martin Donos, professes to account for the closing of the institution.

Rendered more striking by contrast with the riches and luxury but a stone's-throw away are the poverty and misery enshrined in the warren of dark and smelly narrow streets and squalid alleys of—

The Old Town.

That part with which visitors generally first make acquaintance is the **Rue St. François de Paule,** which opens from the Avenue des Phocéens, bordering the Jardin du Roi Albert I. It is a portion of a quarter built in the eighteenth century upon waste land and convent gardens outside the old rampart. Until the middle of last century, it was the aristocratic street of Nice. It is the site of the **Mairie,** originally a hospital; the **Church** of St. François de Paule, begun in 1736 at the same time as the neighbouring houses; the **Municipal Opera House ;** and the ancient prefecture, No. 8, in which Napoleon stayed for five days in 1796, and which received Pope Pius VII in 1809 and 1814.

During the winter the street is the site of the wonderful **Flower Market,** held every forenoon. The stalls, laden with glorious blooms, extend into Cours Saleya, occupied by the **Vegetable and Fruit Market.** In the eighteenth century this area was so treated that it became the most beautiful quarter of Nice and the rendezvous of the town's most fashionable inhabitants, who had also as their promenade the **Terraces** formed by the level roofs of the two parallel rows of low buildings on the seaward side.

Opposite a wide opening on the northern side of the Cours Saleya is the **Prefecture,** dating from 1611 and originally the palace of the Duke of Savoy. Just westward of it is the **Palais de Justice,** inaugurated in 1891. By passing eastward before the northern side of the Prefecture, one soon has on the left the narrow Rue Ste. Réparate. A tablet on the corner house, an extensive building, commemorates the death there, in 1840, of *Paganini*, the celebrated Italian violinist.

The side street leads to the **Cathedral.** In 1658 its dome collapsed : among the many victims was the bishop. It was rebuilt in 1737 and restored in 1901. There are very fine monuments in honour of bishops Colonna d'Istria and Sola, ancient heads of the diocese of Nice, and the Treasury contains many objects of great interest. Place and Rue Rossetti, on the opposite side of Rue Ste. Réparate, soon lead to **Rue Droite,** running north and south, once occupied by the goldsmiths, and the finest street in the town. No. 15 is **Palais Lascaris,** dating from the seventeenth century, and formerly the sumptuous dwelling of the great family whose name it bears.

The Château Hill.

If a visit to the **Château Hill** is combined with a visit to the old town, go southward along Rue Droite to the stepped **Rue du Château,** which leads to the Montée du Château. An alternative route for pedestrians is up steps at the eastern end of the Quai des Etats-Unis. The steps pass the Tour Bellanda, now a belvedere of the adjacent hotel, but originally part of the fortifications. For those who go by carriage or car the route lies along the Quai des Etats-Unis and the eastern side of the hill, the site of the imposing **War Memorial,** or along Boulevard MacMahon and Boulevard des Italians to **Place Garibaldi,** with its interesting statue of that general, a native of Nice, and thence for a short distance along Rue Catherine Ségurane.

Of the castle from which the hill takes its name there are only a few masses of masonry among the trees which adorn the height, now ascended for the very fine view from its summit, some 315 feet above the sea. As a picture, the prospect is seen at its best in the morning or towards the close of the day. The prominent points in the panorama, to which no words can do justice, can be recognized by the aid of an orientation table erected by the Touring Club of France. A short distance below the summit is a **Cascade** fed by the River Vesubie. One of the most notable monuments in the neighbouring **Cemetery** is that of Gambetta, who was buried in 1880 beside his mother. Another tomb of more than local interest is that of the mother and the wife of Garibaldi.

The cemetery is used now only by families owning tombs in it.

Sports and Amusements.

The second day of January sees the first of the **Horse Races,** which are among the most important in France. Steeplechasing takes place in January, trotting in February, and flat-racing in March. The course is near the mouth of the

Var. In the second week in April there are international military races on ground adjoining the hippodrome.

In January is the first of the international tennis tournaments in the Parc Imperial, the centre of the game in Nice. International regattas are organized by the Club Nautique de Nice. At Peïra Cava and Beuil are ski-ing competitions organized by the French Alpine Club. There is a local **Golf Club** which has an 18-hole course at St. Véran, adjoining Cagnes-sur-Mer and easily reached by bus.

As for amusements, there is no other Riviera resort which makes better provision. The casinos, the opera, the theatres and the numerous cinemas have tempting programmes throughout the winter season, and some of the places of amusement are open in summer also. On every hand there are opportunities for dancing, the large municipal band plays daily in the open air, and fêtes succeed one another almost without interruption. Of these the most popular and attractive is—

The Carnival.

Carnem-Vale, "good-bye meat," because it ends on the eve of Lent. The festival, said to be a remnant of the Bacchanalian and Saturnalian festivals of the ancients, begins with the entry of the fatuous and gargantuan King Carnival into the beautifully and profusely illuminated town. On the two following Sundays, afternoon and evening, with many bands of music and a train of courtiers with whose appearance newspapers and cinemas have made all familiar, the King of Folly parades certain streets, and on the evening of Shrove Tuesday he is burnt at the stake after a torchlight procession. To each royal progress the king's subjects are invited by a herald attended by trumpeters all duly apparelled and on horseback. During the processions there is throwing of unlimited paper confetti—except on the second Sunday afternoon, when, in compliance with the clamour of the veritable Nicois, the Mayor permits the use of pellets of plaster, making prudent the wearing of old clothes and a wire mask.

Other towns on the Riviera and elsewhere have their carnival, but none equals that of Nice.

In England a carnival as understood on the shore of the Mediterranean is impossible. The southern sunshine and light-hearted temperament are necessary to make such a festival a success. How many respectable British fathers of families, eminent citizens and functionaries could, with unselfconscious joy, parade the streets in broad daylight wearing a false nose or otherwise absurdly disguised, dancing, singing, and playing the fool?

During the Carnival the fêtes of the day are followed by the *Veglione* of the Opera House, and the *redoutes* of the municipal casino—masquerade fancy-dress balls worth attending for the spectacle.

Historical Note.

The band of Greeks who disputed possession of this part of the coast with its primitive inhabitants came from Marseilles. Somewhere in the neighbourhood of Corsica they encountered a hostile fleet which they defeated, and then they made for the bay which is now the Bay of the Angels; and there, at the eastern extremity of what is now the Castle Rock, they drew up their boats on the shore of a small cove, the little cove of the Ponchettes, a name derived from a Nicois word signifying "little point." Having conquered the Ligurians who had their stronghold on the crag rising above the point, they established themselves in the coves, on one side of which was Mont Boron, and on the other the Castle Hill of to-day. On the ruins of the native encampment they erected a temple dedicated, probably, to Artemis. They called their settlement *Nike*, commonly said to signify victory. In course of time Nike became changed into the softer Nice.

The Greek colony flourished until the coming of the Romans, and then, although it was left undisturbed, it began to decline. When the settlement lost the protection of the Romans, it was harassed by the barbarians and was destroyed by them in the sixth century. Then the summit of the rock became inhabited and fortified. In time stout walls enclosed the castle of the governor, a cathedral, a bishop's palace, a town hall and residences of nobles. At the foot of the rock were humbler dwellings. These formed the Low Town; the settlement on the rock was the High Town.

In the twelfth century the inhabitants of the Low Town surrounded it by ramparts and bastions, which have almost entirely disappeared. In 1518 another great change occurred. The civil buildings on the summit of the rock had to be abandoned in order that the whole of the site might be occupied by military works. These in their turn were levelled in 1706 by order of Louis XIV, and were never rebuilt. It must be remembered that in those days Nice was not a

French town. It was taken and retaken again and again
by the kings of France and the princes of the House of Savoy,
successively entitled Counts of Savoy, Dukes of Savoy, Kings
of Sardinia.

The onerous conscription which the population suffered
under Napoleon led to the acclamation of the new king of
Sardinia upon Napoleon's overthrow in 1814. The third
Napoleon wished the town and county to be returned to
France, and in 1860 a plebiscite ratified the return. Only
159 votes were cast against it ; over 26,000 for it. Since
that important transfer was made the history of the town
has been that of its extraordinary growth due to its popularity by reason of its beautiful situation and its winter
sunshine.

Walks and Excursions.

The neighbourhood of Nice is singularly charming, and the
pedestrian may spend many happy hours in exploring it.
As the country has been pushed farther and farther off by
the expansion of the town, the walks must often begin by
a bus ride, if the pedestrian would spare himself a tramp of
the best part of an hour before getting to the lanes and roads
which run into the semicircle of hills shutting in the town
and commanding a succession of delightful prospects.

From St. Sylvestre, a northern quarter reached by way
of Avenue Borriglione (p. 90), or Boulevard de Cessole, a
continuation of Boulevard Gambetta (p. 89), a path leads
through the **Vallon Obscur,** a picturesque little ravine, muddy
after rain, to which the stream that comes from it is a sufficient
guide. As it is sunless, it is prudent to take something to
put over the shoulders when going through it.

The summit of **Mont Gros,** the peninsula **St. Jean-Cap-Ferrat ;**
the high ground of **Le Piol,** reached by a road near the upper
end of Boulevard Gambetta ; the **Vallon des Fleurs,** entered
from St. Maurice (p. 89) ; the **Cascade de Gairaut,** farther
north ; **Saint André** (p. 97) and the village of **Falicon,** which
can be made the object of a walk from Cimiez—are among
the spots within easy walking distance of Nice or from the
end of a short bus ride. For these and other jaunts, the
maps in a guide in English, published by the Tramway
Company, will be exceedingly useful. Really good walkers
should join the outings arranged by the Touring Club of
France. Its local headquarters are at 43, Boulevard Dubouchage (p. 89).

Motor Coaches go westward as far as Marseilles, eastward to San Remo in Italy, and visit all the northern points of interest within range of a day's run. No other resort in the French Riviera gives such a choice of outings. Certain coaches are accompanied by an English-speaking guide.

Visitors whose time is very limited will do well to take a seat in a coach which, each morning and afternoon, with an English-speaking guide, makes the tour of Nice and its surroundings.

TO MENTON BY THE GRANDE CORNICHE.

The Grande Corniche is the highest of the three roads between Nice and Menton, the others being the **Moyenne** (Middle) **Corniche** and the **Corniche du Littoral,** the coast road. An elevated route was followed by the Phœnicians, by the Roman armies and by armies in the Middle Ages. This was in places so steep and narrow that only a mule could pass along it. Dante traversed it as an exile, and it suggested to him an image of a road out of Purgatory.

Finding the coast route too narrow for the passage of his army, and the old high route quite useless for his purpose, Napoleon in 1806 constructed the Grande Corniche as we see it to-day. No visitor at Cannes, Nice, Menton or any intervening place should omit to travel along it from end to end.

The Grande Corniche commands glorious views in every direction, and the aspects and outlooks are ever varying. On one side are the rugged spurs and offshoots of the mountains, the lower slopes bearing olive trees, the upper slopes showing their grey rock, and on the distant horizon, the Maritime Alps with snow-crests. On the other side, far below, the varied coast tract—steep precipices, cultivated terraces, curved bays and far-projecting promontories, embosomed in a wilderness of olive, pine and other greenery— and stretching away to the southern horizon, the sapphire plain of the Mediterranean.

Perhaps the best time for the passage is when the sun casts its radiance over the scene from the south-west.

The route from Nice begins at **Place Risso,** on the east bank of the Paillon, from which it lies along the Avenue des Diables Bleus. At the end of the avenue it goes to the left and takes the right branch at the fork. It climbs the side of Mont Vinaigre, affording a view over Nice. After passing

Ballance,] [*Menton.*

THE FLOWER MARKET, NICE.

Ballance,] [*Menton.*

A FOUNTAIN AT SOSPEL.

Riviera.

Ballance,] [*Menton.*

EZE.

Ballance,] [*Menton.*

SOSPEL.

a little chapel it soon has, on its right, the Observatory, and there opens out a view of the Paillon Valley. On one side is **St. André,** with its seventeenth-century château; on the other, **La Trinité Victor.** High above the latter is Falicon. A patch of grey in the mountains, 7 miles away, is **Peille** (p. 113). Where the Paillon is lost to view is **Drap** (p. 112). At 3¾ miles from Nice are the **Col des Quartre-Chemins** (1,130 feet), and a monument to Masséna, who is there said to have breakfasted ! One of the four ways zigzags down to the Middle Corniche.

The Grande Corniche goes straight on, and discloses on the south a beautiful panorama in which are Mont Alban with its ruined citadel, the Bay of Villefranche, St. Jean-Cap-Ferrat, St. Hospice with its tower, and Beaulieu. Farther away is Mont Bastide, on which are the remains of a Roman camp, and beyond is the Château de Eze.

At the **Col d'Eze** (1,694 feet) is another panorama, beautiful and extensive. There is a stretch of coast from Tête-de-Chien eastward to St. Tropez westward. There is the old town of Eze with its charm and bay. Inland, snow-clad Alps. Westward, Vence, the Gorges du Loup, the Baou (rock) de St. Jeannet with the village at its foot. Eastward, Mont Agel, recognizable by its scar.

About a mile farther is the **Capitaine,** where the Corniche attains its greatest height (1,772 feet), and a footpath goes to Eze (p. 98). There follows a gentle descent to La Turbie (p. 128) (1,585 feet), beyond which there comes into view Monaco, Monte Carlo, Cap Martin, and the coast of Italy to Bordighera. Still descending, the Grande Corniche passes below Roquebrune (p. 137) and shortly afterwards joins the common highway which is followed to Menton.

BY THE MIDDLE CORNICHE TO EZE AND SOSPEL.

The Middle Corniche, La Corniche Moyenne, is much the most modern of the three roads between Nice and Menton. It was many years in the making and was not completed until 1921. Its construction was undertaken to relieve the heavy traffic along the coast road between Nice and Monte Carlo. It is a fine, broad thoroughfare, and is much more sheltered than either of the other routes. At Nice it is entered from **Place Saluzzo,** reached from Place Masséna by Avenue Felix Faure (on the north side of the Casino), crossing

the covered-over Paillon to Place Garibaldi and thence
following Rue Bonaparte eastward.

The Middle Corniche soon mounts to the **Col de Villefranche,**
from which there is a fine view of Villefranche and of the
coast eastward of it, while on an elevated site in front are
the ruins of **Olivula.** Its history is unknown, but on its
site have been found coins and other objects of Greek,
Roman and Carthaginian origin, as well as Neolithic stone
weapons and implements.

A tunnel carries the road under the ruins. At the end is
the Vale of St. Michel, and the old town of Eze (*aise*) (5½
miles) is seen. It is reached after a deep ravine has been
crossed. It is **Eze-en-haut** to distinguish it from **Eze-le-bas**
or **Eze-sur-mer.**

Ancient Eze

is one of the most curious of the old hill-towns of the Riviera.
Its only entrance is by the Moor's Gate. Miserable dwellings,
many of them deserted, line the tortuous streets, often
vaulted, forming a veritable maze—and electrically lighted !
There are stone doorways with Moorish ornamentation,
doors worth looking at, and beautiful stone windows. The
Church, enlarged and restored in 1765, is of little interest.

In spite of the strength of its position, Eze was again and
again successfully attacked. In 1543 its thirteenth-century
Castle was blown up. In February, 1887, it was damaged
by an earthquake, and in May of the same year its walls were
split by lightning. Some three or four years after the Great
War it was bought by Mr. Barlow, the American composer,
and was converted into a summer residence. Less in keeping
with its surroundings is a residence built by the Crown
Prince of Sweden.

In 1929 there was inaugurated a fountain, by which Mr. Barlow
provided the town with pure water. Until then, apart from rain-
water cisterns, the only water supply had been a fountain at the
foot of the final ascent by the path from the shore. The Greeks,
who are supposed to have formed the first settlement here, and
from the name of whose goddess, Isis, is supposed to have come
the name of the place, had no water, and in the centuries that
have elapsed no government, no private individual, had taken
measures to provide it.

The fortunes of Eze are curiously linked with the town of
Southampton, for in 1338, during the war between France

and England in the reign of Edward III, a fleet of Spanish
and Genoese galleys, aiding the French, burnt and plundered
Southampton. With his share of the booty the leader,
Carlo Grimaldi of Monaco, bought the town of Eze.

Beyond Eze the Middle Corniche reaches its highest point,
1,200 feet. At 9½ miles from Nice the Observatory of
Monaco is passed. At 2¼ miles farther Monte Carlo and
the Little Corniche are reached, and the route is thence
eastward to **Menton,** 18½ miles. *See* pages 131–4. For the
route thence to **Sospel,** *see* page 138.

The Nice–Coni (or Cuneo) Railway

affords an alternative route from **Nice to Sospel.** The line,
opened in 1928, links Nice with the Italian Cuneo– (or Coni)
Ventimiglia line, and thus there is now direct railway communication between Southern France and Northern Italy.

The route is rich in mountain scenery and picturesque
villages. It crosses deep valleys, runs on the side of precipices, and is carried through tunnels having a total length of
nearly a fourth of the length of the line.

Out of Nice it climbs the valley of the Paillon to the village
of L'Escarène, and thence passes under the Col de Braus,
in a tunnel nearly 3¾ miles in length. From the tunnel it
traverses the picturesque **Vale of Sospel,** beyond which it
passes the frontier by the Mont Grazian tunnel, some 2¼ miles
long. At the northern end is the valley of the *Roya,* in
which is the international station and junction of *Breil.*
From this a branch, 14 miles long, goes southward to **Ventimiglia,** while the main line follows the valley of the *Roya*
northward towards Fontan and Saorge. Hereabouts are
two interesting structures, the **Saorge Bridge,** spanning the
Roya at a height of 197 feet, and the **Scarasson Bridge,**
131 feet above the bottom of the valley.

At 39 miles from Nice the Italian frontier is reached and
then begins the 24-mile section constructed by the Italian
government.

LA BASSE CORNICHE.

The Coast Road between Nice and Monte Carlo.

Between Nice and Monte Carlo the railway passes through
countless tunnels, so that passengers by train miss much of
the marvellous scenery that is enjoyed by those who travel
along the high road. Although the journey from east

to west has few rivals, it is when going in the opposite direction that there is presented one of the most beautiful scenes that the world can offer. The road hugs the coast in parts so closely that it runs on precipices against which the sea dashes. It is an exceedingly busy thoroughfare, as along it lie highly favoured resorts.

Nice can be left by way of **Place Garibaldi** and **Rue Cassini** on its eastern side, or by passing round the extremity of the **Château Hill** (p. 92) and then along the western side of the harbour. At the northern end of the port it meets the route *viâ* Place Garibaldi, and then both go eastward, passing the Church of the Immaculate Conception, beyond which they enter Boulevard Carnot. Beyond the Octroi post (one of some twenty-five at which taxes have to be paid on a long list of articles brought into the town) is the **Queen Victoria Memorial Hospital,** and then soon there comes into view the renowned harbour of Villefranche and the coast of St. Jean-Cap-Ferrat.

Forward and backward the view is superb. The picturesque old town of **Villefranche** (p. 117) on the shore is backed by precipitous hills, and by a turn of the head the curve of the bay may be followed towards Antibes.

Extending southward from **Pont St. Jean** is Cap Ferrat (p. 114). Beyond Pont St. Jean the coast road opens up another beautiful panorama. On the right are the east coast of Cap Ferrat, the village of St. Jean and the old tower on St. Hospice. Ahead is Cap d'Ail. Above it is the **Tête-de-Chien** (1,700 feet). The rock is not so called on account of a supposed resemblance to a dog's head, but through the corruption of the original name which signified head of the camp.

In the immediate foreground, ½ mile from Pont St. Jean, is **Beaulieu** (p. 119). The coast road traverses it from end to end. On leaving that part which is known as the **Petite Afrique** (p. 120), it passes through a tunnel cut in Cap Roux, and ½ mile beyond it reaches Eze Station, with the houses of **Eze-sur-Mer,** a comparatively new resort at the foot of the lofty rock on which ancient Eze (p. 98) was founded centuries ago. The modern portion is composed of villas in gay gardens, and is sheltered from all winds except those from the sea. Near the station there starts a steep and difficult path, which winds through olive groves and amid pines to ancient Eze. A better approach from the coast road is by a carriage road, 3 miles long, branching off 1½ miles farther eastward at **St. Laurent d'Eze.**

Eastward also the coast road crosses a viaduct where are, on the left, an ancient Benedictine Monastery, and on the right the Gulf of St. Laurent, where the Phœnicians and the Romans had a port.

Ten miles from Nice is—

Cap d'Ail,

(Hotels—*Eden; du Soleil*)

a charming little beflowered resort adjoining the Principality of Monaco and within easy reach of the gaieties of its renowned neighbour. Here, as elsewhere along the coast road, the garden walls of the villas are draped with red and pink ivy-leaved geraniums and bougainvillæa prodigal of its purple flowers. Cap d'Ail has sheltered little beaches, admirable for sun- or sea-bathing, and more attractive to some dwellers on the neighbouring territory than is their own beach of Larvotto. Along the coast there is a pleasant footpath to Monaco, and a road winds up to **La Turbie,** 3¾ miles (p. 128).

The coast road crosses the frontier a few yards from the cemetery and 11¾ miles from Nice reaches Place d'Armes of **Monaco** at the foot of the rock. The road to **Monte Carlo** follows the sea-shore, fronting the **Condamine,** passes before the Church of Ste. Dévote and ascends a steep gradient to the world-famed Casino.

To the Gorges of Daluis,

situated to the north-west of Nice, in the upper part of the *Var.*

For a short distance the route runs westward, as for Cagnes. At Californie it turns to the right for the carriage road along the left (eastern) bank of the *Var* (p. 75). On the opposite bank is seen St. Laurent du Var, and then come into view the slopes of **La Gaude** (p. 80) and the Baou of **St. Jeannet** (p. 79), both farther away from the river and farther north. At 3¾ miles from the Nice–Cagnes main road, a branch road goes eastward to St. Isidore, about ½ mile distant. The route crosses fertile land recovered from the *Var,* and some 2 miles from the Isidore turning one has, on the hills on the right, **St. Roman de Bellet,** in the heart of the Bellet vine-growing district, especially famed for the Château-Bellet wine. In the church of St. Roman is a miraculous sixteenth-century image of the Virgin.

A short mile beyond St. Roman is the **Pont de la Manda,** nearly ¼ mile long, which carries the light railway and a carriage road across the river. The village on the opposite side, perched on a rounded hill covered with vines, olives and orange-trees, is **Gattières,** 14½ miles from Nice (p. 116). Continuing, one has on the right **Mont Chauve,** seen from many parts of Nice. On its flank are Aspremont (p. 110) and Castagniers, marked by its steeple.

On the western side of the river, opposite Castagniers, is Carros, where the Romans had a station. The Château of the Blacas now crowns the height. A mile or more to the north is **Le Broc,** which was also a Roman station, and long after the departure of the Romans was a fortified village.

It is situated near the confluence of the Estéron with the Var, and commands a delightful panorama. The village has a church dating from 1563 and a fifteenth-century hostel, and is noted for the delicacy of its olives. Its name has nothing to do with the French word for jug, but is said to be derived from the Provençal word for grafted olive-trees.

Next on the eastern side of the river is **St. Martin du Var,** on a rocky spur dominating the valleys of the *Var* and the *Estéron.* A short distance farther is **La Roquette,** situated on a conical peak from which there is a most beautiful view.

The route crosses the river by the **Pont Charles Albert** and ascends through olives and pines to **Gilette,** 1,380 feet above sea-level. By fortifying the southernmost of the two rocks on which it is situated, the Counts of Provence protected the valley of the *Estéron.* In 1793, its defences having been opportunely strengthened, it checked the advance of an Austro-Sardinian army, and the garrison having been reinforced, the attackers were put to flight. The conflict was so important that a picture of it was placed in the Gallery of Battles at Versailles.

For some time the route runs along a level tract below which the *Estéron,* full of fish, flows through gorges amidst high mountains, and then the route descends to the charming little village of **Roquesteron-Puget,** with cemented streets lighted by electricity. It is situated at the foot of Mount Long and is connected by a bridge with **Roquesteron-Grasse,** dating from Roman times.

Then the route rises to **Sigale,** situated between two rocky points which seem to bar the way through the valley. It was a stronghold of the Romans, and in the Middle Ages the Counts of Provence made the site almost impregnable, by erecting a castle on the highest point. It was demolished in 1744. Where the keep stood is now an incongruous square tower erected by the municipality in 1903.

Here the route leaves the Estéron and ascends northward.

It passes **La Penne,** whose quarters are named Salomon, Uriel, Manasses, and the Valley of Canaan, from which it is surmised that the village was founded by a band of Jews. Soon is reached the **Col St. Raphaël,** 3,000 feet high. From the pass the road descends to **Puget-Théniers** (1,460 feet), a summer station in the midst of gardens wrested from the bed of the *Var.* The village is divided by the *Roudoule,* a torrent reddened by the rocks over which it passes. Under the Romans, Puget-Théniers was an important trading town.

The *Var* is crossed and one is then in the Basses Alpes. The road passes the ruins of the ancient town of **Glandèves.** After it had been several times destroyed by the flooding of the *Var* or by barbarian invaders, the inhabitants migrated to a spot on the opposite side of the river and there founded the fortified town of **Entrevaux**—between vales—4½ miles from Puget-Théniers. Its church was the cathedral of the diocese of Glandèves. It is noted for the beauty of its choir. The fortifications remain as they were constructed in 1693.

From the bridge of Gueydan, at the confluence of the *Vaïre* and the *Var*, the route changes its direction. It now runs along the western side of the *Var*, which is coming from the north-east. Shortly after passing **Castellet-les-Sausses,** on the heights, the route leaves the Basses Alpes to re-enter the Alpes Maritimes and arrive at **Daluis.** About 1¼ miles from Daluis a sphinx carved by nature out of a red rock guards the entrance of the **Gorges.** "The vegetation becomes rare and then disappears ; to the white calcareous rocks, the grey schists, succeed the red schists. All is sombre red in this savage defile. The narrow winding road to the summit of the gorge buries itself in tunnels. Down below, the *Var* splashes from cascade to cascade, roars, froths and precipitates itself into the ever-deepening abyss."

Then the gorge widens, the red pales, the sun shines afresh, the mountains resume their familiar tints, the vegetation reappears, cultivated fields, a chapel with an alpine-like wooden roof, an avenue of poplars, and in the narrow space between the *Var*, the *Suébie* with its black waters, and the mountain, is **Guillaumes,** over 2,600 feet above the sea and 60½ miles from Nice, but lighted by electricity and with running water in the rooms of its principal hotel. High on a rugged rock are the ruins of the castle constructed in the eleventh century by Count William II, who gave his name to the town. Forming the background of the picture is the valley of the upper *Var*, dominated by the majestic **Mounier,** often snow-clad.

Guillaumes is the limit of the excursion. The return is generally made by the outward route as far as Puget-Théniers and thence by the eastern side of the Var.

To the Gorge of the Cians and to Beuil.

This excursion passes through most wonderful mountain and river scenery and reaches an elevation 364 feet above that of Ben Nevis, the highest mountain in the British Isles, but while the summit of Ben Nevis is generally cloud-capped, it will be a very exceptional day, either summer or winter, if Beuil is not found bathed in sunshine.

In places the road is cut out of the rock, and as it is not everywhere suitable for charabancs, the excursion has to be made in small cars.

As far as **Pont Charles Albert** (p. 102), the route is identical with that to the Gorge of Daluis. In the district called the **Plan du Var** the *Var* receives the *Vésubie* (p. 107). On the opposite bank is the village of **Bonson,** on an elevated site surrounded by a hollow making a natural fosse across which, in troubled times, was a drawbridge, but in these peaceful days there is a permanent passage.

Continuing along the eastern bank of the *Var*, the road lies through the defile of Ciaudan and the *Gorge of Mescla*, at the junction of the *Tinée* with the main stream. So enclosed by the mountains and so deep is the gorge that the sun never fully penetrates it. Beyond it the valley broadens out, and having crossed the *Var*, which is now coming from the west, the route lies for some distance along the southern bank and passes the small and ancient village of **Malaussène,** situated in a fold of Mount Vial, just south-ward of the road.

If an old chronicler may be believed, the name is a cor-ruption of Mala-Cena (bad supper), a name given to it by its feudal lord in revenge for the unsatisfactory meal with which he was served when bad weather compelled him to spend a night in the place. The village is about 25 miles from Nice, and stands at a height of 810 feet above the sea.

Upon the other side of the river is the village of **Massoins,** which has been well described as " a little oasis in the midst of rocky precipices."

A mile or so beyond Malaussène the road crosses the river opposite **Villars,** on a table-land covered with orchards, olive groves, and vineyards which produce an esteemed wine. Its church possesses a retable on which is a representation of the Annunciation, considered one of the best works of

Louis Bréa. Another treasured possession is a wooden statue of St. John the Baptist, carved in 1524.

The castle, the favourite residence of the Grimaldis of Beuil, was destroyed by the Duke of Savoy in 1412. The Grimaldis rebuilt it, making it more comfortable and even luxurious. Two hundred years later (1618) the Count de Beuil, carried away by pride during the festivities accompanying the marriage of his daughter to the Count de Bar, marshal of France and the sworn foe of the Duke of Savoy, effaced from the walls of the castle the shield of Savoy and substituted his own arrogant device, " I am Count de Beuil.   I do what I will."   Three years later the duke's forces made him prisoner in his castle of Tourette, between St. Martin du Var and Malaussène. As he had boasted that he would rather die at the hand of a Turk than recognize the authority of the Duke of Savoy, he was strangled by two Turkish slaves, brought from Nice for the purpose.   Then the duke caused all the castles that the count had held to be razed to the ground and took possession of all his lordships, which occupied a great part of the county of Nice.

Some 5 miles westward the road reaches the vicinity of the small village of **Touët-de-Beuil,** 1,400 feet above sea-level, half-way up a hill on the right. Amidst the houses are open-sided structures, recalling Dutch barns, used for the drying of figs and other fruit. Its church spans a torrent which can be seen through a grating in the nave. The village owes its name to a rude building which the Grimaldis built as a shelter when hunting. In the language of the country it was a " touët," meaning a hospitable roof. Beuil was added to indicate the owner.

A very short distance farther the road crosses a stream, the *Cians,* which comes from the north, and the route turns in that direction. At the mills of **Rigaud** the valley widens. Half-way up a hill is the village, said to have been the stronghold of a brigand bearing the name borne by the village. On the opposite bank is **Lieuche,** of which only the church steeple is visible.

At **Pradastie,** on the same side of the stream as the road and facing the Valley of Pierlas on the other side, is the lower end of the famous **Gorge of the Cians,** through which " the torrent leaps from rock to rock, splashing with white foam the chaotic mass of enormous rocks of violently contrasting colours. As one ascends, the mountains close in and the road as it creeps up becomes embedded in the slatey rock through which it has been cut."

In winter one looks upon " a fairy palace of crystal with mighty stalactites of ice ; in summer, upon a symphony of

red and flamboyant shades. Overhead only a small strip
of blue sky can be seen through the narrow gap separating
the lofty mountains. Then, as by the touch of a magic
wand, all this disappears, and one finds oneself in open alpine
country ; vast stretches covered with grass or snow, according to the season, and forests of fir and larch.'' The outward
journey is nearly ended. Not far ahead, on a hillock in the
centre of a broad tableland is—

Beuil.

Hotels.—*See* p. 29.
Inquiries.—Syndicat d'Initiative. For inquiries by post, *see* p. 32.
Water Supply.—Abundant.

Situated 4,770 feet above sea-level, Beuil is a summer
resort and a centre for winter sports. Early in the season
the snow becomes deep. The ice for skaters covers nearly
3 acres. Skis, etc., can be obtained at the office of the
Syndicat d'Initiative.

At the entrance of the village houses and hotels have arisen
to meet the needs of visitors. The streets of the older part
are irregular, and for the most part are formed of flights
of steps lined by dilapidated houses with great wooden,
steeply sloping roofs.

Summer visitors see little life in the village, as the inhabitants are then feeding their flocks on the mountains or
cultivating the small plains and valleys in the neighbourhood.
But there are many attractive walks, and guides of the
Club Alpin Français and muleteers can be engaged for excursions on which they are necessary. Of the castle which
occupied the summit of the hill there are only very slight
remains. Its disappearance has been accounted for in connection with Villars.

On **Mont Mounier,** which dominates the village, is an
observatory dependent on that at Nice. It is at an elevation
of 8,970 feet. The principal peak is nearly 200 feet higher.

From October to March the return to Nice has to be
made by the route followed in the morning, but from March
to October it is made by the Gorge of Daluis, the road
between the two being then practicable.

For this Beuil is left by a road which ascends through
grass land and forests of firs and larches to the **Col du Quartier,**
at a height of 5,915 feet, where a comfortable refuge has
been constructed by the Winter Sports Club. From this

pass the road descends to Peone, 8¼ miles from Beuil and
63 from Nice, situated at the foot of sharp-pointed rocks.
The route thence runs south-westward, alongside a streamlet,
the *Turbie*, which joins the *Var* at **Guillaumes** (p. 103).
Thence the route lies through the **Gorges of Daluis.** It is
described in the reverse direction on pages 101–103.

To St. Martin Vésubie.

Access.—Chemin de Fer de la Provence, 4 hours. Motor-coaches 2 hours (*see*
      below). Motor-buses.
Hotels.—*See* p. 31.
Inquiries.—Syndicat d'Initiative.—At the Mairie.
Population.—About 2,000.

An alpine station often called the capital of the Switzerland
of Nice.   It is situated at an elevation of 3,120 feet above
sea-level, 37½ miles from Nice, at the confluence of the two
torrents, Fenestre and Boréon, whose united waters form the
River Vésubie.   In summer it is a very popular resort of the
permanent residents of Nice ; in winter it is the terminus of
a very attractive excursion.

A streamlet rushes down **Rue Droite** or Rue Centrale,
which goes through the town from end to end.   In it are
old houses, sculptured doors, churches and covered passages.
Entering the street from the square and descending, there is
almost at once on the right the church of the Penitents
Blancs, with three modern reliefs on the façade.   Where the
street forks there is seen ahead on the right the ancient
residence of the Comtes de Gubernatis with a pointed arcade
and machicolations.   The left branch leads to the **Parish
Church,** built by the Templars.   Among the treasures of
the sacristy are a fourteenth-century processional cross of
silver, a velvet cope said to have been the gift of the Duke
of Savoy in 1564, and two panels, one of which is attributed
to Louis (Ludovic) Bréa.

A niche is the winter resting-place of the *Madone de Fenêtre*,
a Moorish statue of the Virgin brought from Palestine.   In
summer she is in a shrine 6,120 feet above sea-level near the
Col de Fenêtre, one of the three chief pilgrim resorts of the
district of Nice.   Against the shrine a hospice was erected for
the succour of pilgrims and travellers.   Now for their accommodation there is the *Hôtel-de-la-Madona*.   It is a three-
hours' walk up the valley named after her.   The fenêtre is a
window-like aperture in the Col de Fenêtre which has an
elevation about 1,200 feet above that of the sanctuary.

Through it the souls of the devoted adherents of the madonna fly upward.

But for most tourists the great attraction of St. Martin Vésubie is the magnificent scenery amidst which it stands. There are extensive forests and cherry orchards, lofty wooded cliffs, and ravines which afford glimpses of snow-capped peaks, a striking contrast to the flower-bedecked fields and laden cherry orchards among which the spectator stands. With the beautiful panorama before one's eyes, Maeterlinck's description of St. Martin Vésubie as "the central pearl, the purest and most perfect of the magnificent crown which nature has placed upon the region of Nice," seems not hyperbolic.

From the town may be made a variety of excursions, appealing to climbers, botanists, geologists, natural historians of all kinds no less than to the ordinary holiday-maker or tourist. (*Passports must be carried when the frontier is crossed, and cameras should not be taken.*)

One hour south by road, 45 minutes by path, is **Venanson** (4,760 feet), with a church containing fifteenth-century panels and frescoes.

A walk of 1¾ hours up the **Vallon du Boréon** should take one to a waterfall 110 feet high with a restaurant by its side.

The Coach Route.

Coaches usually follow the route to **St. Blaise** (p. 110) as far as the Traverses and then go straight on to **Levens**, 1,850 feet above the sea and 13¼ miles from Nice. The church is a thirteenth-century structure with a thirteenth-century screen. In a corner of the neighbouring market-place —the Place de la Liberté—is the Boutade, a large round stone taken from the castle and preserved as a souvenir of the downfall of the feudal lord, that Annibal Grimaldi strangled at Tourette Revest. On September 1 and at any other time when the farandole is danced, the men as they pass the stone place a foot upon it to show that they are free men ; the girls place both feet on it. Rue Masséna claims to be the site of the birthplace of André Masséna (p. 87).

Soon after leaving Levens, the road winds along a precipitous side of the base of Mount Férion. Almost hidden by olive trees on the opposite side of the valley is the hamlet of **Cros d'Utelle.** At 18¼ miles from Nice is the straggling village of **Duranus,** 600 feet above the bed of the river. It was founded in the seventeenth century by some of the inhabitants of Roccaspàrviera (the hawk's nest), destroyed by an earthquake. A few ruins may be seen by giving a backward glance. In front, on the opposite mountain, is the sanctuary of Notre-Dame-des-Miracles, to the south-west of Utelle.

Just outside a tunnel, an iron cross on the parapet marks the *Saut-des-Franfais*, a perpendicular cliff from which, at the time of the Revolution, brigands known as barbets precipitated French prisoners into the torrent with the cry, " Saute Français "—" Jump, Frenchman."

A steep descent, dangerous when snow is on it, takes one into St. Jean de la Rivière, the site of the reservoirs from which Nice is mainly supplied. From near the dam a winding road mounts to **Utelle.** " No village of the Alpes Maritimes occupies a site more fantastic," says V. E. Gauthier in his historical novel *Les Bandits des Alpes.* The church dates from the twelfth century and has many interesting features.

Farther up the valley is **Lantosque,** picturesquely perched on the brow of a hill. Beyond it there is soon seen on the right the agreeable summer resort of *La Bollène.* The route crosses the valley of the *Gordolesque,* a torrent which comes from Italy. Then the route passes **Roquebillière** (the rock of the bees).

The Romans found it on a peak on the right bank of the *Vésubie.* After the departure of the Romans the barbarians destroyed it. The surviving inhabitants established themselves on the bank of the river. With the exception of the Church of St. Michael, dating from the twelfth century and still standing, the village was destroyed by a flood at the end of the fourteenth century. The inhabitants re-established themselves on the opposite bank. That village was destroyed by an earthquake in 1564. In various wars also Roquebillière suffered, and in November, 1926, the elements once more scourged it. Unusually heavy and continued rain caused a landslide on the mountain north of Belvédère, and this destroyed the whole of the southern part of Roquebillière, which was reconstructed on a new site.

Belvédère is a summer station, 2½ miles from Roquebillière. It is at the extremity of a plateau, 2,723 feet above the sea and overlooking the *Gordolesque.*

Just beyond Roquebillière a road goes off to the right to **Berthemont,** a thermal station at which the wife of the Emperor Gallien took the cure, A.D. 261. The waters are still in high esteem. The site is 3,000 feet above sea-level. The bathing establishment is open from May 15 to September 25.

Olives now disappear. Chestnuts, oaks and cherries become increasingly abundant and there is a multiplicity of rivulets.

The return from St. Martin Vésubie is usually made by the same road as far as St. Jean de la Rivière and thence by a road, which is a masterpiece of engineering, alongside the *Vésubie* to its confluence with the *Var.* In the course of this passage the Saut-des-Français (*see* above) is again seen, but from below. The Vésubie is crossed by the Durandy Bridge, near which is the bust of Alexandre Durandy, who as a member of the Conseil Général (comparable to a County Council), promoted many useful public works. The rest of the route is along the east bank of the *Var* (p. 101).

To Tourettes, Saint Blaise and Aspremont.

The first part of this route lies along the western bank of the *Paillon* until St. Pons (p. 90) is passed, and then alongside the torrent of the *Garbe*. On the right are the church and castle of **St. André,** dating from the closing years of the seventeenth century. The torrent is crossed by a natural bridge and the route lies between heights of from 900 feet to 1,300 feet.

The **Gorge of St. André** gives place to a cultivated valley, and 7½ miles from Nice the road reaches the **Tourettes,** Tourette-le-Bas below, and above, Tourette Levens. Here are a twelfth-century church and the remains of the castle, which had three towers—hence the name of the place. When the Romans were here Tourettes was a market town.

The heights draw near again, then again recede, and a forest gives place to orchards. The village of **Levens,** on an elevated site, comes into view. At the **Traverses,** the route branches off to the left and soon goes zigzagging down between olive groves, pinewoods and oaks. It passes the chapel of **St. Antoine de Siga,** having a steeple faced with coloured earthenware, and then the " palai," a large decrepit building, the birthplace of the celebrated Masséna, says an unfounded local tradition.

Finally the road reaches the suspension bridge of **St. Blaise,** 260 feet above the bottom of the gorge which it spans. The tiny village from which it takes its name has a pink-tinted church.

Following the irregular outline of Mont Cima, the road arrives at **Aspremont,** at an elevation of some 1,700 feet, sheltering itself behind Mont Chauve. When the Romans held the country the village was on the summit of Mont Cima.

The scanty ruins may be reached in an hour's walk by a mule-path. The inhabitants first migrated to a lower site, marked by the ruins of a church. A plague in 1327 drove them away. They fled to Mont Chauve and some twenty years later founded the present village of narrow winding streets with inclines and steps, bordered by very old grey houses. The public square was the site of the lord's castle,

pillaged and destroyed in 1792. The square affords a splendid view.

From Aspremont the road runs down to the **Cascade of
Gairaut,** and thence enters Nice by way of St. Maurice.

To Peïra Cava.

Hotels.—*Bellevue Victoria; Truchi.*
Syndicat d'Initiative.—Villa Les Lys Rouges.

One of the surprises which the Riviera provides is the
contrast between the blue sky, roses, palms and orange and
lemon trees of Nice, Cannes or Menton, and the alpine setting
of pine trees and snow at **Peïra Cava,** the Riviera headquarters
of winter sports, where one can skate, ski, luge and bobsleigh.
One can climb by coach or one's own car, and setting out
about 9 a.m. can go and return within the daylight hours of
a winter's day.

Peïra Cava, the hollow stone, as its name signifies, is situated
5,138 feet above the sea and 12½ miles to the north-east of
Nice as the crow flies, but double that distance by road.
Upon the plateau on which it stands are barracks for a
detachment of the Chasseurs Alpins, the " blue devils " as
the Germans called them, a soubriquet they have adopted.
At Peïra Cava is their school of ski-ing, and if your visit coin-
cides with competitions, you will see that the zeal and daring
of the little chasseurs lead to deeds which make almost
insignificant the performances of the civilians.

About 2½ miles through the great forest of Turini, a thick
growth of pines, firs, larches and aspens, is a military post at
Turini at an elevation of 5,250 feet (cameras forbidden).
From it an hour's climb takes one to the summit of the great
peak of the **Aution,** 6 miles north of Peïra Cava, crowned by
one of the strongest forts in the country and one of the
highest in Europe (6,825 feet), but this excursion is for those
who stay more than one day and who have the necessary
permission. In the forest is the Hôtel Corniglion, 3½ miles
north of Peïra Cava.

So popular is the excursion to Peïra Cava that the resources
of its hotels are sometimes incapable of meeting the demands
of an unusually large crowd with sharpened appetites, and
it is a wise precaution to take a picnic lunch with one. When
dressing, one should also bear in mind the keen air of a
snow-resort in winter.

Peïra Cava is in the happy position of having two seasons.
When the snow has melted on the plateau and the permanent

residents down below go holiday-making, Peïra Cava is one
of the summer resorts to which they betake themselves.

The route generally followed by the coaches goes through
medieval villages, plunges down into the valley of the
Vésubie and from it mounts to a yet higher crest. For the
greater part of the distance the scenery is unsurpassable.
There is a wonderful view of the coast and the Alps, a view
ever extending and into which new features are continually
being introduced.

From Nice this route runs along the east bank of the
Paillon. At the end of 3¾ miles it reaches the little village
of **Trinité Victor,** and 1¼ miles farther, the village of **Drap,**
interesting to geologists as one of the best spots for the
examination of modern marine deposits. Since 1238 the
bishops of Nice have been Counts of Drap.

Twelve miles from Nice the route reaches the interesting
village of **L'Escarène,** at an elevation of 1,150 feet. It is
built in a kind of funnel at the confluence of the *Braus*
with the *Paillon*. The name of the village is a patois word
for *escalier*, that is, staircase.

Thence for nearly 4 miles the route lies almost due north
through a winding narrow valley with sides here bare and
there covered with pines or with olive trees, and the stream
at the bottom bordered by market gardens and orchards.
Then comes the ancient village of **Lucéram** about 2,200 feet
above sea-level. It was once a Roman colony. On some of
the ancient houses which line the stepped streets are inscriptions. As in most of the old hill towns, there are cat-holes
in some of the doors. At the summit of the village is an
ancient tower almost intact. The church was originally a
Gothic building. It contains four sixteenth-century retables
classed as historic monuments. Other treasures are a sixteenth-century silver statuette, representing St. Margaret
striking down a monstrous animal (la tarasque), and a fifteenth-
century monstrance containing relics of Ste Rosalie of
Palermo, renowned for the efficacy of her intercessions in
times of plague.

A succession of steep gradients and hair-pin bends charac-
terizes the road from Lucéram. At 20½ miles from Nice,
the **Col-de-Saint-Roch,** 3,281 feet, is attained. The road
onward from this pass is the property of the French Foreign
Office. Along it by zigzags one arrives at the **Cime du
Rocaillon** (summit of the Rocaillon, 4,657 feet). From the

[*Menton.*

LUCÉRAM.

23

Ballance,]

VILLEFRANCHE.

[Menton.

24

wooded crest there is a beautiful view of the *Var* valley westward and the *Roya* valley eastward. During the winter months one comes to the snow, patches of it at first, and finally to its deep carpet, through which a road has been cleared for vehicles.

An alternative route is by L'Escarène (p. 112) and the Col-de-Braus to Sospel, thence to La Moulinet, the road from which affords an admirable view over the valley of the upper *Bévéra*, and the solid mass of the Aution. It mounts to Turini and thence descends to Peïra Cava.

To Peille.

An interesting place, 14½ miles north-east of Nice. It is said to have been founded by a Roman colony from Mont Pellius, whence its name, and it claims to have been the birth-place of the Emperor Pertinax, after whom a street in Nice has been named. In the eleventh century it was allied with Lucéram and Utelle in a republican confederation sufficiently powerful to defy the Counts of Provence. Even at work the men of the federated villages were armed, being bound always to carry with them an unusually large knife. The people of Peille remained independent of any feudal lord until the territory was granted by the Duke of Savoy to Lascaris de Castellar, who built a castle dominating the village.

Peille is generally reached by following the shortest road to Peïra Cava (p. 111) as far as the **Bridge of Peille.** Thence the route is through the **Grave de Peille** to the foot of the conical rock on which is perched the little village of **Peillon.** Then after the mountains have come closer to the bed of the torrent, the valley widens and on the right, far up the slope of the **Baudon,** is seen the old borough of Peille.

Zigzagging through a grove of olives and crossing gorges, the road mounts. Suddenly vegetation disappears and Peille is reached. The road is continued by the principal street Rue St. Sebastian, to the square, Place Mont St. Agel. Here among the ancient houses is the house of the Lord Justice. Upon it is a mutilated bull's head, a sign of power. On some of the ancient houses are inscriptions committing them to the protection of the Most Highest, or embodying a good maxim or proverb. The church is on an eminence outside the village. It dates from the eleventh century. Its pillars are of rough, almost shapeless, stones. The holy-water basin and the font are of rough granite.

Riviera (*h*)

Interest has been added to the village by J. C. Campbell's story, *The Miracle of Peille*.

To Laghet, Eze and Cap Ferrat.

Laghet is situated in a hollow among mountains about 13 miles north-east of Nice. It is the site of a monastery and a place of pilgrimage by reason of its possession of a miraculous image of the Virgin. Once upon a time a small lake, a " laghetto," was there, hence the name of the place.

It can be reached from Nice by the Grande Corniche and a road which leaves the great highway in the vicinity of La Turbie. Another route lies along the valley of the Paillon to Trinité Victor, and thence to the right along the valley of Laghet. Milestones found upon it show that it was a Roman road.

The spot became celebrated through the discovery in the valley of an image of the Virgin, which was taken in great pomp to La Turbie. The next day it was again in the valley, by which the people understood that it was to be venerated there. They therefore erected a chapel in which to place it. Miracles began to be wrought there by the Virgin and have never ceased. That they have been very numerous and varied is apparent from the votive offerings—crutches, models of parts of the body that have been healed, pictures, generally naïve and crude, of miraculous incidents. Pilgrimages are made to Laghet during the greater part of the year, but chiefly at Whitsuntide, Trinity, and the Fête of Notre-Dame-du-Mont-Carmel.

The present chapel was built as a thank-offering in the seventeenth century by a lady of Menton who, suffering from a disease regarded as incurable, was carried to Laghet and there was cured, after praying without ceasing for three days. In 1656 the present monastery was commenced and was confided to the barefooted monks of Mount Carmel.

Facing the monastery is a fountain with an inscription which has been translated :—" Pilgrim, you find here two streams ; one descends from heaven, the other from the top of the mountains. The first is a treasure which the Virgin distributes to the piety of the faithful, the second has been brought here by the people of Nice : drink of both, if you thirst for both."

From the Grande Corniche the route descends rapidly to the Moyenne Corniche, at the foot of the village of Eze

(p. 98). The coaches stop near the fountain to which the villagers had to descend.

From Eze the coaches descend to Beaulieu and thence make the tour of Cap Ferrat (p. 118).

To Tenda (or Tende).

(Passports are necessary to enter and leave Italy.)

The route from Nice is that to Peïra Cava as far as L'Escarène, and thence to Sospel *via* the Col-de-Braus, described in the reverse direction on page 113. From Sospel it ascends gently to the **Col-de-Nieja** and thence through a landscape increasing in austerity to the **Col-de-Braus** (3,020 feet), from which is a descent revealing the steeple of the Madone de Grace and Breil on the *Roya*, before arriving at the hamlet of **Giandola,** northward of which are the **Gorges of Saorge,** taking their name from a village with a castle deemed impregnable, but captured by French troops sent against it by Masséna.

About 1½ miles farther north is **Fontan,** the last French village on the route, and after passing through impressive gorges, the Italian frontier is reached and passports are examined. Some 4 miles from the French Fontan is the Italian **San Dalmazzo,** in a chestnut forest. Less than 3 miles farther is the town of **Tende,** at the foot of a long chain of mountains and some 2,650 feet above the sea.

It originated under the Romans, near the end of the third century, and was long occupied by the Saracens. A tower supporting a public clock is almost all that remains of a castle built early in the fourteenth century. The church, dedicated in 1518, has a remarkable façade. The interior ends in a very fine apse, and there is a chapel containing the tombs of the Counts Grimaldi-Lascaris.

Beyond Tende the public road passes through a tunnel, damp, muddy and two miles long, under the **Col-de-Tende.** A military road, closed to the public, goes over the pass, more than 6,000 feet high.

To Gattières, St. Jeannet, Vence and St. Paul du Var.

Nice is left by the Promenade des Anglais, from which the route continues by the road over the *Var*. Just beyond the bridge it turns to the right and goes under the railway at the station of St. Laurent. About a mile north is the old village of *St. Laurent du Var* (p. 75).

From the village the route continues alongside the *Var*, passing market gardens, orange groves, vineyards and olive groves for the most part on terraces on the hillside. The route brings into sight the villages of **Carros** and **Gattières,** the former the more distant and also the more elevated. It is 1,200 feet above the sea, while the elevation of Gattières is not quite 1,000 feet. Carros was a Roman fortified post and Roman inscriptions may still be seen. Later it was a medieval stronghold. The old castle remains intact.

Gattières is 14½ miles from Nice. The rounded hill on which it stands is covered with vines, olives and orange trees. When the visitor has looked, from the top of the belfry for preference, upon the panorama which the site commands—Mont Cima, Mont Chauve, the villages of Aspremont, Castagniers, Colomars, and all the valley down to the sea—he has seen all that the village has to show with the exception of the scanty remains of its once formidable castle.

From Gattières the route goes to the left and passes within sight of the ruins of the Castle of **La Gaude** (p. 80), a commandery of the Templars dating from the thirteenth century. Then in succession are passed the **Baou-de-la-Gaude** and the **Baou-de-St. Jeannet** (p. 79). Between the baous flows the *Cagne*. This the road crosses and goes along the foot of the **Baou-des-Noirs** and the **Baou-des-Blancs** to **Vence** and then to **St. Paul du Var** (p. 78). Thence the route is *viâ* **La Colle, Villeneuve-Loubet** and **Cagnes** (pp. 72–3).

To the Gorges du Loup

viâ Vence, returning viâ Gourdon, Grasse and Villeneuve-Loubet.

One of the most interesting excursions from Nice. The route crosses the *Var*, circles Cagnes (p. 72) and then goes more or less north-westward amidst pines, olives and flower-gardens. Westward are the valley of the *Malvan* and the fortified **St. Paul** (p. 78). Eastward is Villeneuve with its castle.

Vence is described on pages 76–8, and the route thence to the **Gorges,** to **Gourdon,** and to **Grasse** on pages 80–81.

From Grasse the route is *viâ* **Châteauneuf** and the valley of the *Mardaric* to **Villeneuve** (p. 73) and **Cagnes**.

Coaches also run through the **Corniche d'Or** (pp. 56–8), to which the route is *viâ* **Cagnes, Antibes, Juan-les-Pins, Golfe-Juan** and **Cannes**, which have all been described. (*See* Index.) The return is by the **Estérels** (p. 54). The road goes over the Col-des-Adrets (1,020 feet), passes the *Auberge* of the same name, and re-enters Cannes by way of **La Napoule** (p. 53).

CORSICA,

called by the Greeks *Kalliste*, most beautiful, can be pleasantly visited by steamer from Nice, and the excursion on land can be continued by the P.L.M. cars. The passage takes 9½ or 10 hours, depending on whether the landing is made at Bastia or Ajaccio. Those who make the trip for the first time, and desire to do so under the most comfortable conditions, will be well advised to take an inclusive ticket. They will not then have to concern themselves about hotel accommodation, which leaves much to be desired except in four or five towns, or how to get from one place to another.

Of the islands in the Mediterranean, Corsica is the third in point of size. It is 116 miles long, 52 miles broad and abounds in mountains, of which the highest reaches nearly 9,000 feet. They are largely covered with forests of oak, beech, pine, chestnut and cork trees, and with maquis, to which the island is indebted for its names of Scented Isle and Garden of Perfume. The population numbers about 300,000.

Bastia, the commercial capital and military headquarters, is the largest town. It contains little to interest the tourist, but is the base for the circuit of Cap-Corse, the peninsula, 25 miles long at the north-eastern corner of the island, containing scenery which none should willingly miss.

Ajaccio, the next largest town, is more interesting. The Hôtel de Ville has a collection of objects connected with the Bonapartes. The house in which Napoleon was born is a show-place. The museum has a collection illustrating the natural history of the island. The cathedral dates from the sixteenth century.

Northward of Bastia are the **Calanches de Piana,** a most remarkable range of lofty red rocks of fantastic shape, along which the road runs for more than a mile.

Vizzavona, a clean, new-looking place, perhaps the best summer resort, stands at a height of 2,975 feet, in the midst of one of the most beautiful forests.

Bonifacio, at the southernmost point, is a town of narrow streets situated on a narrow promontory with vertical cliffs nearly 200 feet high and containing caves which form the principal curiosity of the place. From the citadel there is a fine view of Sardinia, only 7½ miles away.

The highest road pass is the **Col-de-Vergio,** 4,805 feet above the sea.

The island has had an eventful history, but since 1814 it has been an undisputed possession of France.

VILLEFRANCHE-SUR-MER.

Hotels.—*See* p. 31.
Inquiries.—Syndicat d'Initiative, at the Pavilion de l'Octroi.

A small picturesque town less than 4 miles from Nice,

built on the slope of hills which rise from the very edge of
the water, and which necessitate stepped streets and tunnels
under houses. Here are many quaint " bits " which have
been represented on canvas, for Villefranche attracts artists
and even induces some of them to become residents.

On the outskirts are modern villas, the site being very
agreeable. On the beach are bathing cabins; interesting
walks may be taken. There is a station on the P.L.M. line,
and buses facilitate visits to the neighbouring great resorts.
A little more than 2 miles away is the Chapel of Saint Michel,
used as a **Museum** of objects recovered from Olivula (p. 98).

The harbour shelters fishing boats, and above the town
carnations are extensively cultivated. Villefranche has no
ground suitable for battles of flowers, but its bay makes a
fine arena for a naval battle of flowers, and this gives the
little town its gayest day of the year. Gay days also result
from the presence of warships in the bay, a roadstead in
which the French Mediterranean squadron, and British and
American men-of-war, are often seen. To it also come
pleasure yachts and great liners. The entry is safe at all
times, and the vast expanse of tranquil water has a depth
which permits the largest vessels to anchor at a few cables'
length from the quay.

In the eighteenth century the European Mediterranean
powers combined to maintain a fleet to protect their commerce. Villefranche was its base, and the barracks of the
galle y slaves are still standing opposite the Old Dock, where
are also the more modern barracks of a battalion of Chasseurs
Alp ins. Between this and the quays at the foot of the old
tow n is a seventeenth-century **Citadel,** in which are military
offi ces and stores. When it was built the town was some
30 0 years old, having been founded in the fourteenth century
b y Charles II of Anjou, Count of Provence and King of
Sicily. To attract inhabitants and trade, he made it a free
port. Hence its name.

At 1¾ miles from Villefranche is Pont St. Jean, from which——

Cap Ferrat,

a narrow rocky peninsula, extends southward. It is the site
of many villas, most of whose owners are English, and is traversed by fine avenues which make its exploration a pleasure.
About ¼ mile from the bridge is the **Chapel of St. François.**
Westward of it is the villa called **Les Cèdres,** built by King

Riviera.

Patras,]

MONTE CARLO.

[Paris.

Leopold II, who in the latter part of his life bought a great part of the peninsula and beautified it by the creation of gardens. Hard by the Cèdres is **Les Bruyères,** the villa of H.R.H. the Duke of Connaught.

The highest point of the peninsula attains an elevation of 446 feet and is the site of a semaphore. At the extremity of the peninsula is a lighthouse. From both there is a good view, but that from the semaphore is the better of the two.

The only spot on the peninsula where habitations are grouped is on the eastern side, at the fishing village of **St. Jean,** about 1½ miles from the bridge. It is renowned for its bouillabaisse (p. 47). At the entrance to the village is a statue of a fisherman, the work of Claude Vignon (Madame Rouvier).

From St. Jean the long low tongue of land called **Cap St. Hospice** projects eastward. Near the extremity are a tower and a chapel. The latter since 1655 has replaced the oratory built on the tomb of St. Auspicius, who lived here in the second half of the sixth century and after whom the Cap is named. Over the altar is a picture representing the legend that the arm of a Lombard about to strike St. Auspicius was paralysed and had the power restored to it by the hermit touching it.

The tower, built by the Duke of Savoy in the sixteenth century to check the raids of pirates, stands on the site of a fortress of the Saracens, who called it the *Little Fraxinet,* in contrast to their Great Fraxinet in the Maures. In the top story is a model of a gigantic bronze reproduction of the Madonna of Laghet, standing near the tower, in which it was intended to be placed, but it proved to be too heavy. The work of the Milanese sculptor Galbusiéri, it was cast on the spot.

BEAULIEU-SUR-MER.

Hotels.—*See* p. 29.
Inquiries.—Syndicat d'Initiative, opposite the station (*see* p. 32).

" Beaulieu, the well-named (' beautiful spot '), nestling at the foot of a rocky rampart which protects it from the mistral, exposing to the south its houses, in the Italian style, planted among olive groves and orchards. Beaulieu, the country of mandarines and of roses, from which in April there spreads a subtle fragrance of flowers and of fruit suggesting an

Arcadian paradise," wrote André Theuriet, the poet and novelist. Since then more gardens have been made and more flowers grown as more wealthy people have been drawn to the spot, so that Sir Frederick Treves, writing more recently, could say, " Beaulieu is a super-village of sumptuous villas. It lies on an evergreen shelf of the sea pampered by an indulgent climate, made gorgeous by an extravagant vegetation. . . . It breathes luxury and wealth, languid ease and a surfeit of comfort. It is probably the richest village in the world, and the glory of its gardens is nowhere to be surpassed."

The most sheltered part is a strip at the eastern end, lying between the sea and the hill of St. Michel. On account of its exceptionally warm climate and the character of its vegetation, this quarter has been named **La Petite Afrique.**

The late Lord Salisbury had a villa high up on the hillside, and it was his preference for Beaulieu, together with that of Sir Blundell Maple and Mr. Gordon Bennett, which made it popular with its present class of foreign residents and visitors.

Beaulieu fronts a double bay in which boating and fishing are pleasurable in nearly all weathers. As the water is shallow it is warm enough for bathing even in December and January, but the beach is so overlaid with seaweed that bathing from it is not popular. Of two small twin harbours, one is mainly used by fishing boats ; the other is at the service of pleasure craft. A **Yachting Club** holds a summer regatta and the **Lawn Tennis Club** arranges tournaments in February and April. Evening amusements are provided by a **Casino,** the Villa des Fleurs, which overlooks the beautiful Baie des Fourmis, the Baie de la Fourmigue, as it is called by natives who prefer the old Provençal name.

An **English Church** occupies the site of a Christian Church erected in the sixth century in place of a pagan temple.

The *Réserve of Beaulieu* is a restaurant renowned for the products of its kitchen. " A shrine of the good gourmets," one writer has called it.

Many pleasant walks can be taken from Beaulieu. A footpath goes alongside the bay to St. Jean. A road near the station joins Avenue Leopold II, leading to the Grande Corniche at the Quatre Chemins. The Col of St. Michel with the ruins of Olivula (p. 98) is easily reached. The buses between Nice and Monte Carlo bring those places within easy reach and facilitate other excursions.

MONACO AND MONTE CARLO.

Access.—By the main line of the P.L.M. railway (*see* p. 23). There are two stations, Monaco in the Condamine and Monte Carlo.

Consulates.—British. 24, Avenue de la Costa, Monte Carlo. American, at Nice (*see* p. 84).

Distances.—*By Rail.* Paris, nearly 690 miles; Marseilles, 150; Nice, 10½. *By Road.* Marseilles, 152 miles; Hyères, 106; Nice, 10 by the Middle Corniche, 12 by the coast; Menton, 7.

Hotels.—Monaco town has no hotels for foreigners. Those in the Condamine are more moderate in price than those in Monte Carlo. (*See* p. 30.)

Inquiries.—At the office of the Touring Club of France, Boulevard de la Madone, Monte Carlo.

Money.—French money is used.

Passports.—Those for France. Visitors desiring to remain longer than a fortnight must obtain a " permit de séjour."

Post Office.—The postal rates are those of France, but the principality has its own stamps and *these must be used on letters, etc., posted at the offices in the principality*, but French stamps can be used if the posting is done at Beausoleil, adjoining Monte Carlo on the north-west, or in a box on a French tram-car.

THE Principality of Monaco is surrounded by the French Department of the Alpes Maritimes, except where it touches the sea. It is one of the oldest and also one of the smallest independent states in the world. It extends for some 2½ miles along the coast, and is from 165 yards to 1,100 yards broad. At the last census the population numbered about 25,000, of whom 4,000 were visitors, 9,126 of French nationality and 9,626 Italians. The natives are called Monégasques.

The divisions are **Monaco,** the capital, in which visitors are not likely to find accommodation ; **Condamine,** the quarter of the commercial and middle classes, with good hotels and boarding-houses ; **Monte Carlo,** the *ville de luxe*.

MONACO.

The town is situated on the level top of a promontory with precipitous sides rising 200 feet above the sea, and presenting a most picturesque and striking appearance as one draws near to it from the west.

Visitors who alight at Monaco station and wish to walk to the town will follow the Avenue de la Gare, opening opposite the station and leading to the Place d'Armes—the market-place—from which a steep paved incline and a carriage

road, Avenue de la Porte Neuve, mount to the summit of
the rock. The former leads through a ceremonial gate built
in 1714, through a gate dated 1533 (beyond which was the
drawbridge), through the main gateway, and ends in the
square facing the palace. The carriage road continues to the
Place de la Visitation, from which the Place du Palais
can be reached by Rue de Lorraine, continued by Rue Basse,
both containing ancient houses.

The **Place du Palais** has ramparts on two sides, sixteen
bronze guns given by Louis XIV (*d.* 1715), and two mortars
cast at Strasbourg in the second half of the eighteenth century.

The Palace

(*Admission*. In the absence of the family visitors are admitted daily from
1 to 5)

occupies the entire landward side of the square. The original
building has been much enlarged, and in the middle of the
nineteenth century the palace was so completely restored
and modified that it no longer has the appearance of a fortress.
The main gateway, erected in 1672, is surmounted by the
Grimaldi arms.

On the north side of the courtyard is the chapel of St. John
the Baptist, elaborately decorated. On the right-hand side
are frescoes representing a triumphal procession of Bacchus.
On the opposite side a double white marble staircase leads
to the arcaded gallery of Hercules (1552), where are frescoes
(restored) by Luca Cambiaso, the great Genoese painter of
the sixteenth century. They represent the Labours of Hercules. Here also is the entrance to the State apartments.
The Salle Grimaldi or Throne Room, with walls 30 feet high,
is famed for its finely sculptured chimney-piece, formed of
a single block of marble. The English rendering of a Latin
inscription is, " He who pretends to know God and regards
not His commandments is a liar." In the York Chamber
the Duke of York died in 1767. He was taken ill when
sailing from Toulon to Genoa.

Behind the palace are delightful gardens.

The streets facing the palace are all narrow but clean and
orderly. There are no slums in the principality. In the
Grand' Rue are stone doorways of the seventeenth century
or earlier. Rue du Tribunal is the least ancient. It and
Rue Ste Barbe lead to the **Cathedral**, built in the Romanesque-
Byzantine style, 1893–98, in place of the church of St. Nicholas

MONACO AND MONTE CARLO.

MONTE CARLO.

(1 and 2) The Casino—(3) The Palace.

which dated from the twelfth century. In the right transept is a painting executed in 1500 by Louis Bréa, and over the door of the sacristy is a Pietà painted by him in 1505. The princes are buried in the crypt. The bodies of nearly thirty have been placed there, as have also the remains of Ste Dévote.

Near the western end of the Cathedral is a small **Anthropological Museum** (*10–12 and 2–4 winter, 5 summer*). Among the contents are Roman relics and some of the skeletons discovered in the caves in the Red Rocks (p. 135).

Through the adjacent beautiful gardens of St. Martin, or by the Avenue St. Martin, one can pass to the **Musée Océanographique** (*admission 2 francs. Hours as above*). It is an immense building erected in 1910 under the direction of Prince Albert I, celebrated for his scientific attainments. On the lower floor is an excellent marine aquarium ; the rest of the interior is mainly filled with objects supplied by the prince's various expeditions, with models of his yachts, instruments used in oceanography and fishing implements used in various countries.

THE CONDAMINE AND THE PORT.

The Condamine quarter of the principality is a flat tract little above sea-level, covered with hotels, boarding-houses, business buildings and private houses, situated between the rock of Monaco and Monte Carlo. It is a quite modern district, for early in the nineteenth century all that was not occupied by a dirty little fishing village was a vast garden with orange and lemon trees under which were violets. These last were let for 25,000 francs a year to Rimmel the perfume manufacturer. Now the quarter has about half the population of the principality.

The bay offers excellent shelter for ships, and since the earliest times its shore has been used by traders. In the **Harbour,** Port d'Hercule, may be seen racing and pleasure yachts, motor boats and trading vessels, and not infrequently stately liners landing and embarking tourists. At the end of the harbour are berths for hydroplanes.

Eastward the low plain ends at the **Valley of Gaumattes** or of Ste Dévote. It is a great gorge crossed by a railway viaduct and a bridge 147 feet high. The latter connects both the coast road and the Moyenne Corniche with the road to Menton. Between the two bridges is the modern

Church of Ste Dévote, a Corsican virgin martyr of the fourth century.

At night Christians placed her body on a ship which was to transport it to Africa. A storm plunged the captain into the deepest despair. Then standing out clearly against a black cloud, he saw a figure in the form of the dead girl and he heard it say, "The tempest is passing away. Follow a dove which will fly from my mouth. It will lead you to a quiet haven, and there by the beach bury my body." That which was foretold came to pass, and that which was commanded was done. Many miracles were wrought at the grave of the saint. In 1070 a pirate tried to carry away the body, but the vessel remained motionless. The fête of the saint is celebrated on January 27.

MONTE CARLO

is situated on broad terraces on the rocky ridge of the Spéluges, the eastern horn of the bay that forms the road-stead of Monaco. Its climate is one of the finest on the Riviera. The spot is sheltered from cold winds, is exposed to the sun, and being higher than the Condamine its air is more invigorating. October and November are generally the months of greatest rainfall.

Monte Carlo is seen at its best from October to January and from April to June. It is then a garden of flowers. But at all times it is the cleanest and trimmest town on the Riviera, and in this respect has perhaps no equal.

Very few, if any, will disagree with the writer who has said, "Take it all in all, Monte Carlo is the most beautiful and fascinating part of the Riviera. Nature and art have done their utmost to enchant the eye and stimulate the imagination."

The world-famous **Casino** is a large pretentious building facing a square to which it gives its name. On entering one has at once on the left the office for tickets. (A passport or a carte d'identité must be shown. The price of a day ticket is 10 francs.) On the right is the cloak-room where gentlemen *must* leave hats and overcoats. Going forward, stairs are passed on the left leading to a spacious reading and writing room well supplied with newspapers. In the main hall, a door in the wall facing the entrance opens into the theatre. To the right are a smoking-room and buffet. Opposite are the public gaming rooms, profusely decorated. Here are tables for roulette and for trente-et-quarante. From noon till 11 o'clock at night, the roulette wheel is spun and the cards are dealt.

Serious punters note the winning numbers and colours, and on these records base their future play. Records covering a long period are on sale in the shops, as are also books, containing ''infallible'' systems which, if followed, will give the player a steady income, or will enable a person who commands only a very modest sum to become a millionaire. So the authors profess, and so fools believe.

Although Monte Carlo lives and moves and has its being in gambling, it contains people who never go into the gambling rooms, people who are attracted to the place by its climate, by its gardens, by the friends and acquaintances they will meet, or by its series of concerts, its ballets and grand opera, all alike unrivalled. It organizes an International Exhibition of painting and sculpture, battles of flowers, a dog show in which the animals are not staged but are led about by their owners, and a motor-car competition in which elegance alone is considered. Its outdoor sports include golf, on Mont Agel at a height of 2,665 feet, where almost every tee affords one of the most beautiful sights in the world ; tennis, regattas and bathing. The Thermal Baths, on the upper terrace of the south side of the casino, offer salt-water baths and medical baths of every description. For sun and sea-bathing there are two beaches—the **Plage de Larvotto,** the greater part of a mile north-east, reached by bus or by following the road that goes from the station yard and winds round the Terminus Hotel, and a beach of fine sand below the Club House of the Country Club at **Saint Roman** (the site of a cave with a few stalactites), beyond Larvotto. On the grounds of the club are numerous tennis courts, of which one is reserved for tournaments and championship play. There is seating accommodation for 5,000 spectators.

At the foot of the extensive public pleasure grounds facing the main entrance of the casino and maintained in highest beauty by the gamblers is the **Café de Paris,** the favourite rendezvous of the smart set. On the left are the huge *Hôtel de Paris* and the new **Sporting Club** which in 1929–30 supplanted the Palais des Beaux Arts ; in the background the mountains and La Turbie (p. 128), of which the wonderful tower is just visible. In *Things Seen on the Riviera*, Captain Richardson is not guilty of exaggeration when he says, '' To miss this view is to miss one of the most beautiful sights that it is given to human eyes to behold. Poets have sung it and painters have depicted it.''

The **Terrace,** on the opposite side of the casino, also offers a delightful prospect. To the right is Monaco, to the left Cap-Martin with Italian mountains beyond it. On a fine day with little wind, the Terrace is generally crowded. It is Monte Carlo's promenade. Not a few who appreciate its charms are, however, often driven from it by the popping of guns on a grassy plateau just below, on the opposite side of the railway. It is the site of the pigeon-shooting, which some call sport, but in which very few Englishmen take part.

Of man's handiwork Monte Carlo has nothing which goes back so far as 1850. Before that date and for some years later its site was a rock to which a few goats were brought to graze on the scanty herbage.

The reigning prince, Carlo III, was poor. As a means of raising money, a casino had been established on the rock of Monaco. From there it had been removed to the Condamine, and finally the concessionaires were under covenant to construct their shrine of the Goddess of Chance upon the naked rock. They had not sufficient funds for the purpose, but they found a purchaser, Mr. Blanc, the successful exploiter of a casino at Homburg, which would close in 1863. Under him was formed the Society of the Sea Baths and of the Foreigners' Club to take over the concession granted to the Monaco Casino Company.

The signing of the lease conveying the use of the rock to the new society was the waving of a fairy wand which made stately buildings arise, gave wealth to prince and people, and for a prince's exactions substituted princely largesse. With the change in the appearance of the rock came a change of name, Spélugues giving place to Monte Carlo.

The original concession was granted for fifty years, expiring in 1913. An agreement for a fresh concession for fifty years was signed in January, 1898, and the ordinary 500-franc shares at once rose to 4,770. The society has to pay into the Treasury of His Most Serene Highness the Prince, a yearly tribute of 1,250,000 gold francs, plus a periodically increasing percentage of the excess of revenue from the games at the casino and sporting club, over and above the yearly figure of 25,000,000 francs. A further percentage of the total receipts is turned over to the government " to be spent on works of public utility." Other cash payments include the cost of a printing works and the upkeep of an official newspaper, each issue approved by and placed partly at the dis-

posal of the government. The society must hand over 50 per
cent. of the takings of the tobacco monopoly, guarantee two-
thirds of the cost of maintaining the postal service and the
sum of 25,000 francs to cover each of eighteen operatic performances given every season under the prince's patronage.
And there are numerous tributes in kind. These comprise
a water-supply equal to 300 litres (about 65 gallons) per head
of the population daily, the supply of gas and electricity,
not forgetting " à alimenter à ses frais les becs de gaz posés
dans le palais " (that is to say, free gas for the palace), the
drainage of the principality ; the building, maintenance, and
cleaning of all necessary highways and byways, the upkeep
of and equipment and barracks for the *corps de garde*, the
firemen and the carabiniers.

Thus the inhabitants of the principality are exempted from
rates and taxes. Finally, the casino employs 3,800 servants,
most of whom are doing ordinary municipal work. Of the
others, 525 are croupiers.

Historical Note.—Phœnicians, Phocéens from Marseilles,
Romans and Saracens are said to have established themselves
in turn upon the rock of Monaco. Of their presence there
are no remains, and the modern history of the principality
began in the twelfth century with the coming of the Genoese,
of whom their family of Grimaldi in the fourteenth century
became established as lords of the territory under Carlo I,
one of the opponents of the English at the Battle of Crécy.
In 1715 the reigning prince gave his daughter and heiress in
marriage to a Norman noble, Jacques de Matignon, who was
obliged to adopt the name of Grimaldi. From him and his
wife the subsequent princes of Monaco have traced their
descent, and from his wife the right to rule. The present
prince is Louis II, born 1870, who succeeded his father in
1922.

In 1848 the area of the principality was diminished by the
revolt of Menton and Roquebrune. They maintained their
independence until 1861, when they voted for incorporation
with France.

Apparently forming part of Monte Carlo is the French
commune of—

Beausoleil,

situated on the lower slopes of the mountains. The boundary
runs along the Boulevard de France and, excluding the
Banque Crédit Lyonnais from the taxless land, there turns
inland, as shown on our plan. Beausoleil has a population
approaching 12,000, a casino, and good hotels (p. 29).
Letters posted here must bear French stamps and visitors

who remain here or elsewhere in France more than two months must obtain their French Carte d'Identité (p. 36).

The nearest railway station is Monte Carlo.

EXCURSIONS FROM MONACO, MONTE CARLO AND BEAUSOLEIL.

The first excursion which suggests itself is that to—

La Turbie.

(**Hotels,** p. 3. *Syndicat d'Initiative.*—At the Mairie.)

It is situated by the side of the **Great Corniche**, some 1,600 feet above the sea, and has a population of 1,300. It can be reached by a good road leaving the principality of Monaco by way of the Boulevard Princess Charlotte and the Boulevard de l'Observatoire, or by a funicular railway. From Cap d'Ail a steep bridle-path mounts to it.

The railway is most generally used. The lower terminus is opposite the casino of Monte Carlo, but some 400 yards from it. The ascent occupies twenty minutes. The upper terminus is on a level plot commanding an immense panorama, which sometimes includes the summits of the mountains of Corsica.

Hard by the upper station was the highest point on the Roman road between Rome and Arles, on the bank of the Rhône, and on that elevation the Roman senate ordered the construction of a tower, completed in the year 6 B.C., commemorating the subjugation by the Emperor Augustus of the last of the Alpine tribes. Researches have led to the discovery of fragments of statues, columns and sculptured stones, all testifying to the importance and magnitude of the work which, in the main, was a lofty square structure surmounted by a gigantic statue of Augustus—that Cæsar Augustus from whom there went out " a decree that all the world should be taxed " (Luke ii. 1).

The barbarians who overran the region did not respect the monument. Later there were Christians who wished it overthrown on account of its pagan origin. In the Middle Ages the fallen stones were used in the construction of a watch-tower and a fortress, blown up early in the eighteenth century by order of Louis XIV of France, and it is rather the remnant of that tower than of the original monument upon which we look to-day. Some of the best of the marble was carried off to Genoa and to Nice, and builders went to it for material, notably for La Turbie's church, as recorded by an inscription in the nave. Further destruction was stopped in 1866 when the French Government classed the remnant as an historical monument.

From the name of the monument, **Tropœa Augusti**, the trophy of Augustus, the neighbouring town is said to derive its name.

One of the gates, the Portail du Recinto, the gate in the enceinte, or main wall, as distinguished from the wall of the fort with which it communicated, is close to the monument. On the inner side is the tiny Place Mitto, from which a passage leads under the former Hôtel de Ville] to the small Place St. Jean. From this goes Rue du Four (bakehouse street), owing its name to a public bakehouse long disused. The street leads to the Corniche. On the way it forms an angle with Rue Droite, containing fine old houses and passing through the town from the Nice gate to the Roman gate on the eastern side. The church, built in 1777, contains two beautiful pictures.

From a short distance east of La Turbie a military road zigzags up to the fort on *Mont Agel*, 3,805 feet. Vehicles may not go beyond the golf course, 3¾ miles.

There is a wide choice of **Motor-coach Excursions** from Monaco, Monte Carlo, and Beausoleil, among them being the following :—

La Mortola, for the famous Hanbury Gardens (p. 154).

Laghet, p. 114.

Sospel, p. 138. This may be either a half-day excursion in which the shortest route is taken, or a whole-day excursion which includes, in addition to Menton and Castillon, the Col-de-Braus, L'Escarène and Nice.

Nice, *viâ* La Turbie and the Grande Corniche and returning by the coast road (pp. 96, 99).

San Remo, *viâ* La Mortola, Bordighera and Ospedaletti. (*See* the Italian section.)

Peille, p. 113, returning *viâ* La Trinité Victor, Laghet, Eze, and the Moyenne Corniche.

Tenda, p. 115. The route may be Menton, Vintimille, Breil, Fontan Tenda (or Tende), the Col-de-Braus, Sospel, Castillon, Menton, or it may be followed in the reverse direction.

Cap d'Antibes, p. 68. The return is sometimes made *viâ* Juan-les-Pins.

Levens. The tour includes Nice, Saint André, Gorges-de-Tourettes, St. Blaise, Aspremont.

Cannes, pp. 59–65, *viâ* Nice, Antibes, Juan-les-Pins.

Riviera (*i*)

Peïra Cava, p. 11, *viâ* Sospel, Col-de-Braus, L'Escarène, Lucéram ; returning *viâ* Laghet and La Turbie.

Grasse and the Gorges du Loup, pp. 80–82.   The outward route is generally *viâ* the Grande Corniche, La Turbie, Nice, Cagnes, Vence, the Gorges du Loup and the Pont du Loup; the return by Cagnes, Nice and the coast road.

Alassio.   *See* p. 173. .

St. Martin Vésubie, p. 107, *viâ* Laghet, Levens, Duranus, Saut des Français, and returning *viâ* the Gorges de la Vésubie, the Var Valley and Nice.

St. Raphaël, p. 52, *viâ* Cannes, the Corniche-d'Or and Le Trayas, and returning by the Estérels.

For the excursions into Italy, a passport must be carried.

The Index will indicate notes on the principal places along the respective routes.

MENTON.

Access.—*See* pages 23–7. There are two stations on the P.L.M. main line, Menton, the principal station, and Menton-Garavan for the eastern part of the town.

Consulate.—British, 9 Avenue de Verdun; American, at Nice (*see* p. 84).

Distances.—*By rail*: Paris, nearly 700 miles; Marseilles, 155½; Nice, 15.

Hotels.—*See* p. 30.

Inquiries.—At the Pavillon of the Syndicat d'Initiative, at the seaward end of the public gardens.

Population.—About 23,000.

Motor-coach Excursions *daily* to Nice, La Turbie, Laghet and Sospel, and *frequently* to Cannes, Grasse, Gorges du Loup, St. Raphaël, Peïra Cava, Tenda, San Remo, etc. (It is better to go to Tenda *viâ* Vintimille (Ventimiglia) and to return *viâ* Sospel.) Details of the excursions are obtainable at the *Pavillon Mentonnais*, occupied by the Syndicat d'Initiative. For information respecting places visited see Index at end.

M ENTON, " the Pearl of France," as Elisée Reclus, the great French writer, has called it, occupies one of the most picturesque spots on the French Riviera. It stands between the sea and a succession of encircling hills and mountains. Owing to the protection from cold winds, the reflection of the heat from the adjacent limestone masses, and its southern exposure, it is the warmest town on the coast, and its subsoil, consisting of coarse sandstone, which rapidly absorbs the rain that falls upon it, helps to give this favoured spot the dry air which is one of its characteristics. Named in the order of the number of their rainy days, beginning with the highest number, the months are May, November, March, April, October, December, February and January.

By reason of its dry, sunny, equable climate, Menton was originally an invalid station, but it has become more and more a pleasure resort. It is less gay than Nice or Monte Carlo, but the latter can be reached in a quarter of an hour, and for many the comparative tranquillity of the town is one of its charms. It must not, however, be thought that Menton does not offer indoor amusements or make provision for outdoor sports. There are two casinos in which concerts, balls, and theatrical performances are frequent. Once on Sunday and

131

Thursday, and twice on each of the other days of the week, the
Municipal Band plays on the sea-front. Winter and summer
golfers have a course at Sospel (p. 138), and for them a free
omnibus service is provided by the Hotel Keepers' Association. There are numerous tennis courts, and annual tournaments are arranged. Regattas, a dog-show, motor-races on
the sands, an American horse-show, horse-races, carnival
processions, battles of flowers, and the Fête de Nuit at
Garavan (a fairy-like spectacle in March), are among the
items in each season's programme.

The two portions into which the modern town, the town
of visitors, is divided by the hillock on which the old town
is perched are known from their respective positions as **East
Bay** and **West Bay.** The former is the warmer; it is the
site of some of the largest and finest hotels and boarding-
houses, and it was in the East Bay that Queen Victoria
resided in the spring of 1882. On the other hand, direct
sunlight is cut off from it early in the winter afternoons,
and its only level walk is by the side of the main road.

At the extreme east of East Bay is the suburb called **Les
Cuses.** It has a south-west aspect and is too far from the
old town to be shaded by it. Eastward also of East Bay
is the suburb of **Garavan** (*gare-a-vent*), in the opinion of many
the most sheltered spot between Marseilles and Genoa. It
is the site of a railway station, of hotels, pretty villas in
beautiful gardens, orange orchards and lemon groves.

So sheltered, warm, and fruitful is Garavan, that there
has become attached to it the legend which accounts for
the presence of the lemon along the southern shore of Europe.
It is said that Eve, arriving here with Adam, after years of
wandering, during which she had carefully guarded a lemon
stealthily plucked in the garden of Eden, threw the fruit on
the ground, exclaiming as she did so, " This is the place.
Grow and increase, oh golden fruit, in this garden worthy
of thee."

Following its incorporation with France in 1861, as related
on page 127, there came a change in the spelling and pro-
nunciation of its name, the Italian Mentone (*men-to-neh*)
giving place to the French Menton. About this time also
there occurred a more important change. From having
been but a small fishing town with a few scattered villas for
visitors, it began to take high rank as a health resort. The
claims of Menton in this respect were first brought to the

notice of English people by the late Dr. Bennett, who is commemorated by a statue in a square named after him.

The best view of the old town is obtained from the lighthouse at the end of the harbour. Small it is, but very
picturesque. It is a closely packed collection of lofty old-
time houses, built in the Italian style with loggias on the
top, balconies and terraces. The streets, of course, are
narrow, many are steep, some are stepped, there are vaulted
passages as in other ancient towns, and numerous arches
supporting walls, a feature due to Menton's experience of
earthquakes and of the best method of strengthening the
buildings.

A good point at which to begin the exploration of the **Old
Town** is opposite the Place du Cap, on Quai Bonaparte.
Here one enters the stepped Rue des Logettes, from which
there goes off Rue de Bréa, named after one of Napoleon's
generals, who was born at No. 2. At No. 3 Napoleon lodged
when on his way to direct his Italian campaign, and at No. 1
Pope Pius VII stayed in 1814 when returning to Rome, after
his exile. A tablet in the garden wall commemorates the
event.

From this street can be reached the **Church of St. Michel**,
erected in 1619, modified in 1675 and again in 1890, when
it was reconstructed, through having been almost destroyed
by an earthquake in 1887. It is in the Italian Jesuit style.
Upon its façade is a crude coloured statue of the archangel.
The most notable features of the interior are the graceful
lightness of the columns, the rich frieze above their capitals,
the frescoed and richly ornamented vault of the choir, and
the altar of the original building. It has beautiful bas-reliefs,
and is surmounted by a statue of St. Michel. The shaft
of a processional cross is that of a Turkish lance, captured
by Prince Honoré I at the battle of Lepanto, 1571.

The neighbouring church of the White Penitents is of little
interest.

From the square in which these churches stand, the Montée
de Souvenir, partly cut in the rock, leads to the **old cemetery,**
which is in four tiers, each appropriated to the members of
a particular denomination. Here stood the **Castle,** built
1492–1505. There are traces of its enceinte in the wall
extending from the cemetery to Porte Julien, now but an
arch at the end of **Rue Longue,** originally part of the Roman
road, Via Julia, and until 1810 the only carriage-way between

Provence and Italy. The narrow gates guarding its ends so
delayed the passage of Napoleon's military transport that
he constructed the road called Quai Bonaparte.

Rue Longue is still bordered by buildings, which were the
palaces of the nobles and the houses of the rich. That which
is now No. 123 was the Palace of the Princes of Monaco.
It is dated 1650. Over the portal of another house is 1542,
and 1543 is upon a third. Before their houses the fine ladies
used to sit in the open air and work, just as more humble
persons do now.

Going westward from Rue de Bréa is Rue du General
Gallieni, which passes a bust of Longfellow and is continued
by Rue de la République, from which there goes to the right
the broad Rue Lorédon-Larchey, leading to the **Museum
and Library** (the former open daily except Sunday and Monday, 10–12 and 2–4; the latter Tuesday, Thursday, Saturday).
Farther along Rue de la République is the **Hôtel de Ville**,
containing a fine Assembly Room. Beyond the Town Hall
Rue Villarey leads to the original casino.

The **Municipal Casino** faces the public gardens in the West
Bay quarter of the town. Their site was obtained by covering the lower portion of the Torrent du Careï, which is here
conducted through tunnels to the sea.

Walks and Excursions.

At the office of the Syndicat d'Initiative there can be obtained a small publication containing minute directions for between 70 and 80 walks from Menton.
A map, specially drawn for the purpose, accompanies the booklet.

A passport must be carried when the Italian frontier will be crossed.

Even for the most indefatigable pedestrian, the attractive
walks Menton offers are almost inexhaustible, and those who
are not good walkers can make excursions among the hills
by using donkeys—active, sure-footed animals upon whose
back the most timid may mount in perfect confidence.

One of the first walks the visitor should take is to follow
the Route Castellar, over the railway bridge (*see* plan) and then
to enter upon the steep ascent which rises before him. The
path soon leads into a pine wood and then goes through
an olive grove, continually revealing new aspects of that
mountain panorama which does so much towards making
Menton a delightful spot.

Pont St. Louis, 1½ miles, spanning the Gorge of St. Louis, the
boundary between France and Italy, should also be the goal
of an early walk. One route to it is by the Boulevard de

[Paris,

Patras,]

MENTON.

THE HARBOUR, MENTON.

THE CASINO, MENTON.

Garavan. Another is along Quai Laurenté to the **Hanbury Fountain,** erected by Sir Thomas Hanbury as a memorial of Queen Victoria's Jubilee and of her visit to Menton. From the fountain one follows the Avenue de la Frontière.

The bridge was built by Napoleon I in 1806. Previous to its construction travellers had to follow the Roman road below. On the farther side of the gorge post cards and Italian stamps may be bought so that the cards may be posted in Italy.

The Caves of the Red Rocks (*Rochers Rouges*). The caves, known also as the St. Louis Grottos, are in Italian territory. They are about twenty minutes' walk from the Hanbury Fountain, whence one takes the road along the sea-shore. The caves are remarkable for the relics of early man discovered by excavating the earthy matter, nearly thirty feet deep, upon the floor. Whole families had dwelt together, had allowed to accumulate the refuse of that which had served for food, and had buried their dead in it. The animal remains included the bones of the rhinoceros, the cave lion and the mammoth. Some of the skeletons and other relics are in the **Prehistoric Museum,** against the caves (*daily 8–12 and 2–6 ; 2 francs*).

The Hill of the Annonciade, 2½ miles. About 60 yards beyond the railway bridge north of the Avenue de Verdun the route lies along a cemented path on the left and leads to the rear of the Riviera Palace Hotel, from which there is a steep rise to the summit of the hill, about 700 feet above sea-level. **The Monastery of the Annonciade,** rather more than 3 miles away, can be reached by following the above-mentioned path to the entrance to the property of the monastery, marked by two white gate-posts. An easier ascent is by the funicular railway, of which the lower station is approached by the road which goes to the left from the Sospel road immediately beyond the electricity works. The ascent takes eight minutes and is made whenever required. The Church of the Annonciade is the tomb of the Monléon family, In the seventeenth century Stations of the Cross were constructed along the path to it, as a thank-offering by a princess of the house of Monaco.

The **Gorbio Valley,** the westernmost of the three principal valleys, owes its name to the ancient village at its head, at an altitude of about 1,150 feet, and 5½ miles from Menton. The church bears the date 1683. On the highest ground is the square tower of the old castle, portions of which have been converted into humble dwellings and stables. From the vicinity of the Place a path leads to a view-point, marked by a cross and reached by climbing for half an hour.

From *Gorbio to Ste Agnes* is a rough mule-path. The passage occupies 1¼ hours, distance just over 3 miles.

From *Gorbio to Roquebrune*, slightly over 3 miles distant, there is an excellent path which crosses the Lanzon torrent and the Col de la Tuilerie.

Castellar, a hill village of some 600 inhabitants, 5 miles due north of Menton. There is a good road on the eastern side of the Valley of Menton. From the chapel of the Penitents Noirs at Menton, the Castellar road goes to the left. The time can be shortened half an hour by making use of the bridle-path which starts from the Rue de la Marne on the eastern side of the Mairie.

Castillon is the name of two villages, one the child of the other. The modern village is 9½ miles by road and 7½ miles by tram up the Valley of the Careï. From it a steep cart-road and a steeper mule-path go winding up to the old village, 2,527 feet above the sea. A great part having been overthrown by an earthquake in 1887, the inhabitants deserted it and built the modern village.

Ste Agnes. Looking at the summit of the mountains northward of Menton, one may discern a speck of white. It is the Righi Hotel of Ste Agnes, perched at a height of 2,200 feet and 6¼ miles from Menton. The route begins by the Avenue Cernuschi, westward of the Borrigo bridge.

The town grew up under the protection of a castle, said to have been erected in the tenth century by a Saracen chief called Haroun, who was so enamoured of a Christian slave named Agnes that he embraced her faith in order to obtain her consent to be his wife. The church, dated 1744, is dedicated to Notre-Dame-des-Neiges (Our Lady of the Snows). The rejoicings on the occasion of her festival tempt many visitors at Menton to climb to the village.

Hanbury Gardens. The late Sir Thomas Hanbury's beautiful grounds at La Mortola, in Italy, 3 miles. *Admission 5 live or 6 francs, Monday and Friday, from 1 p.m.* (*see* pp.154–5). The motor-bus between Menton and Vintimille sets down passengers for the gardens and picks them up on its return, but it is preferable to make use of one of the excursion cars which leave Menton at 2 o'clock.

Cap-Martin.

Access.—By tram from Menton. By train to Cap-Martin-Roquebrune station. By the coast road.

Cap-Martin, the long low promontory between Monte Carlo and Menton, is one of the most delightful places of residence on the Riviera, as is attested by its charming villas and by the record of the notable persons who have resided upon it.

There are good roads along each coast and through the centre. At the eastern point of a hair-pin loop made by the tramway is an unfinished triumphal arch, and near the western point is a structure supposed to be a tomb and the sole remnant of the Roman town of Lumona or Limone. The coast roads unite at the huge *Cap-Martin Hotel*, near the extremity of the promontory. At the point where the east coast road turns to the west one can enter upon a charming corniche path which closely follows the shore.

Roquebrune.

By the Grande Corniche. By train to Cap-Martin-Roquebrune station. By tram and road.

Roquebrune lies about $4\frac{1}{2}$ miles westward of Menton and nearly 1,000 feet above the sea. To reach it by way of the Grande Corniche, follow westward the line of Avenue Carnot to the Chapel of St. Joseph and there bear to the right. At the next fork go to the right again.

If the tram is used for part of the way, alight about a third of a mile past the *Hôtel Riva-Bella* at a branch road by which the village can be reached in less than half an hour.

Roquebrune is a quaint rock village which looks as if it had slipped down the hill. Tradition indeed says that it originally stood 130 feet higher and that one night its site went sliding seaward. It is clean and tidy and its situation makes it tempting to those who prefer a higher level than that of Menton. Of course, the streets are narrow and steep, so that everywhere almost there are flights of steps. Some of the miniature thoroughfares pass under houses and one, Rue Pié, passes under another street. The ancient church of Ste Marguerite contains a beautiful statue of Christ. From the summit of the old castle there is a magnificent view.

If instead of going to the right at the second fork of the road from Menton to Roquebrune one took the left branch and followed it over the *Ramingau* streamlet, one would then arrive at **Cabbé,** situated on a pretty sheltered bay whose clean water tempts bathers.

Sospel.

Hotels.—*See* p. 31.

By Road from Menton. Up the narrow valley of the Careï, at the foot of which is the public garden. After the hamlet of Monti, 3¾ miles, is passed, the road climbs by hair-pin bends. At the foot of the village of Castillon, the road runs through a tunnel. On emerging one is among the mountains. Behind are the ruins of old Castillon (p. 136). From the tunnel there is a rapid descent to Sospel.

By Tram. The start is made from the Square St. Roch. The route is along the valley of the Careï and is remarkable for the daring manner in which it makes an ascent of 900 feet in the course of 4 miles. The celebrated **Viaduct of Caramel** comes into view when one is still 1¼ miles from it. It has the form of an Omega, has thirteen arches, is 130 yards long and about 45 feet high. The centre is nearly 1,400 feet above sea-level and commands a delightful prospect down the valley.

Sospel is situated at the bottom of a basin-shaped valley traversed by the *Bévéra*, spanned by two bridges, one built in 1908, the other some seven hundred years earlier. Upon the latter is an ancient toll tower now used as a dwelling-house.

Place St. Pierre is the site of the Mairie and a fountain. White marble capitals in the avenue bordering the Square belonged to the ancient church of Saint Pierre, destroyed during the French Revolution. Leading from the Square is **Rue St. Pierre,** once the finest and most important street, although in places less than six feet wide. The hotel on the right was the cloister of a Franciscan Monastery. Beyond it is the façade of the ancient **Préfecture :** the most notable feature is a rampant lion facing a lamb.

The street leads to the Piazza and the carefully restored *Church of St. Michael*, with a Romanesque tower of the seventeenth century. In the Square dozens of the Christian sect called the Albigenses were burnt at the stake in the sixteenth century.

In the fourteenth century Sospel became the seat of a bishop. Later it became a circuit town with its court of justice and public prosecutor. It came to have four parishes, as many brotherhoods and convents and two academies. In those days it was surrounded by high walls with five gates and many strong towers. In 1702 it had 15,768 inhabitants. It now has between 3,000 and 4,000. Its downfall dates from 1792 when the French Revolution took from it its court of justice and other privileges by creating the Department of the Alpes Maritimes.

Sospel has an excellent 18-hole golf course—some say the best on the Riviera.

ROQUEBRUNE.

[Patras.]

[Paris.]

WHERE FRANCE MEETS ITALY :
THE FRONTIER NEAR MENTON.

THE ITALIAN RIVIERA.

THE greater part of the Italian Riviera has been named after the Ligurians, who, as mentioned on page 20, were in possession of it at the dawn of its history. When during the Second Punic War Hannibal made his famous march across the Alps, Gauls and Ligurians swelled his force. On the conclusion of the Carthaginian campaign the Romans began to punish the Ligurians, who so stoutly opposed them that in eighty years the Romans could obtain possession of little more of the Ligurian territory than sufficed for a road along the coast. It was not until 31 B.C., as mentioned in connection with La Turbie (p. 128), that the conquest was completed.

The Ligurian Riviera is divided into two parts separated by Genoa, and named, according to their position with respect to that city, the **Riviera di Pomente,** that is, the Western Riviera, and the **Riviera di Levante**, the Eastern Riviera.

The western portion is very similar to the French Riviera, the main difference being the absence of large resorts with their parade of wealth and fashion. The high grounds here, as there, are nowhere far from the coast. There is the same vegetation, the same abundant sunshine and dry air.

Along the Riviera di Levante also the highlands are not far from the sea, and the resorts are not overgrown towns, but the coast is more rocky and the rainfall is slightly greater. On account of this difference in the rainfall the atmosphere is less stimulating, and is therefore suitable for persons of nervous temperament or suffering from certain ailments, for whom the air of the Riviera di Pomente and of the driest parts of the Côte d'Azur is too exhilarating.

The Mistral is hardly felt on the Ligurian Riviera, and not at all eastward of Saint Remo. The most unpleasant wind comes from the east, but it never blows long at a time.

The principal English colonies are at **Alassio, Bordighera, San Remo** and **Rapallo.** The largest of these resorts is San

Remo, but its population is only about one-fifth of that of Nice, and a wise law ordains that new buildings cannot be erected where they would cut off the sun's rays from an existing house, or completely block the view which has been enjoyed from its windows.

Under a law made by the Fascist Government, the local authorities have not only to see that the plans of a proposed building satisfy the necessary hygienic conditions, but they are to regard the proposed structure from an artistic point of view and are to consider its effect upon the amenities enjoyed by the inhabitants of neighbouring dwellings and by the public. It must have a pleasing elevation, must harmonize with its surroundings and must not prevent the neighbouring inhabitants or the public generally from continuing to enjoy a beautiful prospect. If there are trees on the property, only those which it is absolutely necessary to remove may be cut down.

Southward of the Ligurian Riviera is the **Tuscan Riviera,** taking its name from its department, formerly a grandduchy. Here sandy beaches are the rule, and the sun is more powerful than on the coast at which we have already glanced.

A very great charm of the Italian Riviera is the friendliness of the people. You do not feel that your presence is tolerated for the sake of the money you will leave behind, but you feel that the people like you and wish you to like them. Only those who have experienced the two atmospheres can appreciate the effect they have on a visitor's enjoyment.

In Italy there are no taxes levied specially on foreigners. There is nothing equivalent to the hundred francs exacted in France for an Identity Card.

Within three days of their entry into Italy foreigners must report to the police authorities to make their prescribed declaration and to take delivery of the proof of statement made. The declaration entails no more inconvenience than does the registration on taking a room at a British hotel. Hotel managers are authorized to facilitate the above formalities by causing the visitor to fill in and sign a declaration form, which is then presented direct to the police authorities against a receipt to be delivered to the visitor. There is nothing to pay.

As in France and some other Continental countries, there

is a visitors' tax, a small sum varying in amount with the class of hotel or boarding-house. The proceeds are used to improve the resort and is levied on foreigners and natives alike.

Those who exchange the Côte d'Azur for the Ligurian Riviera will remark the absence from the streets of vendors of lottery tickets, and gambling has been suppressed at the casinos with the exception of that at San Remo. At other places the casinos are simply social centres. They have refreshment-rooms and reading-rooms, and halls suitable for concerts, dramatic performances, and dances.

From the notes on the routes to the coast, it will be seen that Milan can be conveniently reached from the Ligurian Riviera. Florence is but a short distance from the Tuscan Riviera, and Rome and Naples can be conveniently reached from it.

NOTES FOR TOURISTS IN ITALY.

Notes applicable to both the French and the Italian Riviera will be found on pages 32–9. The following relate only to Italy.

Information Offices.—The services which the Syndicats d'Initiative render to tourists in France are performed and amplified in Italy at the offices of the Compagnia Italiano Turismo, commonly called the C.I.T. They have a complete information service placed gratuitously at the disposal of travellers. They have also special facilities for issuing tickets, reserving places in trains and rooms at hotels, insuring baggage and exchanging money. There are offices at London (16, Waterloo Place, Regent St., S.W.1), New York, and Paris ; on the French Riviera at Cannes, Nice, Monte Carlo and Menton ; at Genoa ; and on the Ligurian Riviera at Ventimiglia, Ospedaletti, San Remo, Nervi, Alassio, Rapallo, Santa Margherita Ligure, as well as in the principal cities in Italy.

Time.—The time in Italy is that of Central Europe, which is one hour in advance of that of Greenwich.

Cost of Visit.—In pre-war days Italy was one of the most inexpensive countries for the English or American tourist or resident. Since 1914 the cost of living has increased more in Italy than in England, but travel or residence on Italian soil is still inexpensive for those with British or American funds. At the larger resorts are fashionable hotels where the charges are fairly high, but there are also hotels where one can have cleanliness, comfort and excellent cuisine at a very moderate figure. The cost of a visit is greatly reduced by staying long enough at an hotel (generally five days) to obtain *en pension* terms (room, breakfast, lunch and dinner for a sum much below that charged when each item is priced) ; and when not moving rapidly from place to place less expense is incurred for cabs, porterage, etc. For identical accommodation the cost of living on the Ligurian Riviera is not greater than on the French Riviera.

Railways.—Corridor coaches are the rule on the main lines of the Italian railways. Third-class carriages are inferior to third-class carriages on the English lines ; second class is equivalent to English third.

Carriages for smokers are labelled "*Fumatori.*" Some compartments are labelled "*Non-fumatori*" to indicate that smoking in them is forbidden.

The trains run on Sundays as on other days.

Return Tickets.—At certain festivals the time during which a return ticket may be used is extended. Ordinarily the validity of those issued for a distance not exceeding 100 km. is 2 days ; from 101 to 200 km., 3 days ; from 201 to 300 km., 4 days ; for more than 300 km. (187½ miles), 6 days.

Reservation of Seats.—Travellers may reserve 1st- or 2nd-class seats at the railway station on the day previous to the journey, up to two hours before leaving in the case of trains specified in the Official Time Table. The fees are 5 lire for a 1st-class place, and 3 lire for a 2nd-class place.

Luggage.—Bags not weighing over 20 kilogrammes (44 lb.) are allowed free of charge in the compartment occupied by the traveller. Luggage weighing over 20 kilogrammes must be registered and paid for. (*See* p. 147.)

A railway porter (facchino, *fahk-keé noh*) who is asked to carry luggage to or from a cab and the train, or to or from a cloakroom (ufficio bagagli, *oof-feé choh, bah-gahl' yee*) is entitled to payment, 1, 2 or 3 lire, according to the weight or quantity.

The cloak-room fee is paid when the luggage is withdrawn.

At the principal stations is a *ristorante* (restaurant). At some of the less important stations is a café or buvette (refreshment bar).

Time-Tables.—In addition to a time-table (*Orario Generale* or *Orario Ufficiale*) for the whole of Italy, there are time-tables for large sections of the country and also for smaller regions. The time-table for the Ligurian Riviera is the *Indicatore regionale di Piemonte e Liguria*, price 50 c.

Time is reckoned from midnight to midnight.

Language (*see* p. 34).—The following are among the Italian words seen at Stations : *A Pagamento*, to pay ;

Bagagli, luggage ; *Biglietti*, tickets ; *Capo Stazione*, station master ; *Cessi*, public conveniences ; *Donne*, ladies ; *Distribuzione Biglietti*, booking office ; *Magazzino*, store ; *Movimento*, staff ; *Ristoratore*, *Ristorante*, restaurant ; *Ritirata*, public conveniences ; *Sala d'aspetto*, waiting room ; *Sala de Ia e IIa classe*, 1st- and 2nd-class waiting room ; *Telegrafo*, telegraph office ; *Ufficio bagagli*, cloak-room ; *Ufficio Merci*, goods office ; *Uomini*, gentlemen ; *Uscita*, way out ; *Vietato fumare*, do not smoke ; *Vietato sputare*, do not spit.

Money.—Money is reckoned in Italy by the *lira*, which is represented by a nickel coin, and for all practical purposes may be considered as worth $2\frac{1}{2}d$. in English money. There are also nickel coins of 20 centesimi ($\frac{1}{2}d$.), 50 centesimi ($1\frac{1}{4}d$.), 1 lira and 2 lire. There are bronze coins of 5 and 10 centesimi ($\frac{1}{8}d$. and $\frac{1}{4}d$.).

There are silver coins worth 5, 10 and 20 lire and notes for 50, 100, 500 and 1,000 lire.

" L " placed before a number stands for lira.

The lira has been stabilized at 92·46 to the pound sterling, instead of 25·20 which was its value before the Great War.

In English money the value of L 5 is nearly 1s. 1d. ; of L 10, nearly 2s. 2d. ; of L 20, nearly 4s. 4d. ; of L 100, about £1 1s. 6d.

Weights and Measures.—As in money, so in weights and measures, the decimal system is followed and except in nomenclature is identical with that in use in France (*see* p. 38). Mètre, décamètre, kilomètre are replaced by metro, decametro, chilometro (ch = k) ; décimètre, centimètre, and millimètre by decimetro, centimetro and millimetro ; litre, décilitre, centilitre, décalitre and hectolitre by litro, decilitro, centilitro, decalitro and ettolitro ; gramme and kilogramme by gramma and chilogramma. For the measure of length the unit is the *metro*, and its square and cube are taken as standards of surface and capacity. The *metro* may be compared with the English yard, to which it approximates. It is slightly longer than the yard, measuring $39\frac{1}{3}$ inches, or in decimals, 39·371 inches. The *decametro* is 10 *metri* or almost 11 yards ; the *chilometro* (ch = k), 1,000 *metri*, by which distances are measured, may be taken as $\frac{5}{8}$ of a mile. Thus by multiplying a distance stated in chilometri by 5 and dividing the product by 8, one gets the distance in English miles.

Going downward from the metro there are the *decimetro*, or one-tenth of a metro, nearly 4 inches, the *centimetro*, two-fifths of an inch, and the *millimetro*, one-tenth of a centimetro.

The standard measure of capacity is the *litro*, about $1\frac{3}{4}$ pints. The *decilitro* is the one-tenth of a litro, say $\frac{7}{10}$ of a gill, and the *centilitro* the one-hundredth of a litro. Going upwards there are the *decalitro* (ten litres) or 2⅕ gallons, and the *ettolitro* (100 litres) or 22 gallons or 2¾ bushels.

In weight the unit is the *gramma*, equal to about 15½ grains Troy, so that 10 grammi are equal to about ⅓ of an ounce avoirdupois. The *chilogramma*, or 1,000 grammi, is the standard weight. It equals 2¼ lb. avoirdupois and is mainly used for wholesale business or heavy goods.

The centigrade thermometer is used for the measurement of temperature (*see* p. 39, French section).

Postal Information.—Post offices are generally open from 9 a.m. to 12 and 2 p.m. to 7 p.m. on weekdays. Branch offices are closed on Sundays. The principal office is open until noon on Sundays for a limited service.

All post offices are closed on New Year's Day, Easter Monday, the Fête de Dieu (Corpus Christi), the first Thursday after Trinity Sunday, the National Festival, September 20, All Saints' Day, November 1, Christmas Day.

In Italy.—For letters and closed packets posted and delivered in the same district the postage is 25 c. for every 15 grammes (grammi) or odd fraction ; for delivery outside the district in which it is posted, 50 c.

For illustrated post cards with only date, signature, and address of sender, 10 c. ; with five words of greeting in addition, 20 c. For illustrated or plain post cards used for correspondence, if delivered in the district in which they are posted, 15 c., if delivered elsewhere in Italy, 30 c.

For printed matter the postage is 10 c. for every 50 grammes.

The fee for registration is L 1·25. There is no form to fill up as in France.

For a telegram not exceeding ten words, the charge is L 2. For every additional word, 25 c.

For an urgent telegram, the charge is three times the ordinary rate.

Money telegram, ordinary rate L 3 ; urgent L 9.

ABROAD.—For letters sent abroad the postage is L 1·25 up to 20 grs. inclusive, and 90 c. for each additional 20 grs.

For post cards (plain or illustrated), 75 c.

For printed matter, 25 c. per 50 grs.

For telegrams to Great Britain the charge per word is L 1·15, to New York L 4·65.

Stamps may be obtained at tobacconists' shops. They are there compulsorily on sale.

Correspondence to be called for at a post office should be addressed to the " poste restante." To obtain it the addressée must give proof of identity by the production of the passport. A fee of 25 c. is payable on each letter and 10 c. on each newspaper.

The name should be very clearly written and should not be followed by Esq., which is on neither a visiting-card nor a pass-port and is a title unknown in Italy.

Another point to remember is that the name of the department should form part of the address. These are indicated in the list of hotels on pages 148–51.

Registered letters are delivered only to the person to whom they are addressed and on proof of identity.

Parcels are taken to the post office as in England.

Motoring in Italy.—From end to end of the Ligurian Riviera, and also on a great part of the adjacent Tuscan Riviera, a main road runs along the extremely irregular coast. It is almost always in company with the railway, but never for long do the two ways occupy the same relative position. Long a narrow, dusty and bumpy highway, it has recently been in great part remade, corners being " opened " and level crossings replaced by bridges. Straight stretches of road are few and short.

The rule of the road is the opposite of that in force in Britain.

The *Motoring Map of Italy* in two parts, Northern Italy and Southern Italy, shows all the roads suitable for motoring, distances, gradients, heights, custom stations, railways and railway stations, mountains, valleys and numerous town plans. Paper, 3s. 4d., postage 3d. per part, or canvas, 5s. 6d., postage 6d., from the Italian Travel Bureau, 16, Waterloo Place, Regent Street, London, S.W.1. There is also a map of Italy in 58 parts, scale 1/250,000, showing all highways, byways, rivers, lakes, mountains, railways, etc., 6d. each, postage 2d. For the Ligurian Riviera, the sections are Nos. 15, 16, 17.

Motorists and cyclists derive many advantages from membership of the *Italian Touring Club.* Upon other tourists, also, member shipconfers advantages. The form of application for membership contains details of the various privileges. It can be obtained from the British Consul of the Club, 16, Waterloo Place, London, S.W.1. The club has many thousands of British members. Entrance fee, 1s. Annual subscription, 5s.

See also the note for motorists on pages 26–7 of the French section.

Clothing.—The notes in the French section, page 32, apply to the Italian Riviera. It is only necessary to add that in Italy the dress of ladies is less décolleté than in England, except at big balls. At many hotels the only change is made for dinner.

Bathing.—The chief resorts for summer bathing are Alassio, Rapallo, San Remo, Spotorno and Levanto. At the large resorts are bathing establishments with cabins, a café, etc., and usually with verandahs and roofs on which one can lounge in the sun. There are diving boards, rafts, chutes, see-saws, etc. Where the shore is rocky, steps lead down

Riviera (k)

into deep water. At some resorts moonlight bathing is popular.

The costumes of the ladies, whether severely plain or ornamental, will survive immersion.

Peignoirs (which can be bought locally) and one-piece suits of gay-coloured towelling are the most popular wear out of the water. At some resorts they are worn all day.

The bathing season is at its height in July and August, but bathing is enjoyable from April to November.

Books to Read.

Italian Highways and Byways from a Motor-Car, by Francis Milloun ; Wordsworth's *Tour in Italy* and *Italian Journeys,* by W. T. Howell ; *Rock Villages of the Riviera,* by W. Scott, and *The Hill Towns of Italy,* by Egerton R. Williams ; *Among Italian Peasants,* by Tony Cyriax ; *Fair Italy,* by W. Cope Devereux ; *San Remo,* by Dr. Lee, and *Genoa,* by E. A. Le Mesurier ; F. F. Hamilton's *Bordighera and the Western Riviera,* and *The Levantine Riviera,* by W. T. Beeby and Eustace Reynolds Ball ; *Along the Rivieras of France and Italy,* by Gordon Home ; *The French and Italian Rivieras,* by H. L. Waters ; *The Rivieras,* by Augustus Hare, and also by Baring-Gould ; *Things Seen on the Riviera,* by Capt. Leslie Richardson ; *The Romans on the Riviera,* by W. H. Bullock ; *The Story of Ventimiglia,* by Miss Briggs. The novels placed in this corner of Italy are too numerous to mention.

ROUTES TO THE ITALIAN RIVIERA.

By Rail.

There are two principal railway routes :—

1. *Viâ* Paris-Marseilles-Nice-Ventimiglia for Bordighera, Ospedaletti, San Remo, Porto Maurizio, Diano Marina, Alassio, Spotorno, Pegli, Genoa.

2. *Viâ* Paris–Mt. Cenis–Turin.

2(*a*) For Genoa, Santa Margherita, Rapallo, Levanto, Sestri Levante, Spotorno, Viareggio. This route can also be used for travelling to Alassio, Bordighera, Ospedaletti, and San Remo *viâ* Genoa.

2(*b*) *Viâ* S. Dalmazzo and Cuneo for Ventimiglia, Ospedaletti, Bordighera and San Remo.

2(*c*) *Viâ* Bra and Savona for Spotorno and Alassio.

Other routes are *viâ* Paris–Lausanne–Simplon Tunnel and Milan to Genoa ; *viâ* Lausanne–Berne–Lötschberg–Simplon and Milan to Genoa, and *viâ* Ostend–Brussels–Basle–Milan–Genoa. The last-named route is somewhat longer than the others mentioned, but there is a through carriage from Ostend to all destinations on the Italian Riviera from Genoa to Ventimiglia, and there is also a first and second-class sleeping coach from Ostend to Milan.

The route *viâ* Marseilles and Ventimiglia is for those visiting Italy *viâ* the Côte d'Azur, the journey from London to San Remo taking about 27 hours and to Alassio about 30 hours. That *viâ* Turin and Genoa is more direct for travellers to the eastern side of the Italian Riviera and the journey from London to Rapallo and Santa Margherita takes about 30 hours, to Levanto 31 hours and to Viareggio, 33 hours. The route from London to San Remo *viâ* Cuneo is an interesting alternative and the line from Turin to Ventimiglia, which has only recently been opened, passes through some fine scenery. The time taken from London to San Remo is about 30 hours, and from London to Alassio, *viâ* Bra and Savona, the time is approximately 33 hours. The times stated are for the express trains, but several hours can be saved by travelling either by the Calais-Mediterranean train de luxe for San Remo, etc., or by the Boulogne-Rome train de luxe for Rapallo and destinations south of Genoa. For further details regarding the route from London to Ventimiglia *viâ* the Côte d'Azur *see* pages 23–5.

Viâ the Mt. Cenis route there is first and second class sleeping car accommodation from Paris to Turin, Genoa, Rapallo, etc., and by the Simplon route similar sleeping car accommodation from Calais or Paris to Milan.

Luggage can be registered from London to all the places mentioned by routes (1) and (2*a*). Travellers by routes (2*b*) and (2*c*) are recommended to register as far as Turin, claim their luggage there, and re-register it to the final destination. There is a free allowance of 66 lbs. registered baggage by the English and French Railways, but there is no free allowance by the Swiss and Italian Railways. Travellers proceeding to small resorts along the Italian Riviera to which there are no through registrations from London should register as far as the frontiers (either Ventimiglia or Modane), clear their baggage through the Customs at those stations, and re-register to their final destinations.

Customs.—Baggage registered from London to Italian destinations is usually examined only at the Italian Frontier stations (Ventimiglia or Modane), or else at one of the following Customs houses :—San Remo, Genoa, Turin, Milan.

Although the French Customs authorities have the right to examine baggage entering their country at the port, they very rarely exercise this prerogative, but travellers are recommended to make inquiries before they get into the trains. When luggage is registered to destinations other than San

Remo, Genoa, Turin and Milan, Customs examination takes place at the Italian Frontier station, and after being cleared there is free to proceed to its destination without further attention on the part of the traveller. In the case of luggage registered to those towns where there are Custom-houses, it should be borne in mind that it is only possible to obtain possession of the luggage during the usual business hours, i.e. from 8 to 12 and 2 to 6, and that Custom-houses are not always at the station. Hence if it is the intention to stop at Turin, for example, for the night in order to break the journey, ample time should be allowed for clearing the baggage before proceeding by the morning train the next day.

Luggage registered from Italy to other countries is subject to Customs examination before leaving Italy, as it is forbidden to take valuable works of art out of the country. This examination should either take place at one of the Custom-houses mentioned above (San Remo, Genoa, Turin or Milan) or else the passenger must clear it at the Frontier. This is *most important*, for failure to comply with this regulation may result in the baggage being detained pending inquiries.

Further details with regard to time of trains, reservations, fares, etc., can be obtained from the London Office of the Italian Travel Bureau, at 16, Waterloo Place, London, S.W.1.

By Air or Sea.

There are air services between London (Croydon), Paris and Genoa. Particulars can be obtained on application to the Air Union, 52, Haymarket, London, S.W.1. (*See* p. 26.) From Marseilles to Genoa the flight takes three hours.

As noted on page 26, many fine liners call at Genoa, and for those not pressed for time they provide an admirable approach to the Riviera. In addition to the liners mentioned on page 26 there are the steamers of such well-known Italian lines as the *Navigazione Generale Italiana* ("N.G.I.").

By Motor.

See pages 26–7 of the French section and the sketch-map facing page 23.

During the winter the only road into Italy open for motorists is that *viâ* the French Riviera, crossing the frontier at Vintimille (Ventimiglia).

See also the note on Motoring in Italy, page 145.

HOTELS AND TARIFFS.

Owing to considerations of space it is impossible to include here a complete list of hotels, with their charges.

Hôtels de luxe and also those with very low prices have therefore been omitted, and one or two others.

Each year a list of the hotels in Italy with their tariff is compiled by the Italian State Tourist Department in collaboration with the National Fascist Confederation of Hotels and Tourist Traffic. The hotel keepers undertake to adhere strictly to the prices they have quoted. Space permits mention of only a few of the hotels on this and following pages. The complete list is published at 1s. (1s. 3d. post free), and the section for any particular district can be obtained on application to the Italian Travel Bureau, 16 Waterloo Place, Regent Street, London, S.W.1, where rooms for any hotel can be reserved and travel arrangements made.

As the tariffs are open to revision annually, the exact charges can be known only by consulting the list for the current year. Therefore the following figures must be regarded only as an indication of the grade of the establishment, and as giving an idea of what hotel expenses are likely to be at the places named.

The percentage for service (included in the bill) is fixed for all hotels at 15 per cent. on hotel bills up to 200 lire and 10 per cent. on all other bills. No other tipping is expected.

NOTE.—The word after the place-name in the following list is the name of the district and should form part of the address.

The figures enclosed in brackets ( ) indicate the number of rooms ; the Roman figures represent the months and the figures in italics the visitors' tax. The tax marked with an asterisk (*) covers the entire stay. The main figures represent the minimum and maximum charges per day for board and lodging. The difference in price depends upon the room selected. The meals are breakfast (coffee, etc., and roll and butter), lunch and dinner. Wine and other drinks are not included. In some hotels (perhaps most) heating (*riscaldamento*) is not included in the charge for a room, and an extra charge of from 2 to 5 lire per day and per person is made. The price for full board refers usually to a period of not less than 5 days. There are no hotels charging such *luxe* tariffs as on the French side. For example, the very best hotels at San Remo and Rapallo charge in the neighbourhood of £1 per day.

Alassio (*Savona*).

Bristol : (50) V–VI, IX–XI, 30–40; XII–IV, VII, VIII, 35–45 ; *1.50.*

Europa e Concordia : (95) V–VI, IX–XI, 30–40 ; XII–IV, VII, VIII, 35–45 ; *1.50.*

Grand et Alassio : (120) I–XII, 50–70, *2.*

Lido : (100) V–VI, IX–XI, 30–40; XII–IV, VII, VIII, 35–50 ; *1.50.*

Mediterranée : (100) I–XII, 40–60, *2.*

Moderne Suisse : (60) V–VI, IX–XI, 30–37; XII–IV, VII–VIII, 35–50 ; *1.50.*

Nettuno : (45) V–VI, IX–XI, 30–40; XII–IV, VII–VIII, 45–50 ; *1.50.*

Palace : (100) V–VI, IX–XI, 40–50 ; XII–IV, VII, VIII, 50–60 ; *1.50.*

Salisbury : (60) V–VI, IX–XI, 30–40; XII–IV, VII, VIII, 32–45 ; *1.50.*

Val' D'Oliva : (27) I–XII, 24–36 ; *1.50.*

Victoria : (100) I–XII, 35–50, *1.50.*

Pensione dei Fiori : (35) V–VI, IX–XI, 25–35 ; XII–IV, VII–VIII, 30–45 ; *1.50.*

Arenzano (*Genova*).

Genova : (80) I–XII, 35–45, *30**.
Grand Hôtel Roma : (70) I–XII, 30–50, *30**.
Gd. Hôtel Arenzano : (125) IX–VI, 30–48; VII–VIII, 35–50; *30**.

Bordighera (*Imperia*).

Angleterre : (50) V–XI, 30–40; XII–IV, 30–45; *1.50*.
Aurora : (40) V–XI, 35–40; XII–IV, 40–50; *1.50*.
Belvedere : (110) V–XI, 35–65; XII–IV, 45–75; *2*.
Britannique : (60) XI, 35–45; XII–IV, 35–50; *2*.
Continentale : (120) XI–V, 35–56, *2*.
Hesperia : (100) IX–XI, V, 35–50; XII–IV, 40–60; *2*.
Londres : (90) X–V, 35–70, *2*.
Miramare : (80) X–XI, V, 35–45; XII–IV, 38–55; *1.50*.
Parc : (100) X–V, 40–56, *2*.
Splendid : (36) V–XI, 32–38; XII–IV, 38–46; *1.50*.

Chiavari (*Genova*).

Moderno : (70) V–IX, 35–40, *10 per cent*.
Negrino : (80) V–VI, 30–35; VII–IX, 35–40; *10 per cent*.

Diano Marina (*Imperia*).

Pardiso : (76) I–XII, 30–34, *15 per cent*.

Finale Marina (*Savona*).

Boncardo : (80) IX–VI, 20–**25**; VII, VIII, 28–35; *30**.

Genoa (= Genova).

Britannia, 38 *Via Balbi :* (110) I–XII, 65–70, *10 per cent*.
Gênes, 42 *Piazzi di Ferrari :* (100) I–XII, 75–80, *10 per cent*.
Grand et des Princes, 36 *Via Balbi :* (120) I–XII, 55–70, *2*.
Isotta, 7 *Via Roma :* (100) I–XII, 60–80, *10 per cent*.
Italie et Minerva, 14 *Via Carlo Felice :* (110) I–XII, 40–50, *10 per cent*.
Londra e Continentale, 2 *Via Balbi :* (90) I–XII, 50–70.
Orlandine, 45 *Via Balbi :* (38) I–XII, 45–55, *10 per cent*.
Pensione Petracchi, 36B *Via Assarotti :* 35–45 ; *1*.
Stella, 2 *Via Andrea Doria* (close to the station) : (100) I–XII. Room, 14–18. Breakfast, 5.50. Other meals not supplied. *1*.
Terminus Milano, 34 *Via Balbi :* (70) I–XII 40–50 *10 per cent*.

Genova—Nervi.

Giardino Riviera : (45) I–XII, 35–45, *1*.
Nervi : (50) I–XII, 30–45, *1.20*.
Pagoda Schweizerhof : (60) VI–X, 28–35, *1* ; XI–V, 35–50 ; *1.40*.
Vittoria Grand : (120) VI–X, 35–45 ; XI–V, 45–60 ; *2*.

Genova—Pegli.

Mediterranée : (140) V–VI, X–XI, 35–40 ; XII–II, VII–IX, 35–45 ; *10 per cent*.

Grimaldi (*Imperia*).

Miramare : (32) XI, XII, 30–32 ; I–IV, 32–45.

Imperia I (Porto Maurizio).

Miramare : (15) I–XII, 30–45, *10 per cent*.

Imperia II (Oneglia).

Concordia : (32) I–XII, 24–35, *10 per cent*.

Laigueglia (*Savona*).

Lalgueglia : (60) IX–VI, 25–27 VII–VIII, 30–35 ; *1*.

Lerici (*Spezia*).

Palmes : (35) I–XII, 25–35, *10 per cent*.

Levanto (*Spezia*).

Excelsior : (80) X–VI, 35–45 ; VII–IX, 35–50 ; *1*.
Grand : (100) X–VI, 25–30 ; VII–IX 40–45 ; *1*.
Stella d'Italia : (100) X–VI, 30–35 VII–IX, 38–40 ; *1*.

Loano (*Savona*).

Vittoria : (70) IX–VI, 23–28 ; VII, VIII, 25–35 ; *20**.

Ospedaletti (*Imperia*).

Harboë pensione : (40) X, XI, V, 40–60 ; XII–IV, 45–65 ; *1.80*.
Reine : (120) V, XI, 40–55 ; XII–IV, 45–65 ; *2*.
Suisse : (80) IX–V, 32–45, *1.80*.

Portofino Mare (*Genova*).

Splendid : (70) V–XII, 40–50 ; I–V, 40–60 ; *30**.

Portofino Vetta (*Genova*).

Grand : (100) IX–II, 40–45 ; II–IX, 40–50 ; *30**.

Rapallo (*Genova*).

Bellevue : (60) V–XI, 25–35 ; XII–IV, 30–40 ; *10 per cent.*
Belvedere : (60) V–XI, 28–45 ; XII–IV, 30–50 ; *10 per cent.*
Bristol : (100) V–XI, 40–60 ; XII–IV, 50–65 ; *10 per cent.*
Canali : (30) V–XI, 30–33 ; XII–IV, 33–40 ; *10 per cent.*
Elisabetta : (58) V–XI, 30–35 ; XII–IV, 30–40 ; *10 per cent.*
Europa : (150) V–XI, 35–50 ; XII–IV, 40–55 ; *10 per cent.*
Moderno : (85) V–XI, 36–40 ; XII–IV, 40–50 ; *10 per cent.*
Riviera Splendid : (30) I–XII, 35–45, *10 per cent.*
Rosa Bianca : (35) V–XI, 32–35 ; XII–IV, 35–40 ; *10 per cent.*
Villa Serena : (28) V–XI, 30–35 ; XII–IV, 35–40 ; *10 per cent.*

San Remo (*Imperia*).

Belvedere : (46) V–XI, 40–50 ; XII–IV, 45–55 ; *1.05.*
Cosmopolita : (60) V–XI, 30–40 ; XII–IV, 35–45 ; *1.05.*
des Etrangers : (100) I–XII, 35–45, *1.40.*
Europa e Pace : (110) V–XI, 40–50 ; XII–IV, 45–55 ; *1.40.*
Fleurie pensione : (23) V–XI, 30–35 ; XII–IV, 35–40 ; *1.05.*
Imperiale pensione : (40) V–XI, 35–50 ; XII–IV, 42–60 ; *1.40.*
Londres.
Morandi's : (45) V, X, XI, 45–50 ; XII–IV, 48–58 ; *1.40.*
Nazionale et Hungaria : (70) V–XI, 30–35 ; XII–IV, 30–50 ; *1.40.*
Paris : (47) V–XI, 40–50 ; XII–IV, 45–55 ; *1.40.*
Royal.
Savoy.
Vittoria et de Rome : (100) V–XI, 30–40 ; XII–IV, 35–65 ; *1.40.*
West End.

Santa Margherita (*Genova*).

Centrale Moderne : (60) I–XII, 30–45, *1.*
Continentale : (60) V–XI, 40–45 ; XII–IV, 50–55 ; *10 per cent.*
Internazionale pensione : (30) V–XI, 30–40 ; XII–IV, 40–50 ; *1.*

Lido Grand : (80) I–XII, 35, *10 per cent.*
Mignon : (50) I–XII, 35–60, *1.50.*
Regina Elena : (80) V–XI, 35–45 ; XII–IV, 40–50 ; *1.*
Santa Margherita : (70) V–XI, 35–40 ; XII–IV, 40–45 ; *1.*

Savona.

Riviera Palace : (70) I–XII, 29–36, *10 per cent.*
Suisse : (75) I–XII, 45–55, *10 per cent.*

Sestri Levante (*Genova*).

Miramare Europe : (80) IX–II, V, VI, 30–40 ; III, IV, VII, VIII, 35–50 ; *30*.*

Spezia.

Croce di Malta : (220) I–XII, 35–70, *10 per cent.*
Italia : (90) I–XII, 30–45, *10 per cent.*
Savoia S. Giorgio : (130) I–XII, 30–35, *10 per cent.*

Spotorno (*Savona*).

Lilian : (50) IX–VI, 22–30 ; VII, VIII, 25–35 ; *1.*
Palace : (180) IX–VI, 28–35 ; VII, VIII, 47–75 ; *1.70.*

Varazze (*Savona*).

Eden Parc : (70) I–XII, 25–45, *30*.*
Toretti : (80) I–XII, 30–45, *.75.*
Varazze Grand : (70) VII–IX, 55–60, *30*.*

Ventimiglia (*Imperia*).

Francia : (50) I–XII, 28–36, *10 per cent.*
Suisse Europa : (76) I–XII, 35–45, *10 per cent.*

Viareggio (*Lucca*).

Continental : (35) IX–VI, 25–35 ; VII, VIII, 30–45 ; *1.50.*
Mediterranée : (100) IX–VI, 30–50 ; VII, VIII, 40–65 ; *2.*
Miramare e Pineta : (80) V–VI, IX, 30–40 ; VII, VIII, 35–55 ; *1.50.*
Pini pensione : (80) I–XII, 35–55, *2.*
Regina : (120) I–XII, 45–65, *2.*
Riviera Golf : (100) IX–VI, 30–35 ; VII–VIII, 40–52 ; *2.*
Splendide des Palmes : (80) I–XII, 25–50, *2.*

VENTIMIGLIA.

Access.—By a *train rapide*, Ventimiglia can be reached from Paris *viâ* Marseilles in 18 hours, and from Turin in 5 hours. It is the terminus for all trains arriving from Paris, with the exception of the Calais–Mediterranean express (*train de luxe*) which the French allow to go on to San Remo.

Distances.—Bordighera, 2½ miles; Menton, 7 miles.

Hotels.—*See* p. 151.

Population.—15,000.

Tramway.—To Bordighera. Travellers who are going on immediately to Bordighera will usually save much time by going on by tram or by a taxi, instead of waiting for a train. Via della Stazione, opposite the centre of the station, leads down to the tramway. A stopping-place is opposite the church a short distance to the left.

Railway Station is shared by the French P.L.M. Railway and by the Italian State Railways, which connect the town with Tenda and Turin and with the coast towns as far as Genoa. It has a good refreshment room and a C.I.T. Information Office.

VENTIMIGLIA, or Vintimille, as the French call it, is the westernmost town of the Ligurian Riviera, but is neither a pleasure nor a health resort. It is situated on the slope of a hill overlooking the River Roja, the old town being on the right bank, the modern town on the left.

About 185 B.C. the town which then stood where the tram-lines cross the railway was taken by the Romans, who fifty years earlier had invaded the district. There are remains of a theatre and baths, and traces of other Roman constructions, and the Roman burial-ground has yielded many relics of Roman days. As elsewhere Saracen pirates ravaged the coast from time to time, and from the quantity of charred material on the site it is thought that the city was finally burnt. It was rebuilt on the western headland overlooking the right bank of the *Roja*, where there was already a settlement with Christian churches. A castle and walls guarded it and it became powerful. Many villages acknowledged it as their overlord and paid tribute to it.

Between it and Genoa, its nearest powerful neighbour, there was intense rivalry and jealousy. Again and again Genoa obtained the rule over it. At different times it also owed allegiance to France, Savoy, Provence, Spain, Milan, Modena, Monferrato, and Naples. From the year 1222, when after an heroic struggle it was obliged to surrender to the Genoese, until 1814, when the Congress of Vienna gave it to Victor

Emanuel I, King of Sardinia, Ventimiglia suffered nearly 40 sieges and changes of suzerainty, the greater number being accompanied by sack and destruction.

The old town is reached by going westward along Via Cavour, the tramway route, which leads to the *Roja*, spanned by a bridge of five arches. From it there is a fine view northward embracing the Roja Valley and the adjacent mountains. Beyond the bridge is the Piazza (square) Vittorio Emanuele, the site of the tramway terminus, from which Via Biancheri, ascending on the left, and then Via Falerina going sharply to the right, half-way up the hill, lead to the **Cathedral.** It dates from the eleventh century and stands on the site of a very early church that supplanted a temple of the Goddess Juno, to whom an inscription may be seen on an inside wall on the right. On the opposite side are chapels added in the fourteenth and fifteenth centuries. By these and other additions and alterations, the architectural value of the building has been much impaired. Above a twelfth-century doorway with defaced carvings are pilgrims' plates.

The adjoining *Baptistery* dates from the fifth century. Its font was used for total immersion, a method of baptism followed at Ventimiglia after it had been abandoned at nearly all other places. The semicircular recesses by the side of the font were occupied by the officiating priests, and the steps in the interior of the font are the usual feature of fonts used for immersion.

On the same square stands a fine building with a double flight of steps. This was a monastery built in 1668 on the site of the castle.

Going from the square is **Via Garibaldi,** which still preserves many ancient features. In it stand the Town Hall, containing many relics of the Roman times, the Church of the Neri, with eighteenth-century frescoes, and the Church of the Minori Osservanti, with a high altar upon which is sculptured a representation of the Annunciation.

Thence by the Piazzetta del Canto, which descends on the right, and the Via Piemonte, which is followed leftward, one reaches the **Church of S. Michele**, with an unusual square tower. The church is said to have been erected on the site of a temple for the worship of Castor and Pollux. It was rebuilt in 1885, but near the west door are Roman columns, and in the crypt there is another which seems to have been a milestone. The crypt, the apse, and portions of the walls are probably remnants of the original structure.

Ventimiglia's Flower Market.

When Alphonse Karr, about 1880, had shown that floriculture might be a profitable industry, a German named Ludwig Winter, seeing that the climate and soil of Bordighera were suitable, began to grow flowers for sale and succeeded in establishing a large business. His example was followed by the peasants of the neighbourhood, and now over a large area of the western part of the Ligurian Riviera, in place of the olive groves of former days, there are miles of flower-beds and acres of glass-houses.

Some eight thousand tons of flowers are sent from Western Liguria annually, and of that quantity about one-fourth goes from Ventimiglia, where it has been exposed for sale in a special flower market held daily, and that market is one of the sights which visitors within easy reach of it should not willingly miss. The display is particularly beautiful during the eight months in which carnations are being cut. The market opens at a fixed hour, generally 3.30 in the afternoon, and not until the signal is given can a flower be seen. Then at the first sound the coverings are removed and the whole area blazes with colour produced, according to the season of the year, by carnations, stocks, wallflowers, marigolds, rosebuds, mimosa, freesias, marguerites, lilies, violets, asparagus fern. Carnations are sent to every country of Europe, except Russia and Poland, but marguerites and violets form the principal part of the export to England, and roses and bulbs of that to France.

The market-place can be reached from Via Cavour by going a few yards seaward along Via della Stazione (opposite the centre of the railway station).

The Hanbury Gardens.

About 4½ miles from Ventimiglia, 8 from Bordighera and 15 from San Remo. **Admission.**—Mondays and Fridays from 1 o'clock. Tickets 5 lire or 6 frs. The receipts are distributed among charitable institutions. Picnicking is not allowed. Tea may be obtained at a restaurant near the entrance. A small pamphlet obtainable from the gate-keeper calls attention to the most interesting features. The visit to the gardens occupies about two hours, but if the walk through a mossy glen to the sea and through the pine woods along the valley is included, the whole afternoon will be needed. Stand cameras are not allowed as they interfere with the free circulation of visitors.

Motor-coaches run from places within a reasonable distance. The visitors are often 500 in number.

From Ventimiglia the route to the gardens—among the most famous in the world—begins by a steep ascent to the barracks, ½ mile from the town. Then there is a long, gradual descent to the foot of the gorge and through the small village of Latte. The Val di Latte, the Vale of Milk, was much in favour with wealthy Romans. The mother of the Roman General, Agricola, who completed the conquest of Britain, had a palace here, and here she fell in a massacre ordered by the Emperor Otto. From Latte the road zigzags up to La Mortola, where, near the Fontane dell' Olivo, is the entrance to the Gardens.

The villa (*not open to the public*) is the ancient Lanteri palace erected in the fifteenth century, known after 1620 as the Palazzo Orengo, from the family which then obtained it. It was restored by Commander Hanbury, who bought the property in 1867. A grandson is the present owner. The scene of H. G. Wells's *Meanwhile* is laid here, but the villa has been given another name.

The grounds are about 100 acres in extent and contain over 5,000 species of plants cultivated in the open air.

Upon a garden seat marked A. E., King Edward VII, then Prince of Wales, sat and talked with his sister, the Empress Frederick, who had come from San Remo. On a wall tablet seen at the end of a great pergola east of the house is inscribed, " They heard the voice of the Lord God walking in the garden."

To the Colle di Tenda, 40 miles (p. 115). A good motor road runs up the beautiful valley of the *Roja* to Cuneo, and thence to Turin, 108 miles from Ventimiglia. It begins near the bridge. Through the valley passes also the railway between Turin and Ventimiglia, affording an easy means of access from the centre of Europe to Bordighera, Ospedaletti and San Remo. There is a motor service twice daily from Ventimiglia to Tenda and Pigna.

The Red Rocks (p. 135). The best route is from Menton, but at the Miramar Hotel, a short distance from the frontier, there is a public lift between the level of the main road and the shore, on which are the caves and the museum.

BORDIGHERA.

Access.—By rail *via* Ventimiglia, 2½ miles distant (p. 152). By bus from Nice (p. 84).
Hotels.—*See* p. 150.
Motor-buses.—To Ospedaletti.
Trams.—There is a frequent service to Ventimiglia.

HOUSES line nearly the whole of the road between Ventimiglia and its near neighbour Bordighera, widely known by name as one of the Riviera resorts to which English people go to enjoy winter sunshine. It claims to have a rainfall smaller than that of Nice and much smaller than that of Cannes. It also claims that within its bounds the fall in the temperature at sunset is less in degree and less sudden than on the French Riviera.

Another feature which helps to give it its English colony is the absence of artificiality, but there is no lack of the aids to enjoyment or of the amenities which visitors expect in a place of its size. A casino provides music daily. The Union Club has bridge, chess, billiard, and reading rooms. There is an excellent International Library. The Lawn Tennis Club has a number of hard courts. Picturesquely situated a mile from the town is a 9-hole golf course with a club-house containing a restaurant. It is near the tramway and there is a special motor-car service four times a day. Information respecting the course and the attractive competitions will be gladly furnished by the Honorary Secretary, whose postal address is The Union Club. Bordighera has Anglican and Presbyterian churches and English doctors.

The promenade along the mile of beach is gay with flowers and commands fine views of the French coast.

Parallel with and close to the shore runs its single shopping thoroughfare. On the rising ground inland of it are villas and hotels in gardens containing palms, orange and lemon trees and flowers of many kinds. The prevalence of these gardens is one of the great charms of Bordighera. Behind them rise the Ligurian Alps, the lower slopes covered with vines and olives.

A special feature of the neighbourhood is formed by the

groves of palms. The trees are not grown for their fruit, which seldom fully ripens, but for their leaves, which are exported to Rome shortly before Palm Sunday and five or six months later for use in Jewish Synagogues. The leaves of two kinds of palms are used. Those sent away in the spring are longer and more pointed than those exported later in the year. In neither case are the leaves in their natural condition, but are more or less bleached through the light having been excluded from them. Those used in the spring are bound up in the previous July, while the Jewish palms are imprisoned only some four months before being cut and are therefore then slightly green. (*See* under Piazza Bresca, p. 167.)

The patron saint of Bordighera is Sant' Ampeglio, who died in 428. He is commemorated by a small chapel, below the Old Town, built over a cave in which he lived and died, just beyond the reach of the waves. Above the high altar is a statue of him dating from 1655.

The **Old Town,** Bordighera Alta, clusters on a hill on the eastern side of the modern quarter. Large portions of its mediæval walls are still standing and retain the three gateways by which the rampart was originally pierced. From each of them the thoroughfare leads to the **Piazza,** the centre of the life of the place. At the western entrance to the Square are two arches in the base of an ancient watchtower, enlarged and converted into the campanile of the parish church, a comparatively modern building standing on the northern side but apart from it. On the opposite side of the tower is the oratory of S. Bartolomeo, a small ancient building which was formerly the parish church. The narrow streets bordered by lofty houses and crossed by earthquake arches are destitute of fine buildings, as Bordighera never numbered wealthy persons among its inhabitants. There exists no reference to it before 1238, when it received refugees from Ventimiglia who hoped in Bordighera to be free from Genoese tyranny, but their place of retreat was attacked, and in spite of its walls, fortifications and watch-tower and its determined resistance, it was captured and destroyed. The walls now seen were built in 1472.

In 1845 the attention of English people was directed to the Italian Riviera by Ruffini's novel entitled *Dr. Antonio.* Various magazine articles followed, all praising the beauty and the climate of the region. Attention was specially directed to Bordighera by the purchase of a villa by the Earl of Strathmore, grandfather of the present Duchess of York, and the development of the English colony was largely promoted by Dr. George MacDonald and his wife, who settled at Bordighera in 1880. Having a large family and small means, they built a house which they called *Casa Coraggio,* the House of Courage, for the reception of a few paying guests. To Bordighera the preacher-poet-novelist and Mrs. MacDonald drew all the most cultured people of the Riviera. For nearly twenty years their house was a centre of interest.

During the Great War two British hospitals were established at Bordighera, and in the small cemetery in the Sasso Valley are 72 graves.

Walks and Excursions.

A very pleasant morning or afternoon walk is to the isolated **Cima dei Monti,** nearly 750 feet above sea-level, from which a wide and delightful panorama is unfolded.

A longer walk crosses the Vallecrosia Valley and goes to the little chapel of **Santa Croce,** at an elevation of some 1,160 feet. From a rocky knoll behind it the prospect includes a magnificent stretch of mountains on three-fourths of the horizon.

The ascent of **Monte Nero,** nearly 2,000 feet, is mainly attractive because much of the easiest route lies through a thick pine wood, shady and cool even during the warmest hours of the day.

Sasso, about 4½ miles from the town, is a village of some 200 inhabitants delightfully situated 700 feet above the sea. From it a mule-path along the summit of the hills leads in an hour to the larger village of Seborga, a thousand feet higher than Sasso and connected with Bordighera by a good carriage-road (*see* below).

At 2½ miles north of Bordighera is the village of **Borghetto,** which in a very special sense may be regarded as its parent, thirty-two families having in 1470 left Borghetto to rebuild the now more famous town on the coast.

Less than a mile beyond it is the village of **Vallebona,** entered by Porta Madonna, part of the ancient fortifications. The parish church, San Lorenzo, has a Gothic doorway on which the Lamb is sculptured, and a fine steeple said to have been built of the materials obtained by the demolition of certain aisles of the church. In the neighbouring oratory of the Nativity are noteworthy stuccoes, and in Via Scudier, which communicates with the piazza, as well as in other streets, are Early Italian and Gothic stone doorways.

From Vallebona Sasso can be reached in ½ hour and thence to Bordighera is a walk of from 45 minutes to 1 hour. Seven miles from Bordighera is the very ancient village of **Dolceacqua.** It is surrounded by olive trees and stands on both sides of the *Nervia*, over which is a single-arched bridge very steep and so narrow that a wheelbarrow is the only vehicle which can cross it. Towering above the village are the remains of a castle of the Dorias, a Genoese family that long ruled on the Ligurian Riviera. The castle was abandoned after the war in 1748.

At 3 miles south of Dolceacqua is **Camporosso.** Its name, meaning red field, is said by some to have reference to the flower of the oleanders abounding in the valley. A quarter of a mile to the right of the village, and now forming part of the cemetery, is the ancient church of SS. Pietro et Paolo, the first Christian church erected at Camporosso.

Half a mile up the valley is the ancient chapel of S. Andrea. 1¼ miles farther is the small chapel called San Rocco, whence Dolceacqua comes into view.

At 2½ miles beyond Dolceacqua is **Isolabona,** at the confluence of the *Nervia* and the *Merdanz*.

Visitors hurry on to the much more attractive village of **Apricale,** some 1¼ miles eastward, and 900 feet above the sea. It is situated at the summit of a hill down the sides of which its houses seem to flow. Its main street is a flight of steps and leads to the piazza on which stands the parish church. Near the church are the ruins of another of the castles of the Dorias.

Nearly 5 miles northward of Isolabona is the large village of **Pigna** (*motor-bus twice daily from Ventimiglia*). It stands at an elevation of 1,000 feet. Its parish church of San Michele has a Gothic portal bearing the date 1450. The interior has been spoilt by restorers. Over the high altar is an elaborate fifteenth-century painting by the Italian artist Giovanni Banavesio, who also painted frescoes in the chapel of S. Bernardo, near the cemetery and reached in 15 minutes.

Visitors desiring more detailed information respecting the walks than can be given here are referred to the locally published *Path Walks of Bordighera and Ospedaletti* and to *Round About San Remo and Bordighera*.

Sasso and **Seborga** (p. 158) are included in a motor-coach excursion, as are also the **Hanbury Gardens** (p. 154), Perinaldo, Baiardo, **San Romolo** and the following places for which the Index should be consulted—the Tenda Tunnel, Nice, Gorges du Loup.

Perinaldo, a town of 2,000 inhabitants, 9½ miles from Bordighera and about 1,900 feet above the sea, is situated on an isolated hill which affords an extensive view. It was the

birthplace of three astronomers, Gian Domenico Cassini
(*d.* 1712), the discoverer of four of the satellites of Saturn ;
Giacomo Filippo Maraldi (*d.* 1729) ; and Gian Domenico
Maraldi (*d.* 1787), the author of a catalogue of fixed stars.
They were all born in the house called Casa Cassini in Via
Maraldi, where may be seen their scientific instruments.

The parish church contains a valuable picture presented
by Domenico Cassini.　There is a beautiful view from this
spot, and close by is a house, the Casa Allavena, in a street
of the same name, inhabited by Napoleon I in 1797.　On the
opposite side of the town, where an old church and convent
stand in a square, there is another wonderful panorama.

At 3½ miles from Bordighera the road to Perinaldo passes
Vallecrosia, of which the main street is almost covered in
by the arches connecting the houses.　The bed of the torrent
is between the village and the valley road.

Half a mile farther is **San Biagio della Cima,** surrounded
by vineyards and olive groves.　The first half of its name
was given it in honour of a bishop so called : the second
half has reference to the cima or summit of Santa Croce.

The high-road next leads to **Soldano,** about 5 miles from
Bordighera, notable as being built on level ground.　In its
parish church is a painting by Ludovic (or Louis) Bréa.
It is on wood and has a gilt frame with six divisions each
containing a representation of a patron saint of the village.

OSPEDALETTI.

Access.—*Viâ* Ventimiglia, from which it is 6¼ miles by rail.　By motor-coach
　　from Nice (p. 84).
Golf.—Bordighera links, 5 miles.
Hotels.—*See* p. 150.
Motor-buses.—To Bordighera, 3 miles.
Trams.—To San Remo, 3 miles.

Ospedaletti, eastward of the Ariziglia Valley and midway between Bordighera and San Remo, is a charming,
smiling little place upon a small bay on the shore of which
is a fishing village, while standing in gardens on rising
ground are the hotels and villas of the Ospedaletti of visitors
and foreign residents.

In 1860 a medical adviser chose Ospedaletti as one of the
best winter stations for the Empress of Russia, but as at
that time every comfort was lacking, the doctor's choice
could not be accepted.　Now there would be no such bar.
In 1883 two companies began to lay out boulevards, to build
hotels and villas and to create all those modern comforts
which visitors expect.　Admirably they succeeded, and
Ospedaletti soon had an English and American colony which
included proprietors of some of the villas.　Its site is the

OSPEDALETTI.

AN OLD STREET, SAN REMO.

most sheltered spot on the western portion of the Ligurian Riviera. It is encircled by hills which screen it but are not sufficiently close to make the climate relaxing. The atmosphere is remarkably dry.

The new town has fine thoroughfares lined with trees and there is a delightful public garden. The water supply is excellent, being identical with that which San Remo enjoys, and the sanitation is modern. There is a profusion of palms, orange, lemon, and olive trees, and as floriculture is the principal industry there are flower plantations in the immediate neighbourhood.

Ospedaletti has a tennis club and there are daily concerts. During the winter season there is a resident English chaplain. It is an excellent centre for excursions. Those from Bordighera and San Remo can be conveniently joined, and the resort is the starting-point for walks minutely described in *Path Walks of Bordighera and Ospedaletti*, obtainable locally.

As bearing on the claim of Ospedaletti to rank as a health resort of the highest order, it may be recalled that the site was so regarded in the Middle Ages. Here the Knights of Malta founded hospitals to which were brought those on board their vessels who required medical attendance and skilled nursing. In consequence the spot became known as Ospedale (hospital), and from that the present name is derived.

The little chapel of the **Madonna della Ruota,** about a mile west of the site of the hospitals, is said to have been founded by the Knights of Malta, who, it will be remembered, were originally known as Knights of Rhodes—Cavalieri di Rodi, and Rodi has become corrupted into Ruota.

SAN REMO.

" The city of flowers and of sunshine
Where life is joyous,
Where life is a dream."

Access.—*Viâ* Marseilles and Ventimiglia or *viâ* Turin and Ventimiglia or *viâ* Genoa. From Ventimiglia (*see* p. 152) it is a run of about half an hour. By the Rome Express (*train de luxe*) Genoa is reached from London in 25¾ hours. By fast train from Paris to Genoa *viâ* Turin, the travelling time is about 21 hours; from Milan to Genoa *viâ* Villavernia, about 2½ hours; from Genoa to San Remo, 3½ hours. By bus from Nice.

Amusements.—Concerts, dances, the best operas and comedies. (There is an excellent theatre in the town and also one in the Casino.) Carnival festivities. Battles of Flowers. Dog Shows.

Baths.—On the Corso Trento and Trieste. Medical baths at the Hôtel Savoy.

Casino.—Open all the year round. Contains reading rooms, ball and concert rooms, salles des jeux and a cercle privé.

Clubs.—Savoy, Union, Sports.

Consulate.—Great Britain, 8, Via Vittorio Emanuele.

Golf.—An 18-hole course opened in 1930 at Regione Gogna, 3 miles from the centre of the town. There is a comfortable Club House.

Hotels.—*See* p. 151.

Information Office.—18 Via Roma.

Libraries.—21 Via Vittorio Emanuele. English and American Book Club, Corso Umberto.

Population.—Exceeds 32,000.

Post Offices.—Central Office, 14 Via Roma. There are branch offices in the Municipal Casino in Piazza Colombo and Corso Cosvallotti.

Sports.—Bathing, Lawn Tennis at the Sports Club and the principal hotels. Golf (*see* above). The local authorities through special committees organize sporting and social events throughout the year. The former include tennis tournaments, horse, motor and cycle races, and regattas.

Trams.—Frequent service to Ospedaletti.

Water Supply.—Excellent. An aqueduct brings the water from springs at an elevation of 3,000 feet.

SAN REMO is the oldest, largest, and one of the most popular resorts on the Ligurian Riviera. It is situated on an inlet divided into two bays and faces south. On the north it is protected by a double line of hills and mountains, and **Capo Verde,** the eastern horn of the inlet, breaks the force of the east winds which are felt in May. Rain and mists are rare and do not last long. There are only from 40 to 45 rainy days in a year. San Remo claims to be drier than Nice and that its climatic conditions are similar to those at Menton.

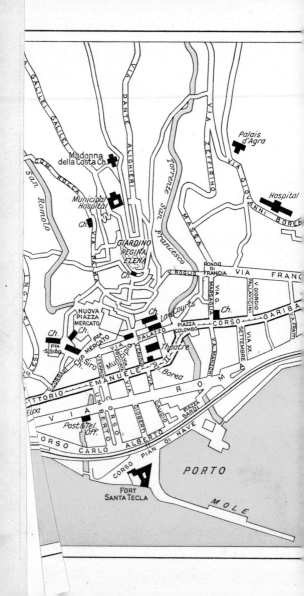

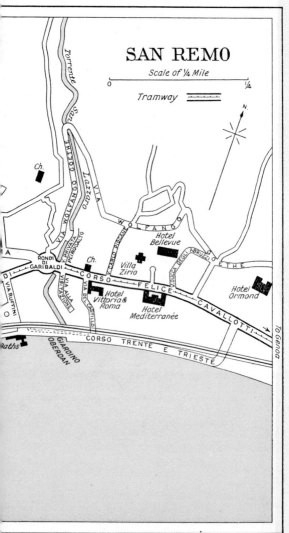

SAN REMO

Scale of ¼ Mile

0   ¼

Tramway ═══════

N.

Torrente S. Giro

Ch.

VIA WOLFANGO GOETHE

VIA Lazzaro

VIA WOLFANG

Hotel
Bellevue

VIA CARLO BRUZZA

VIA DEGLI BRUZZA GOETHE

PRIVATA PIETROSATO

VIA ALLA STAZIONE

Ch.

Villa
Zirio

RONDO
DI
GARIBALDI

CORSO   FELICE

CAVALLOTTI

Hotel
Ormond

DI VIA RUFFINI O

VIA AL CASTILLO

Hotel
Vittoria &
Roma

Hotel
Mediterranée

To Genoa

Baths

GIARDINO OBERIAN

CORSO TRENTE E TRIESTE

WARD, LOCK & C.º LT.º, LONDON. E.C.4.

The old town is almost separated from—

The Modern Quarter,

which has been developed on spacious lines along the sea-front and on the hills which slope gently towards the shore. **Via Vittorio Emanuele,** lined with shops of all kinds, extends for some half-mile eastward from the vicinity of the station. This thoroughfare is an exception to the spaciousness else-where provided. The needs of the future were not sufficiently recognized when it was planned and so it has become too narrow for the traffic. Its side pavements are for one-way use only. " Keep to the left " is the rule. Unheeding pedestrians are requested by the police to cross the road.

Standing above it at its western end is the imposing **Municipal Casino,** the rendezvous of friends and the scene daily of the most varied diversions.

Running southward from Via Vittorio Emanuele is the wide **Corso Umberto,** in which are a *War Memorial* and flower-beds. It cuts **Via Roma** a few yards eastward of the **Information Office** and the principal **Post Office.** Near the farther extremity of the Via Vittorio Emanuele is the **Palazzo Borea,** dating from the fifteenth century. It is now divided and let in flats. In it were entertained, when it was really a palace, Pope Paul III, on his way to Nice in 1538, to make peace between François I and Charles Quint, Pope Pius VII, and Napoleon I. In this direction the thoroughfare terminates at the **Piazza Colombo,** where are the Palace of Justice and the sixteenth-century church of the Madonna degli Angeli.

From this square, eastward of which lies the German quarter of the town, starts the **Corso Garibaldi,** bordered by plane trees and continued by the **Corso Felice Cavallotti.** On the left side is the **Villa Zirio,** which, as the White Villa, was the residence (1887–88) of the Crown Prince Frederick William of Germany. Here it was that the dying prince heard of the death of the old Emperor and of his own accession to the throne, as dramatically described by De Blowitz in his *Memoirs.* The villa stands back from the road and is just westward of the great *Hôtel Bellevue.* The garden wall begins at a small entrance over which is the figure 9. The wall has upon it a number of capital B's and is surmounted by lamp-posts.

On the opposite side of the thoroughfare is the huge *Hôtel Méditerranée.* Its southern windows overlook an extensive and very fine public garden rich in tropical trees, lying between the sea and the railway, which here is in a deep cutting. The southern end of the garden is connected with a palm-bordered thoroughfare, bearing the now common name of *Trente e Trieste*. Between it and the harbour is a sandy beach which in summer is gay with bright costumes and multi-coloured sunshades, when also numerous bathing cabins form a line below a fine bathing establishment which has a large terrace jutting out to sea.

Another public garden in the eastern quarter of the town contains the **Villa Ormond.**

The greater part of the English colony is in the western quarter of the town, a charming district. In line with Via Vittorio Emanuele, there runs the palm-shaded **Corso Impéra-trice,** the most beautiful of San Remo's thoroughfares, named in honour of the Empress Maria Alexandrowna of Russia and to commemorate her sojourn in the city. On its land-ward side are terraces of beautiful gardens belonging to modern hotels and fine villas. Behind these and on higher ground are groves of orange, lemon and olive trees, as there are on the inland side of the buildings of the eastern quarter.

On the seaward side of the Corso is a wide grove of palms with beds of flowers, many seats, a Garibaldi monument and a bandstand.

But a short distance from the junction of this fine Corso with the Via Vittorio Emanuele is the **Scots' Church.** A few yards westward the *Via Regina* leads inland to the **Russian Church,** in which repose the bodies of the King of Montenegro and his queen, Milena. Via Regina leads also to the **English Church** dedicated to St. John.

Where the Corso Impératrice gives place to the **Corso Matuzia,** which like the former runs between hotels, villas and gardens, there stands the **English Church** dedicated to All Saints, and a little farther in this direction are the lawn-tennis courts of the San Remo Sports Club.

One of the earliest walks taken by the visitor should be eastward from the railway station to the harbour, following the lines to a level crossing giving access to it. From the farthest end of its mole, one looks upon the whole of San Remo, its background of wooded hills, Capo Verde on the eastern horizon, and Capo Nero, the western horn of the inlet. The fort at the land end of the mole is **Santa Tecla,** and reminds the Sanremese of some very sad incidents in the history of their city.

G. *Bazzoli*.]

[*San Remo*.

CORSO DELL' IMPERATRICE, SAN REMO.

Riviera.

G. Bazzoli,]   [San Remo.

OLD BUSSANA.

Ballance,]   [Menton.

THE HARBOUR, SAN REMO.

In the centre of the prospect is—

The Old Town,

La Pigna, as it is often called from its resemblance in form to that of a pine cone. Surmounting all is the dome of the church of **Madonna della Costa.**

No visitor to San Remo should omit to walk through the old town. The thoroughfares are as clean as those in any quarter of the modern town, and there is a complete absence of unpleasant smells. There are many curious spots and interesting sights, and the inhabitants are friendly and courteous. Visitors who delight in recalling the past will go again and again, always finding new paths to take. No one need hesitate to wander at will through fear of being lost, as every ascending thoroughfare eventually leads to the church crowning the hill, and every descending street is on the way to Via Vittorio Emanuele.

A convenient route from the harbour to the summit of La Pigna is up **Via Gioberti,** opening opposite the level crossing, then across Via Roma and Via Vittorio Emanuele and up Via Privata. The archway at the upper end covers the site of the hall of the Palazzo Roverizio, erected in 1720, and now let in tenements. From it one passes into **Via Palazzo,** along which a few steps have to be taken to the right to an archway on the left, by which one goes under the **Palazzo Municipio,** dating from the eighteenth century, into the Piazza Alberto Nota and Piazza Cassini. On the right is the **Church of Santo Stefano,** one of the oldest of the local churches. For centuries it was the meeting-place of the Parliament of San Remo. It contains some good tapestry. The **Law Courts** were originally the monastery attached to it.

Via Santo Stefano leads into that part of the town which was enclosed by walls. Immediately after passing through the south gate, **Porta San Sebastiano,** the route lies to the right, up **Via Romolo Moreno,** one of the main thoroughfares. It winds steeply up to the **Porta Candelieri,** one of the two north gates still existing. From it there is a rather stiff climb to the **Church of Madonna della Costa** (of the coast), more interesting from its situation than on account of its statues and pictures, although one of the latter is attributed to St. Luke. The church was built in the seventeenth century and restored after the earthquake of 1887.

In the wall to the left of the church is a small opening from which steps lead down to a carriage-road. This should be followed to the right for a few yards and then a flight of steps on the left should be taken. At a fork the left branch is the one to follow. Thus one is led down to the picturesque **Porta San Giuseppe,** the most interesting of the three gates on this route. Through it Via Palma leads, then turns to the right and in a few yards passes the parish **Church of San Giuseppe.** A short distance below it the Vicolo Balilla branches from Via Palma and leads one to the small **Church of Santa Brigada,** with a fascinating tiny campanile. Via Palma can be regained by Via Capitolo. From the foot of Via Palma Via Morado goes to the right and passes behind the Municipal Library. It also passes the public washing-place, where many housewives are usually to be seen at work.

Various turnings to the left lead down *Via Debenedetti* to the **Piazza San Siro,** the site of four churches. The most important is that from which the open space takes its name. It dates from the twelfth century. Standing outside the walls, it suffered more from invaders than did the churches within the fortification. During the War of the Austrian Succession, cannon balls discharged from English ships made their mark upon it. But the affection of the Sanremese for this church and their pride in it received their greatest blow from the Genoese when that people in the middle of the eighteenth century determined to put an end to the frequent rebellion of San Remo. By forced labour they built the fort by the mole with its gun-holes towards the city, and among other punitive and defensive measures was the removal to Genoa of San Siro's bell, which had again and again called the people to arms. The humiliation was deepened by the bell being taken down on the festival day of San Siro and the reduction of the tower to half its height. Nearly half a century later the French Revolution moved Liguria to reassert its independence of Genoa, and it was in the despoiled church of San Siro that the Sanremese assembled to listen to an exposition of the doctrines of the great movement for liberty and to register their determination to expel the Genoese governor.

The east door, carved with representations of the palm, the olive and the ass, typifying the ancient industries, is one of the few remnants of the original church. The west door is another. In the sixteenth century the church was practically rebuilt ; in the seventeenth the choir was added. The front, in Baroque style, dates from 1897, and in 1929 the building was restored. In the interior are some frescoes and a painting by D. Piola.

The other churches here are S. Giovanni, now the baptistery and supposed to be the first church in San Remo ; the Oratory of San Germano, dating from the seventeenth century ; and the very ancient Oratory of the Conception, which contains frescoes by Merano. The *statue of Siro Andrea Carli*, standing in the market-place, honours the mayor who brought to the town its abundant supply of pure water, and who in other respects did much to promote the health and happiness of the inhabitants.

From the market-place, Via Feraldi leads on to **Via Vittorio Emanuele.** Before this important thoroughfare of the modern town was constructed, the through traffic passed along **Via Palazzo,** the ancient commercial street, a little farther inland. All the land seaward of it was occupied by lemon trees, when modern San Remo began to arise, and the only old thoroughfare is **Via Gaudio,** which connected the town with the port, and now cuts across Via Vittorio Emanuele and Via Roma.

At the lower end of Via Gaudio is an old house with a tablet recording the fact that Garibaldi stayed there in February, 1848. Between this house and Via Roma is **Piazza Bresca,** containing a fountain and a granite obelisk. Probably the column, as well as the name of the square, commemorates a captain of a trading vessel, the hero of an oft-told story.

In 1586, Pope Sixtus V ordered the removal of an Egyptian obelisk from the Circus to the Piazza di San Pietro in Rome. Owing to the difficulty of the work and the danger that the cries of the spectators would bewilder the workmen, the Pope issued a decree that the lifting of the obelisk was to be conducted in strict silence under pain of death. The work went satisfactorily until the column was within a few inches of the perpendicular, when it was in danger of falling, owing to the strain on the ropes, the lifting blocks being now close together. Seeing this, Bresca, a native of Bordighera, disregarding the papal prohibition, cried, " Wet the ropes." The advice was taken, the hempen ropes contracted, and the monolith became perpendicular. The Pope's Swiss Guards took the disobedient man to their master, who, contrary to the general expectation based on his known severity, received the culprit courteously and rewarded him by granting to his family the great privilege of supplying for ever the palms at Easter for St. Peter's.

Historical Note.—On the site of the Sports Club and the Campo Santo (the cemetery) stood the Roman town of Matuta. To convert its pagan inhabitants, the Bishop of Genoa, in the fourth century, sent to the town a bishop who became known as San Romolo. While he was there the barbarians made their first attack on the province. The bishop put aside his pastoral staff and took a sword with which he bravely fought against the invaders. After his unclerical exploit he retired to a cave and there spent the remainder of his days. His body was buried in Matuta, but after another attack on the town, the Bishop of Genoa

ordered it to be taken to his city.   Other invasions followed
and in 934 Matuta was completely destroyed. When, some
sixty years later, the barbarians had been definitely expelled
from Provence, the Matutans rebuilt their town, not on its
defenceless site, but on the high ground, and surrounded
it with walls and fortified gates.   In honour of their warrior-
bishop, they called their new town San Romolo.   Sanctus
Romolus in Eremo was its full official title in Latin, and the
corruption of this is one of the explanations given of its
present name.

In 1794 General Bonaparte arrived in San Remo.   He
made it the capital of a republic established in the Ligurian
Riviera, which he called the District of the Palms.   After
other political changes the whole of Liguria finally became
a part of free Italy.

Walks and Excursions.

Motor Excursions.—Thrice daily to San Romolo. Daily to Monte Carlo *viâ*
Ventimiglia and Menton and to Nice *viâ* the Grand Corniche, returning
viâ Monte Carlo. At intervals to La Mortola and the famous gardens,
and to the Italian Corniche *viâ* Porto Maurizio, Oneglia and Alassio.

On the hills behind San Remo may be taken many interesting walks, some along carriage-roads passing between villas
and gardens and offering uninterrupted views of the town
and its harbour ; but those who confine their excursions to
the roads will gain only a slight knowledge of the country
around San Remo.   No fewer than eight valleys come down
from the hills, and the greater number can be followed by
pedestrians beyond the point which vehicles can reach.
Mule-paths and footpaths run in every direction, and often
to a beautiful view-point.   In spring blossoming fruit trees
and a profusion of wild flowers add their charm to the landscape.

A short selection of the walks and excursions is all that
can be given in these pages, but it will serve to show how
interesting is the country around San Remo.

Coldirodi,

being almost always before one's eyes, is generally made the
object of one of the first walks that a visitor takes outside
the town.   Until 1882 the village was known as Colla, from
Collina, meaning hill.   In the year named it obtained the
permission of the Government to call itself Coldirodi in remembrance of the Knights of Rhodes who founded it.

The village is perched on a ridge. By a mule-path which leaves the main road just beyond the Sports Club, it can be reached in about an hour, but as at every turn of the path the pedestrian will be tempted to halt to admire the view, he will probably be more than an hour on the way.

In the Municipio building—the Town Hall—is a wonderful collection of books and pictures bequeathed to the municipality by Paolo Stefano Rambaldi, born in the village and for some time Rector of the Seminary at Florence. Treasured in the sacristy of the parish church is a beautiful ivory crucifix bequeathed to the village by another of its sons, Stefano Rossi. About ten minutes' walk from the southern end of the village street is the **Chapel of San Bernardo,** reached by following the driving-road past the cemetery. From the vicinity of the chapel there is a magnificent view.

The return from Coldirodi may be made *via* Ospedaletti, reached by a mule-path on the western slope of the hill.

Another walk, generally among the first to be taken, is to—

Old Bussana,

Bussana Vecchia, often spoken of as one of the earthquake villages. It is nearly 5 miles from San Remo, but the walking distance to it may be reduced to 2 miles by taking the tram to New Bussana, Bussana Nuova, eastward of San Remo and south of the old village. This new village was built after Old Bussana had been overthrown by the great earthquake in 1887. As related in connection with Bajardo, the catastrophe occurred on Ash Wednesday at the time of early mass. The roof of the church fell on the worshippers and killed 80 of them.

About 3 miles eastward of San Remo is the **Madonna della Guardia,** Our Lady of the Guard, a chapel standing among cypresses at the extremity of Capo Verdi. It contains numerous objects and paintings relating to the miraculous intervention of the Virgin in favour of the grateful persons who have placed them in the church.

Five miles north-east of San Remo is the village of—

Taggia,

the Tabia of the Romans. It was the port from which François I, as a prisoner, set sail for Spain, but is now cut off from the sea, and is often called " the Village of Palaces." The walk to it may be shortened at will by means of the railway, tramway or bus. It stands amidst orchards in which violets are grown and it contains several points of interest. In the Church of the Madonna de la Misericorde are magnificent fifteenth-century paintings, and in the Church of the Sacré Cœur is the miraculous " Winking Madonna." The village rivals old San Remo in quaintness, and still answers in the main to Ruffini's description of it in *Dr. Antonio*. It was the home of the Ruffinis, who lived in Via Solari (in the first house on the right when entering from the south end). On the ledge of the old Roman bridge Giovanni Ruffini was sitting when the idea of writing *Dr. Antonio* came to him, and in a country house on the hill-side he passed his last years, when the emancipation of Italy enabled him, then an old man, to return from his exile in England.

The distance from Taggia station to the village is 2½ miles. Readers of *Dr. Antonio* who get as far as Taggia will certainly be tempted to go on to **Lampedusa,** as the strange story of its church is told in the novel. On application to the priest its miraculous picture may be seen (a small donation to his fund for the relief of the poor should be offered). The route from Taggia lies along a good mountain path to the village of **Castellaro,** which can be reached in ¾ hour, and thence it will take about ¼ hour to arrive at the famous little church.

An excellent road known as the **Circonvallazione** winds round the hills encircling San Remo. It passes fine villas and gardens and permits the inclusion in the same excursion of **Peirogallo, Baragallo, Borgo Pescio,** and **Berigo.** Each is also directly connected with San Remo and therefore can be the object of an independent excursion. The distances from the town are respectively ½ mile, 2 miles, 2½ miles, 2¼ miles.

The Croce di Para, about 3 miles north of San Remo, is a wooden cross set up to mark the spot where, in 1548, the Mayor of San Remo and his townsmen, fighting with the courage of despair to defend their families and homes, drove back a band of invading Saracens and by their brave stand helped to shatter the power of those foes of the Riviera.

The village of Ceriana, north of San Remo, is 9 miles from it by a road which runs through **Poggia** (4 miles), a collection of old streets and lanes and an ancient square tower.

Ceriana, which can be reached by bus, is mainly attractive by reason of its site, which makes it a village hidden upon a hill. The church piazza commands the whole sweep of the gorge. From the piazza a dark alley leads upward to the crumbling church of S. Andrea, the bell tower of which is seen when the village comes into view. By way of the archway at the foot of the town and across a bridge, one can reach the *Church of S. Spirito*, probably earlier than the tenth century. The lintels of two south doors are finely carved, and before one of them a porch on pillars is a very distinctive feature.

The Chapel of S. Giovanni is the turning-point in a pleasant and easy walk—easy because when the ascent of La Pigna has been made the route is almost level. Over the door of the chapel is a fresco of St. John the Baptist.

San Romolo. Two of San Remo's valleys are those of the Romolo and the Francia. Between them is a ridge climbed by a mule-path. Another route is amidst wild flowers, olives and pines, by a gently ascending carriage-road, some 9½ miles long. It is in the San Romolo Valley that the San Remo golf course is situated. From the vicinity of the Valley there is a superb prospect, and near by is the cave to which the good bishop Romolo retired (*see* p. 167). Little of the original cave can be seen, as it has been converted into a chapel.

For mountain climbers there is **Monte Bignone.** The summit, 4,259 feet above sea-level, is said to command one of the finest panoramas in Europe. It can be reached on foot in four hours, and the ascent can be made on mule-back. It may have been noticed that Monte Bignone is only 147 feet lower than Ben Nevis, the highest mountain in the British Isles, but while the latter has grey water at its foot and is generally enveloped in mist, the former looks down on glittering blue water and has its head uncovered.

SAN REMO TO ALASSIO.

BETWEEN these two centres, each with its large English colony, are places which attract artists and also the general tourist who finds pleasure in leading a simple life among pleasant scenes, where he will learn much about the natives and will find accommodation at a lower price than that demanded in a larger resort.

For a few miles eastward of San Remo, floriculture is continued, but at **Santo Stefano** the fields of flowers give place to a stretch of barren land, $7\frac{1}{2}$ miles in length, quite destitute of beauty.

At its eastern extremity is Porto Maurizio, which in 1923 was united to adjacent Oneglia, the resultant town being named **Imperia.** It is the capital of the province bearing the same name, is a busy and picturesque port, and is the first place of any size that the traveller from the west will pass through which is typically Italian and has no foreign colony or season. **Porto Maurizio** was an important place in Roman times, its name then being Portus Maurici. Partly ancient, partly modern, it is an attractive portion of its town. Its site is on a promontory which forms a picturesque feature of the coast. The country behind it, rising in hills with a background of mountains, is covered with olive groves. **Oneglia** stands on a plain and has industrial features due to the presence of a number of oil establishments. Between it and Porto Maurizio is the torrent *Impero*, but the two are united by a fine avenue, 2 miles long, bordered by villas and gardens.

Imperia is an excellent centre for pedestrians, as inland are many quaint villages within the limit of a day's tramp. And one of the finest trips in Liguria is made twice daily in summer and once in winter by the motor service along the Impero Valley, from Oneglia to the charming mountain resort of **Ormea,** and thence by rail to Turin.

Five miles east of Imperia is—

[*E.N.I.T.*

ALASSIO, FROM SANTA CROCE.

[*E.N.I.T.*

ALASSIO.

Diano Marina,

(Hotel, p. 150)

an unspoilt modern little town on a bay with a beach of
fine sand which attracts bathers. It is modern because it
was completely destroyed by the earthquake of 1887.

Among the hills are many places of interest to which the
keen walker may direct his steps.

With the exception of tennis there is not much organized
amusement. Its pleasant surroundings and its simplicity
form the charm of Diano Marina and with its dry and bracing
climate make it ideal for those seeking a restful spot.

That it attracts a fair number of English visitors is evident
from its possession of an English Protestant church and an
English doctor.

Eastward of Diano Marina are the railway stations of
Cervo (3 miles) and **Andrea** (9 miles), pleasant little nooks
offering good sea-bathing, but with little accommodation for
visitors, who will probably have their quarters either at Diano
Marina or at—

Laigueglia,

(Hotel Laigueglia)

only 4 miles by rail from Andrea. It is a bright little seaside
resort, closely backed by hills inviting walkers. One of the
few old-world features remaining is a gateway at the eastern
end of the main street. Its parish church of St. Matthew,
consecrated in 1807, took the place of one said to have been
built in the fourth century.

Laigueglia is only 2 miles west of Alassio, with which it
is connected by an avenue of palms and has communication
by a bus service, as well as by the railway.

Alassio.

Access.—All the express trains and trains de luxe stop at Alassio, which is
reached from Ventimiglia in little more than an hour and from Genoa in 2½
hours. *See* pp. 146-7.
Amusements.—Concerts, dramatic performances, dances. The Municipal Band
plays frequently in the open air.
Clubs.—British (social). Tennis.
Hotels.—*See* p. 149.
Library.—The English Circulating Library, comprising several thousand volumes,
is housed in a specially designed building, and is one of the best on the
Riviera.
Motor-buses.—To Laigueglia and Albenga.
Population.—9,500, and increasing.
Sports.—Boating (sailing, rowing and motor boats for hire). Tennis.

Water Supply and Drainage.—Pure and abundant drinking water is brought
from mountain springs by a conduit nearly 20 miles long.
The drainage system is modern. The sewers discharge eastward of the
town where the set of the currents ensures a complete removal.

Alassio is a quiet winter retreat very popular with British
people, and in summer it is a popular bathing resort. It is
situated 30 miles east of San Remo on a beautiful bay with
a gently sloping sandy beach which is one of the finest in
Italy and which extends from Capo S. Croce, sheltering
Alassio, to Capo Mele, some 2 miles beyond Laigueglia, and
even in the narrowest part is over 30 yards wide.

There are bathing establishments, and in the summer
numerous separate cabins. The water is not too cold for
a dip throughout the winter, and the agreeable conditions
have led to the bathing season beginning earlier and ending
later than at San Remo or Bordighera.

During July and August the town is thronged with Italians
who come with their children from the large towns of northern
Italy to enjoy the bathing. The proportion of adept swimmers among them is very large. The day clothes of the
summer visitors of both sexes consist, for the most part,
of robes of bright coloured towelling with shade-giving hats
or sunshades of brilliant hue.

The town stretches from the sea to the hills behind, which
keep off cold winds, except those from the east. In September
the weather is almost always superb. October is a rainy
month. November, December and January usually have
settled and genial weather, while February and March are
generally wetter and colder. From April the temperature
rises rapidly. After what has been said about the weather in
February, it is worthy of note that during the exceptionally
cold February of 1929, Alassio was the only place on the
Riviera from Hyères to Spezia at which tennis suffered no
interruption.

The annual rainfall is very low and mists are rare.

During a period of twenty years, Alassio has rejoiced in
an average annual number of 157 perfectly clear days, and
as there are no factory chimneys the air is practically free
from smoke.

The old town forms a narrow band extending along the
shore for nearly a mile. A very ancient square, the **Piazza
del Commercio**, divides the main street, of which one part
is the **Via Vittorio Emanuele,** the other the **Via Umberto I.**
Both portions are narrow and are in the line of the coast

road, cut in great part out of the rock, but the through traffic has been diverted by a modern road.

From a small oratory has been developed the **Cathedral** dedicated to S. Ambrogio. It was erected about the year 1000, and has been twice enlarged, first in the fourteenth century and then in the early years of the sixteenth. In 1896 it was restored and was then given a new façade. Alassio has also the churches of S. Vincenzo, the Salesians and the Capuchins, the Anglican **Church of St. John** and an **International Free Church.** None of the ecclesiastical buildings has features of very special interest.

In the modern part of the town is a **Public Garden,** the site of the **Town Hall** built in 1904. Some of the streets are bordered by charming little houses in gardens, and on the wooded slopes which form a portion of the frame of the town are fine villas in parks and gardens.

Off the coast is the picturesque rocky island of **Gallinaria,** the first island east of Cannes. It rises nearly 300 feet above the water, has steep bare cliffs and two caves which can be entered only from the sea. At the end of the fourth century St. Martin of Tours spent a year on the island, and afterwards the caves sheltered a few Benedictine monks. The island is much visited, especially in summer.

By reason of the beauty of the natural scenery, the mildness of the climate and the salubrity of the air, Alassio has grown very much and is still growing. New thoroughfares have been laid out and the extensive building of houses is still in operation. After gaps have been filled and the avenues and gardens have taken their normal form, the whole of the modern town will present an appearance as pleasing as that of the earlier portion. In the meantime one can be very happy at Alassio, as is demonstrated by the existence of the large English colony, which is soon discovered to be a very friendly community. Most if not all of the new arrivals pay an early visit to the Tennis Club and there meet with such a hearty welcome that they at once feel they are among friends. The Club House, an extensive and well-furnished building, with rooms for various purposes, is a popular rendezvous, as is also the **British Club,** which has a large reading-room, well supplied with newspapers and magazines, and several bridge-rooms. It is housed in the Hanbury Hall, where is also an entertainment hall with a stage for concerts and dramatic performances.

Another scene of indoor amusements is the **Municipal Casino,** on the beach.

Walks and Excursions.

One of the carriage-roads leading up the hills was made by Austrian prisoners of war. From the vicinity of the station it leads under the railway bridge and then divides. The left branch goes to the tennis courts, the right to the small village of **Moglio,** prettily situated rather more than 3 miles from the town. There the road divides, the right branch going to **Vegliasco,** 2 miles farther, and the left to the **Gap,** as visitors call the Colletto di Moglio, 1,235 feet above sea-level, and also to **Testico,** about 11 miles from the town.

Another road, starting from Viale Hanbury, runs only to **Solva,** 2 miles distant. A third, from Via Nizza, goes to the municipal abattoir.

For the pedestrian there are mule-paths and foot-paths in great number.

It is a very short but interesting walk to **Cap Santa Croce,** the eastern horn of the bay. At Santa Croce the road passes under an arch in a wall loopholed for musketry fire, and near by is a tiny church, built about the year 1000 by the monks of the neighbouring island. The chancel was lengthened in the thirteenth century and the porch was added in the sixteenth. From the Cap one looks upon a vast panorama, particularly delightful at sunset.

The summit of **Monte Tirasso,** visible from Alassio as the most conspicuous object on the skyline cut by the mountains, is more than 1,900 feet in height and is the site of the church of *Nostra Signora della Guardia* (Our Guardian Lady), used only on Ascension Day, when it is the centre of a pilgrimage from all the neighbouring villages. The journey to it is made during the night. Looking northwards from the summit one sees the snow-clad Maritime Alps and the Apennines. In the far distance to the eastward, on a clear day, the Apennines may be seen stretching down towards Pisa and Carrara. Also visible are the mountains in Corsica, 120 miles away, and sometimes the island of Elba. Another summit tempting climbers is that of **Pisciavino.** Although this is the highest hill behind Alassio its elevation is not quite 2,000 feet.

Reached *via* Laigueglia is the village of **San Michele,** deserted after its destruction by the earthquake of 1887. Over the porch of its church is an inscription recording that Pope

Pius VII, when returning to Rome from Avignon, halted at the church and gave the people his blessing.

In the Albenga Valley is the old town of **Villa Nuova,** which still retains its walls, bastions and gateways. It spins silk and around it are grown violets and other flowers for market and very beautiful peaches.

Rather more than 3 miles farther up the valley stands the village of **Garlenda.** Green hills covered with trees and flowers encircle it—hence its name.

Extensive ruins known as the **Castello d'Andora** are in the green and fertile valley of Andora, west of Alassio. They may be the remains of a large fort constructed by the Romans, to whom are attributed a bridge over the river, an aqueduct near it, and a well. A Church, dedicated to SS. Philip and James, is protected as a national monument. Some of its pillars may have formed part of a Roman temple.

The village of **San Bartolomeo,** in the same valley, has a church containing models of ships, the votive offerings of sailors. At the head of the valley is the hamlet of **Stellanello.**

The bed of the **River Torsero** offers a walk specially interesting to geologists.

The routes to the above points and to others are fully indicated in *Walks Around Alassio*, by Dr. Maurice Richards. The booklet can be bought at the Anglo-American Agency and Bank.

Motor Excursions

are arranged daily by the Anglo-American Agency and Bank to such places as :—

The Bubbling Springs of the Bormida. The springs owe their name to the intermittent bubbling of sulphurous gas. Their site is ideal for a picnic.

San Remo or **Old Bussana.**

Garlenda and the **Lerone Valley.**

Diano Marina.

The picturesque town of **Pieve de Teco.**

The ancient hill-town of **Ormea,** and **Garessio,** a smiling summer resort from which the route lies over a pass 3,200 feet above the sea.

Albenga, Spotorno, and **Noli.**

The **Andora Valley,** and the **Blackbird Valley,** famous for its beauty and its wild flowers.

Castel Vecchio, which may have been a Saracen stronghold. It has flat-roofed houses, and a castle for centuries the seat of one of the proudest families in Italy.

Riviera (m)

ALASSIO TO GENOA.

O N the long stretch of coast between Alassio and Genoa are about thirty towns and villages. Some are intensely interesting, some if not all have accommodation for visitors, but none ranks among the principal resorts of the Riviera.

First in point of order is—

Albenga,

an agricultural centre, but once a great Ligurian naval station. Its maritime importance was lost through the silting-up of the harbour, and the town now stands half a mile from the sea. It has, however, most interesting Roman and mediæval remains. These include a bridge, a cathedral and a baptistery. The bridge, called the pontelungo (the long bridge), is the largest Roman construction in northern Italy and is in a fine state of preservation.

In the centre of the town is a large square, the **Piazza XX Settembre.** From it Via Enrico d'Este leads to the Cathedral and the Baptistery. Before reaching them there will be passed the Church of **S. Maria in Fontibus,** erected in the eighth century, and taking the distinctive portion of its name from a spring of water under the choir. The devout used to be washed with the water, which was especially valued as a cure for leprosy. In this part of the street, near the War Memorial, is the shop of a pastrycook who makes *Bauxin,* a cake peculiar to Albenga. At a shop elsewhere in the town it is said to have been made for 300 years.

The **Cathedral,** dedicated to St. Michael, was built about 1400 in place of a smaller church. On the ceiling of the central nave is a fresco representing the expulsion of Satan from Heaven. Attached to the cathedral is a library containing many beautifully illuminated church books of the fourteenth and fifteenth centuries.

In a square at the back of the cathedral are carved stone lions which are thought to have formed part of an ancient monument. Here also is one of the brick towers which are prominent features of the town. It belongs to the Palazzo Balestrino.

The **Baptistery** is the octagonal brick building at the side of the cathedral. It dates from about the year 400. Part of it is now below the street level.

The **Roman Bridge** is by the side of the road to Genoa. It is reached by going beyond the baptistery for a few yards, then turning to the right and walking straight ahead for about ten minutes. The bridge, said to date from 414, is constructed of square blocks of stone, is 160 yards long, 10 feet wide and has ten arches. It wears a pathetically deserted air, being heeded neither by water nor by wayfarers. The river which it spanned gradually altered its course between the fifth and the tenth centuries and made for itself a new bed westward of the site of the present town, alongside which it now flows. The original bed silted up, burying a great part of the piers of the bridge over which the road no longer goes, but runs alongside it. At the western end of the bridge is the modern church of the *Madonna del Porte-lungo*. In a triptych above the altar is a painting of the Virgin dating from 1502.

Next to Albenga is the village of **Ceriale,** possessing a small harbour and a picturesque tower. It is followed by **Borghetto San Spirito,** and then comes—

Loano

(*Hotel*, p. 150), a small town typically Italian, standing between the foot of a pretty hill and a sandy beach. Among its more imposing buildings are one of the largest Carmelite monasteries in Italy and a fine palace, an ancient seat of the Dorias. In the vicinity of this small resort, Napoleon gained one of his greatest victories in Italy.

Adjoining Loano is **Pietra Ligure** (*Villa Marina Pensione*), a small place noted for its orange and lemon groves and its palms. Its northern (or eastern) neighbour—

Borgio

(*Hotel Lido di Borgio*), is a picturesque little village with a sandy beach and has long been renowned for almonds, peaches, asparagus and scented stocks. Some of the hill-slopes are natural rock gardens. On a hill-crest to the east are the remains of the Saracenic village, **Verezzi,** reached by steep steps through vineyards and olive groves, or by a winding high road.

Only a mile from Borgio by the coast road is the small but pleasant **Finale Marina** (*Hotel*, p. 150), which has a station at which fast trains stop, and is one of a family of Finale towns, all diminutive. An inland suburb is **Finale Borgo,** a charming little place with a fine cathedral, a town wall and gateway, old-world streets the delight of artists, and the ruins of an ancient castle around which writers have woven romances of mediæval days.

Finale Pia has a richly ornamented thirteenth-century church, classed as a national monument. In it are cannon balls fired by the British into the town, which was miraculously protected by S. Maria di Pia. An *oratory* adjacent to the old church is sacred to the memory of British victims of the Great War. The road tunnels under the ancient castle of Pia, converted into a luxurious modern dwelling.

The last of the family is **Finale Varigotti,** formerly a pirate stronghold. It faces south and has pretty villas surrounded by luxurious vegetation.

The countryside of this group of places is very pleasant. Olives, oranges and vines grow luxuriantly. Through it and around it may be taken many walks and excursions. The high ground offers fine views inland and along the coast.

Next comes—

Noli,

one of the most interesting spots on the coast though it has no accommodation for visitors. This, however, is unimportant as by bus and train there is communication with Spotorno, only 3 miles away and sufficiently supplied with hotels.

Noli is believed by many to be one of the oldest human settlements in the world. Legend attributes its foundation to Noah's nephews. Documentary evidence establishes its existence in 1500 B.C. Long before the Christian era it was a Roman port and arsenal. It took an active part in the Crusades and therein earned special distinction. For nearly six hundred years it was the seat of a bishop. In 1795 its waters were the scene of a British naval victory in which Nelson shared. In 1917 they were the scene of the sinking of the British troopship *Transylvania*, with the loss of 407 lives, by an enemy submarine. As rescuers, Noli fishing

THE CATHEDRAL, ALBENGA.

[E.N.I.T.

NOLI.

boats put out in a heavy sea, and for this brave and humane action, decorations were awarded by His Majesty the King.

The days of Noli's mercantile and military importance are long past, and it is now but an old fishing town, with small fish-curing establishments, without a trace of modernity but with many of ancient times. Perhaps its greatest treasure is the **Church of S. Paragoris,** built in the seventh century over a much earlier subterranean church. It contains a ninth-century marble ambo, a curious Byzantine crucifix, known as the Volto Santo, some thirteenth-century tombs, and paintings. Admission can be obtained on application to the priest, who will show its many features of interest.

The **Casa Ripetta** is a perfect specimen of a thirteenth-century noble's house. On the north side of the town is the ancient gateway with remains of the drawbridge and moat. The more important residents had a tower above their house, but of the seventy-two towers at one time existing there are now very few. The most notable is rhomboidal. Under the houses along the sea-front runs a wide vaulted passage.

Spotorno

(*Hotels*, p. 151), some 22 miles by rail from Alassio and a little farther by road, is much patronized by Italians in July and August, as it has an excellent sandy beach. As it enjoys an equable climate, plenty of sunshine and excellent hotel accommodation, it is beginning to attract English visitors desiring tranquillity and modern comfort. An English chaplain and an English doctor are resident in winter, and there is an English library. Tennis, sea fishing and boating may be enjoyed. There are concerts and dances at the principal hotel.

By easy roads through pine woods and olive groves, picturesque hamlets can be reached on foot. From the semaphore on **Cap Noli** there is a magnificent prospect. At the extremity of the cape is a marble cross marking the nearest spot on the mainland to that where the *Transylvania* went down, and in Spotorno is a monument commemorating the disaster. Both memorials were erected by the Italians.

Interesting **Noli** (*see* above) merits more than one visit. At **Bergeggi,** on the opposite side of Spotorno, is a grotto opening on the sea. A passing desire to be in busy streets and before shop-windows can be gratified by a trip to Savona, only a dozen miles away.

Savona.

Although Savona has good hotels (p. 151), it is not a tourist resort, but a busy port and industrial town. From it the industrial centres of the Lombardy Plain draw their supplies of imported coal, and it is at a junction of the coast railway with a line coming from Turin. By this line Paris can be reached in thirty hours, and visitors to the Ligurian Riviera have an alternative homeward route.

Immediately beyond Savona is **Albissola,** a town of Roman origin. In a rather small way it makes common earthenware goods and artistic pottery. The portion known as **Albissola Marina** is an unpretentious bathing resort.

The neighbouring **Celle Ligure** attracts a greater number of bathers. At the *Villa Adele* the pension terms are about 5s. 3d. to 6s. 3d. a day, according to the time of year.

Very much more popular, as a bathing resort, is **Varazze** (*Hotels*, p. 151), a picturesque little town which faces a lovely piece of coast and as background has hills on which olive trees and vines are cultivated. Italians visit it in large numbers for its bathing, as it has a sandy beach, and at the best points are comfortable bathing establishments. Some of its hotels are open all the year.

Separated from it by **Cogoleto** and only 11 miles nearer Genoa, is—

Arenzano,

" beautiful Arenzano, seated amid cedars and palms, and the smiling Ligurian strand," an unpretentious place, patronized by Italians in summer for bathing, but which has not yet attracted many English visitors. It is well protected on the north, and the air is mild but invigorating. Many pleasant excursions can be made inland and along the coast and there are several tennis courts. (*Hotels, see* p. 150.)

Arenzano marks the end of the true Riviera westward of Genoa. The names of all places which follow it are prefixed by the word Genova, an indication that the places have become part of the great city which in the English language is Genoa. The first is **Voltri,** the site of steel-works, iron foundries, wool and cotton-spinning mills. The next is **Pra,** which has many smoking factories. The third is—

[E.N.I.T.

GENOA.

IN THE PALAZZO REALE, GENOA.

Pegli

(*Hotel*, p. 150), the only one of the six of any interest to visitors. It has steam laundries, a foundry and other works, and yet it is a lively seaside resort, the centre of attractive walks, and from it charming spots are accessible by train or tram. It is sheltered from the north winds by hills covered with olive trees and woods of chestnut and pine. The rainfall is greater than at places farther west. Pegli has a Casino and a Foreigners' Club, an English Library, art and language schools and a Protestant church. An English chaplain is resident during the winter, and there is an English doctor.

Passing tourists should halt at Pegli in order to visit the famous gardens of the **Villa Pallavicini,** which was built for Maria Theresa, Empress of Austria, and is now the property of the City of Genoa. The villa is in process of being converted into a museum. The grounds can be visited in the afternoon. They are interesting for their botanical specimens, their quaintness and their freakishness. There are fountains which can be discharged on an unsuspecting spectator, extensive grottos, in one of which are stalagmites brought from other countries, a lakelet with a white temple of Diana, structures in foreign styles, statues and so on.

The villa is close to Pegli station, the entrance lodge being immediately on the left. Those who arrive by tram should alight at the thoroughfare leading up to the station. The entrance gates are in sight. Application is made at the lodge on their left.

Close by is the **Villa D'Oria,** which, having become a municipal possession, is now a Naval Museum. From the station the museum, a long, low, pink building, can be reached in a couple of minutes by taking the road which goes upward on the left as one faces the station.

An interesting bit of Pegli is its **Villini**—its Villa Promenade. Go westward along the tramway to the statue of Garibaldi and there take the thoroughfare Umberto I, going inland on the left. Almost at once are seen two arches, over which is Villini di Pegli. Follow the tree-bordered road upward past a succession of large villas, each in its own grounds.

Between Pegli and Genoa trams run every two or three minutes.

GENOA.

Access.—*See* pp. 146–8.
Hotels.—*See* p. 150.
Information Office.—In the principal railway station, at the top of the steps
leading *up* from the platforms.

L EGEND assigns the foundation of Genoa to Janus, the
son of Saturn, King of the Itali. Archæologists declare
that it owes its origin to the Ligurians, and that it was built
in the period preceding the Roman civilization.

Its geographical situation assured it increasing importance
and power, in spite of repeated sackings by the barbarians
after the fall of the Roman Empire. In the fourteenth and
fifteenth centuries it furnished France with military and naval
engineers. It gave her her first admirals and it put privateers
and sea captains at the service of England, Portugal and
Spain, towards the end of the fifteenth century and in the
early years of the sixteenth. Its economic prosperity led to
the erection of sumptuous villas and palaces, some of which
remain to excite the pride of the citizens and the admiration
of strangers, as do also the works of the painters, sculptors,
tapestry-makers and silversmiths with which the interiors
were adorned.

Through the annexation of neighbouring communes, Genoa
now extends for more than 20 miles along the shore of the
Mediterranean. It stands between the Eastern and Western
Rivieras of Liguria.

Original Genoa clustered round its harbour, whence the
city has spread up the slopes of the neighbouring hills, making
necessary several funiculars and lifts in addition to gigantic
flights of steps.

The oldest part of the city is strong in its suggestion of
the mediæval, its dark, narrow lanes harbouring palaces of the
nobles and rich merchants of crusading times, now inhabited
by humble citizens. In this section also are some of the
principal churches.

On a slightly higher level is a zone into which the city
spread in the sixteenth century, and which onwards from
then became increasingly populous. Here also are handsome

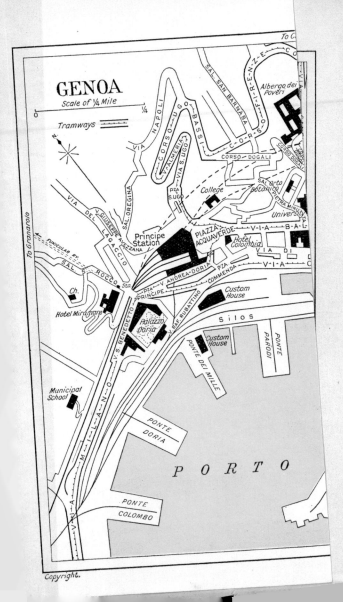

GENOA

Scale of ¼ Mile

Tramways

To C

Albergo dei Poveri

SAL. SAN BARNABA

CORSO · FIRENZE

CORSO DOGALI

CORSO - BASSI

VIA NAPOLI

V. ALMERIA

VIA S. UGO

CORSO DOGALI

SAL. ORTO botanico

PIETRA MINUTA

PZA S.UGO

College

University

SAL. OREGINA

VIA DEL L. GIACCIO

V. GIUSEPPE AVEZZANA

Principe Station

PIAZZA ACQUAVERDE

VIA · BAL

Hotel Colombia

VIA · DI

VIA ·

To Genova

FUNICULAR RY.

SAL. S. ROCCO

Sta.

PZA PRINCIPE

V. ANDREA · DORIA

PZA COMMENDA

Custom House

Ch.

Hotel Miramare

V.S. BENEDETTO

Palazzo Doria

P.F. RUBATTINO

Custom House

Silos

PONTE PARODI

Municipal School

PONTE DEI MILLE

PONTE DORIA

P O R T O

PONTE COLOMBO

Copyright.

palaces, especially in **Via Balbi** and **Via Garibaldi.** Once private residences, they are now chiefly used for public services.

At a still higher level is the modern residential part of the city, consisting of elegant and substantial houses, and with most of the former palaces converted into flats. This section has broad thoroughfares and steep ascents.

On the western side of the city are busy industrial centres, some of which have already been noticed. Eastward the people live under more rural conditions. There are still fine mansions with parks or gardens, and extensive views of mountain, valley and sea.

As a rule travellers spend too little time in Genoa. It is not, it is true, a part of the Riviera, as although it is on the shore of the Mediterranean, it lacks the distinctive features of the district which, by common consent, is known as the Riviera. It contains, however, so much of interest that it should not be regarded merely as a place where one breaks a railway journey, embarks or disembarks.

For a comprehensive description of the city, all the pages of this handbook and more would be required. We can do no more than indicate some of its principal sights.

Through the City.

Even visitors who can speak only English need not fear to set out with no other guide than the itinerary which follows. Sight-seeing parties conducted by an English-speaking guide leave Cook's office, 183–185 Via Balbi, and Wagons-Lits Office, 40 Via Balbi, every weekday at 9.30 a.m. and 2 p.m.

Facing the principal railway station is **Piazza Acquaverde,** where stands a marble statue of *Christopher Columbus*, of whom, it will be remembered, Genoa was the birthplace. Four bas-reliefs on the pedestal show the great navigator at the Congress of Salamanca ; setting up a cross in the New World ; on his first return to Italy ; disgraced and in chains.

From the Place the tramway enters **Via Balbi.** About midway on the right is the **Palazzo Reale** (Royal Palace), dating from the middle of the sixteenth century, and used for various purposes since the king gave up his right to it. Almost opposite is the **Royal University,** built in 1632. No. 1, at the end of the thoroughfare, is the **Palazzo Durazzo Pallavicini** (seventeenth century). Then comes **Piazza Annunziata.** Its church dates from 1228, and yet the façade has not been completed. The interior is highly decorated. No church in the city is richer in marble and pictures.

The tramway can be followed across the piazza and a little beyond it. Then one must enter **Via Cairoli,** on the right, bordered by the ancient residences of patrician families. In the same line is **Via Garibaldi,** called the "street of palaces." One is the **Palazzo Bianco** (White Palace), built 1565–69. Having been bequeathed to the city, it is used as an Art Gallery (*open daily except Monday*). Nearly opposite is the **Palazzo Rosso** (Red Palace), also bequeathed to the city and used as an Art Gallery and Museum. Close by is the **Municipio** (Town Hall), constructed 1560–64, and ceded to the city in 1850 in exchange for the **Palazzo Ducale.** In the Red Room of the Town Hall are favourite violins of Nicolas Paganini and Camille Sivori and facsimiles of letters of Columbus. (The originals are in the pedestal of his bust in the Sala della Giunta.)

From the end of Via Garibaldi one turns to the right and very shortly right again into **Via Carlo Felice,** which leads to **Piazza di Ferrari,** the principal square. On the left are first the **Carlo Felice Teatro** and then the **Ligustica Academy,** containing one of the richest collections in Europe of Japanese works of art. It is open to the public. A circular building on the left, at the farther end of the square, is the Stock Exchange. Behind it is the **Central Post Office** (*Ufficio Postale*).

On the right side of the Stock Exchange and the Post Office building is *Via Dante*, having on the right side an arcade. When walking through this away from Piazza di Ferrari one sees fronting the farther end a mass of ivy. It covers the house in which **Columbus** was born. Within the enclosure is the cloister of the Necropolis of St. Andrew, reconstructed with part of the materials discovered on the neighbouring site of the church.

By following the tramway on the opposite side of the square one is led to the front of the **Palazzo Ducale** (Ducal Palace), dating from 1291 and now containing law courts, etc. Thence the tramway leads to the Cathedral, **San Lorenzo.** It was founded in 985, rebuilt in 1307, and the Renaissance dome was added in 1567. For a small fee the visitor will be shown the treasures, which include the legendary Holy Grail, an ancient cross containing a piece of the true cross, and relics of John the Baptist.

The tramway down Via San Lorenzo and then to the right leads to *Via Andrea Doria*, which followed to the right soon brings one to the starting-point. It would not take much longer to retrace one's steps across the *Piazza di Ferrari* and along *Via Carlo Felice*, etc., and this route would probably be followed with greater ease. Or tram No. 27 can be taken from Piazza di Ferrari to the Piazza Acquaverde in front of the railway station.

From the Piazza di Ferrari tram No. 21, 31, 32 or 33 may be taken to the famous—

[*E.N.I.T.*

THE CATHEDRAL, GENOA.

[*E.N.I.T.*

THE CEMETERY OF STAGLIENO, GENOA.

[*E.N.I.T.*

THE COAST AT NERVI.

Cemetery of Staglieno.

Visitors who desire to be conducted through the cemetery should engage only an authorized guide.

By trams 31, 32 and 33 one passes under a monumental bridge and along the very fine **Via Venti Settembre.** The name commemorates the day on which Italy regained possession of Rome.

The cemetery is one of the most remarkable in the world. It is situated at the foot and on the side of a hill. On three sides of an open space are long lofty galleries in two stories. Along the greater part of the sides of the galleries are remarkable sculptures commemorating those who lie below. Some are allegorical subjects ; others are statues of the dead. Elsewhere the sides of the galleries consist of tombs equal in size and similar in appearance, piled one upon another. The exposed side, which can be removed without difficulty, bears the names of those whose bodies are enclosed. Before many tombs lamps are burning and flowers lie or are attached. Long light ladders are at the disposal of mourners interested in tombs which cannot be reached from the pavement. In the open space are graves which will remain undisturbed for 30 years ; others in which the poorest lie will be used again at the end of 5 years. In this space is a gigantic statue representing Faith. In that part of the cemetery reserved for Protestants is a fine statue of the Resurrection, a monument of the Bauer family. Boundary stones on which is the Star of Italy mark off a group of graves crossed by bands of red, white and green stones. Here also, easily recognizable, is the Altar of the Unknown Soldier. There is also a spot in which were interred American soldiers who fell in the Great War, and whose representatives consented to their burial here.

From the Piazza di Ferrari or from Piazza Acquaverde one can take tram No. 25 in order to traverse the **Circonvallazione a Monte,** a succession of thoroughfares through the highest part of the city. Cook's afternoon excursion combines the passage of this very fine route with a visit to the cemetery and to the site of the *Hôtel Righi* (1,070 feet), commanding magnificent views of the city, the harbour, and the background of mountains.

NERVI.

Access.—By the coast-line or by tram from the centre of Genoa.
Amusements, etc.—Concerts and other entertainments in the Casino. Music
in the open air. Golf (9 holes). Tennis, bathing.
Hotels.—*See* p. 150.
Information Office.—Villa Gropallo. For inquiries by post, *see* p. 32.

NERVI is a charming Riviera resort about 7 miles eastward of Genoa. The Avenue delle Palme, leading
up from the station to the high-road, is bordered by palms
and orange trees, and the trunks of the palms are girdled
by flowering plants. This, however, is but a foretaste of the
floral beauties of the place, for everywhere in profusion are
flowers, palms, orange and lemon trees. The winter climate
is mild, as the site is sheltered by mountains, so that even
during the coldest period the temperature rarely falls below
47° Fah.

A paved promenade, $1\frac{1}{4}$ miles long and quite free from dust,
has been cut out of the side of the cliffs. It faces south and
is for the use of pedestrians only. Here are a bandstand,
cafés and a thirteenth-century tower. Below the esplanade
the shore is rocky, but bathing is possible.

Between the esplanade and the high-road is an extensive
and beautiful **Municipal Park** destined to become the Botanical
Gardens for the fauna and flora of the Mediterranean. It
has been formed by the union of the grounds of two large
villas, Serra and Gropallo. The former houses a modern
Art Gallery; the latter has been converted into a **Casino,** the
scene of musical and other entertainments. Some of the
rooms are appropriated to a **Foreigners' Club,** to which visitors
have free and informal admission.

The Environs of Nervi.

Reached on foot in 20–25 minutes is **San Ilario,** situated
on a plateau, where is also the new **Golf Course.** Thence a
walk of about equal length takes one either to **Monte Gingo**
or to **Monte More,** one situated to the right, the other to the
left. By half an hour's walk from San Ilario along hill-paths
one may arrive at the small church of **San Rocco,** hidden
in olive groves.

PORTOFINO MARE.

little harbour was important as it was on the sea route, the
principal line of communication, between Rome and Gaul.
In those days, and much later, it was a common procedure
of vessels caught in a storm to run for shelter to the little
ports on this coast.   The ship carrying the crusading Richard
Cœur de Lion to Palestine was one of those that did so.   It
sought shelter at Portofino.

For those who wish to pay Portofino more than a flying visit,
there is a hotel (p. 150) on the hill-side above the village.

centre of learning and the cradle of civilizing missionaries.

In the thirteenth century S. Fruttuoso became the
burial-place of members of the Genoese noble family Doria,
whose tombs now show but traces of their original beauty.
As a defence against the corsairs, a tower (still standing)
was built by Admiral Andrea Doria, who commanded in

turn the rival fleets of Charles Quint and François I. In the fourteenth century the prestige of the S. Fruttuoso monastery declined, the place of that institution was taken by the more accessible monastery at Cervara, and in the sixteenth century the monastery at S. Fruttuoso came to an end. The abbey church has become the parish church and holds the treasured ashes.

The road—

Between Santa Margherita and Rapallo,

a short two miles, is traversed again and again, either on foot or by bus, by visitors staying at one or other of the resorts. It passes Santa Margherita's *Imperial Palace Hotel*, where a treaty between Germany and Russia was signed in 1922 ; and the beautiful **Villa Spinola,** on the S. Margherita-Rapallo boundary, where was signed in 1920 a treaty between Italy and Yugo-Slavia. It passes also the small fishing village of **San Michele di Pagana,** which has a permanent exhibition of Umbrian Art, and a church containing a picture attributed to Van Dyck. In this are figures of the Crucified Christ, St. Francis, St. Bernard, and a member of the Orero family, with whom the artist is thought to have stayed.

RAPALLO.

Access.—By rail *viâ* Ventimiglia or *viâ* Genoa. By the Simplon-Orient Express, Milan is reached from London in about 24 hours. From Milan to Genoa, the time is 2½ hours, and from Genoa to Rapallo about ¾ hour.
By the Rome Express (*train de luxe*), Rapallo is reached in about 26 hours. For other trains to Genoa *see* San Remo (p. 162).
By road along the coast to Recco and thence across the promontory of Portofino. On certain days a bus runs from Nice to Rapallo, Santa Margherita and Portofino Vetta.

Amusements, etc.—Concerts and dances at the Casino. Battles of Flowers and other fêtes. Tennis, golf (a new 9-hole course), boating (motor, sailing, and rowing boats for hire). Fishing, bathing (on the rocks are several bathing establishments).

Buses.—To S. Margherita, Genoa, Sestri Levante, Spezia, etc. Starting-place, behind the parish church.

English Club, English Library, English Church (chaplain resident in winter), English doctor.

Excursions.—By motor-car and by steamer (p. 196).

Hotels.—*See* p. 151.

Inquiries.—The manager of the Tourist Office, 2 Corso Italia, will be pleased to give information through the post (*see* p. 32), or to callers.

Population.—14,000.

Rapallo is one of the most beautiful resorts on the Ligurian Riviera, and is the largest and best known of those on the eastern portion. It stands on the shore of an inlet to which it has given its name, in the centre of the Gulf of Tigullio, which has an exceptionally fine coast. In one direction it rises precipitously, in the other less abruptly, but both east and west the cliffs and slopes are luxuriantly wooded.

Riviera (n)

Beyond the valley are ranges of the Ligurian Apennines.   On the other side is the coast-line of the Gulf of Genoa, and on a clear day the Mountains of Corsica may be seen on the horizon.

An easier but slightly longer descent than that afforded by the mule-path indicated above may be made by proceeding by a mule-track to the **Crocetta,** a pass about 1,950 feet above the sea, on the western ridge.   The path can be reached from Monte Rosa without descending to the sanctuary.   From the pass the route is to the Monte Valley and down to the road by a good path.

Motor-car excursions are organized by the C.I.T. and Italian State Railway Tourist Office, 2 Corso Italia.

Steamer trips are made morning and afternoon, by a fast and well-appointed boat, to S. Margherita, Portofino, and S. Fruttuoso.

SOUTHWARD FROM RAPALLO.

THE railway, passing through many tunnels, follows the coast from Rapallo to Spezia, at the extremity of the Ligurian Riviera. A road with many loops follows the coast-line in a general way as far as Sestri Levante and then by a great curve goes to Spezia.

Upon mighty rocks, little more than an hour's walk by road from Rapallo or only 2½ miles by rail, is the quaint village of **Zoagli**, in whose *Palazzo della Seta*, which should be visited, the Genoese velvet originated and then velvet-making became a home industry in the village and its neighbourhood. The church, dedicated to S. Martino, was erected in 1726 by the side of one dating back to the twelfth century. The captain of the ship which conveyed to Genoa the ashes of St. John the Baptist, stolen from a monastery by certain Genoese, at the time of the first crusade, was a native of Zoagli, and he successfully claimed for his church a small portion of the ashes, still its great treasure.

Just over 3 miles by rail from Zoagli is—

Chiavari,

built on the site of a Roman city, at the mouth of the *Entella*, " the beauty stream " sung by Dante. From the station public gardens extend to the Piazza Madonna dell' Orto, the site of the **Cathedral Church,** dating from 1613 (the colonnade only from 1841). Frescoes illustrate the wonders of the Madonna dell' Orto. In the Piazza Carlo Alberto is the **Palazzo di Guistizia**, the residence of the Governor, erected in 1404 and reconstructed, with the exception of its tower, in the second half of the nineteenth century. A tablet on a house in Via Vittorio Emanuele records that Garibaldi was there in 1849. A monument stands in Piazza XX Settembre.

The neighbouring commune of **Nè** was formerly called Garibaldo, and from that the Garibaldis may have derived their name. The descendants of an eleventh-century Captain Paolo di Garibaldo larly interesting to the historian and to the artist, but it is important to remember that forts must not be approached without permission and that sketching and photographing are forbidden.

The most interesting buildings in the city are the fourteenth-century castle of St. George (**Castello di S. Giorgio**) and the **Church** of Santa Maria Assunta, founded in 1371, rebuilt in 1550, and restored and enlarged 1928–29.

Along the shore are beautiful tree-shaded walks, and pleasant trips can be taken to Portovenere and the Island of Palmaria on the western side of the gulf and to **Lerici** on the eastern side.

It will be remembered that Shelley and Byron resided for some time near Lerici and that the former was drowned between Lerici and Leghorn. In describing the situation of the house which Byron and Shelley inhabited, Mrs. Shelley wrote : " The Bay of Spezia is of considerable extent and divided by a rocky promontory into a larger and a smaller one. The town of Lerici is situated in the eastern point, and in the depth of the smaller bay which bears the name of the town is the village of Sant' Arenzo. Our house, Casa Magni, was close to this village, the sea came up to the door, a steep hill sheltered it behind." The Villa is now called Casa Maccarini.

At Spezia the coast scenery completely changes. The cliffs of the Ligurian Riviera give place to the long stretch of sun-beaten beaches of the **Tuscan Riviera.**

The most famous of these beaches is that of—

Viareggio.

Access.—*By rail* : The main Genoa-Rome line, 3 hours' journey from Genoa, 6 hours' from Rome, 6 from Turin and Milan and 2 hours from Florence.
By road : A road suitable for motors runs along the coast from Spezia, connecting with the Ligurian coast road.
Hotels.—*See* p. 151.
Inquiries.—These may be addressed to the Italian Tourist Office in London (p. 141), or to the local information office, " Ente pro Viareggio, Viareggio, Lucca, Italy " (*see* p. 32).

Viareggio is some 35 miles south of Spezia. Little more than a hundred years ago, it was a modest fishing village. Now it is a large, clean, well-planned town with wide avenues, spacious squares and gardens, and a hundred hotels that are open all the year. The air is uncontaminated by factories and there is an abundant supply of excellent water.

The climate is dry and there is the sunshine characteristic of the Riviera winter, but as this portion of the coast is less sheltered than that of the Ligurian Riviera, and is occasionally swept by strong winds, the town is not, during the winter months, suitable for invalids or for most convalescents.

It is as a summer resort that Viareggio has become famous. It is Italy's largest bathing resort, and rivals the Lido as the most fashionable. Quite as definitely as on the Venetian shore is there here a land of sunshine and pyjamas.

Viareggio faces a broad and gently sloping beach of fine, golden sand extending for seven miles along the coast. On this ideal bathing ground are innumerable cabins, and there is a bathing establishment equipped according to the most modern ideas. For more than $1\frac{1}{2}$ miles the beach is bordered by a fine garden promenade beautified by ornamental trees and flowering shrubs, among which are palms, orange trees and oleanders. Facing this charming and popular parade is an equally long range of elegant villas and majestic hotels. On each side of the town and behind it are extensive pine woods, which fill the air with their perfume and offer innumerable shady walks. A short distance inland are the hills, and in the background are the Apennines, snow-clad in winter and early spring.

Sailing, rowing, fishing, water-polo and sea excursions vie with the land attractions, which comprise golf on a course alongside the sands, tennis, clay-pigeon shooting, rail and road excursions, horse races in September, and, during the last ten days before Lent, carnival festivities on the lines of those at Nice. Indoor pleasures are promoted by a casino, a visitors' club, theatres, concert halls, and ball-rooms.

An English church indicates that Viareggio attracts English visitors. A piazza commemorates the poet Shelley, whose body was cremated on the beach.

For those who prefer a quieter resort than Viareggio there is adjacent to it **Pietrasanta,** a very pleasant place with good hotels, and there are other quiet pleasant spots along the coast.

Nine miles north of Viareggio, with which it is connected by electric railway, is **Forte dei Maroni,** a small resort on a flat coast, with a sandy beach bordered by a pine forest, behind which rise the Carrara Mountains. Another similar resort in the same direction is **Marine di Massa.** Trams run between

204 INDEX